Service Worke
Development
Cookbook

Build highly available and performant native web
applications that seamlessly integrate with third-party APIs

Sean Amarasinghe

PUBLISHING

BIRMINGHAM - MUMBAI

Service Worker Development Cookbook

First published: August 2016

Production reference: 1260816

Published by Packt Publishing Ltd.
Livery Place
35 Livery Street
Birmingham B3 2PB, UK.

ISBN 978-1-78646-529-0

www.packtpub.com

Credits

Author
Sean Amarasinghe

Reviewer
Daijiro Wachi

Commissioning Editor
David Barnes

Acquisition Editor
Nitin Dasan

Content Development Editor
Mehvash Fatima

Technical Editor
Siddhi Rane

Copy Editors
Safis Editing
Tom Jacob

Project Coordinator
Kinjal Bari

Proofreader
Safis Editing

Indexer
Hemangini Bari

Graphics
Kirk D'Penha

Production Coordinator
Shantanu N. Zagade

Cover Work
Shantanu N. Zagade

About the Author

Sean Amarasinghe is a software developer from Melbourne, Australia. He is a developer, designer, photographer, and also a blogger. He blogs about development, design, technology, and photography. He is passionate about offline apps and what they bring to the user. He has firsthand experience of how well offline apps work. He has written a couple of blog posts about offline cache manifests, as well as service workers.

About the Reviewer

Daijiro Wachi is a JavaScript developer from Tokyo, Japan. He is passionate about open web and some of open source projects/communities related to JavaScript on a daily basis. He has gained the highest award in Service Worker Hackathon 2015 held by Google Japan.

www.PacktPub.com

eBooks, discount offers, and more

Did you know that Packt offers eBook versions of every book published, with PDF and ePub files available? You can upgrade to the eBook version at www.PacktPub.com and as a print book customer, you are entitled to a discount on the eBook copy. Get in touch with us at customercare@packtpub.com for more details.

At www.PacktPub.com, you can also read a collection of free technical articles, sign up for a range of free newsletters and receive exclusive discounts and offers on Packt books and eBooks.

https://www2.packtpub.com/books/subscription/packtlib

Do you need instant solutions to your IT questions? PacktLib is Packt's online digital book library. Here, you can search, access, and read Packt's entire library of books.

Why subscribe?

- ▶ Fully searchable across every book published by Packt
- ▶ Copy and paste, print, and bookmark content
- ▶ On demand and accessible via a web browser

Table of Contents

Preface

The service worker feature of the browser will enable you to build highly available and performant native web applications that seamlessly integrate with third-party APIs. Whether you want to create an offline web app or a proxy, this book will show you how to do it.

What this book covers

Chapter 1, *Learning Service Worker Basics*, covers setting up the service worker in your environment, and how to get up and running using service worker development. This chapter includes registering a service worker and debugging.

Chapter 2, *Working with Resource Files*, provides several recipes on how to handle resource files with the service worker, including loading CSS and fonts.

Chapter 3, *Accessing Offline Content*, takes a look at how to cache resources and serve content offline.

Chapter 4, *Accessing Offline Content with Advanced Techniques*, explores advanced techniques, including templating and Google Analytics, when working with offline content.

Chapter 5, *Reaching Beyond the Offline Cache*, provides recipes beyond the offline cache and explores topics ranging from getting network responses offline to how to use the service worker as a load balancer.

Chapter 6, *Working with Advanced Libraries*, talks about Google Analytics, circuit breakers, and dead letter queues.

Chapter 7, *Fetching Resources*, covers various techniques on fetching resources from different sources.

Chapter 8, *Experimenting with Web Push*, talks about different ways of implementing push notifications.

Chapter 9, Looking at General Usage, provides various recipes on general usages of the service worker from slow responses to a live flowchart.

Chapter 10, Improving Performance, talks about how to optimize your service worker application to perform efficiently and in a performant manner.

What you need for this book

This book was written using a Mac with Google Chrome as the browser, running Node.js. However, Node.js can be run on a Windows or Linux machine as well, along with Google Chrome.

All the software used in this book is free and open source. You will definitely need to be running Node.js and Google Chrome for most of the recipes.

Conventions

In this book, you will find a number of styles of text that distinguish between different kinds of information. Here are some examples of these styles, and an explanation of their meaning.

Code words in text, folder names, filenames, file extensions, pathnames, dummy URLs, user input, and Twitter handles are shown as follows: "The `skipWaiting()` method is used inside the active event handler, which in turn uses `Clients.claim()`."

A block of code is set as follows:

```
self.oninstall = function(event) {
  event.waitUntil(
    fetch(zipURL)
      .then(function(res) {
        return res.arrayBuffer();
      })
      .then(getZipFileReader)
      .then(cacheFileContents)
      .then(self.skipWaiting.bind(self))
  );
};
```

Any command-line input or output is written as follows:

```
$ git add –all
$ git commit -m "initial commit"
$ git push -u origin master
```

New terms and **important words** are shown in bold. Words that you see on the screen, in menus or dialog boxes, for example, appear in the text like this: "Finally, in the sidebar on the left-hand side, select **Credentials**."

Reader feedback

Feedback from our readers is always welcome. Let us know what you think about this book—what you liked or disliked. Reader feedback is important for us as it helps us develop titles that you will really get the most out of.

To send us general feedback, simply e-mail `feedback@packtpub.com`, and mention the book's title in the subject of your message.

If there is a topic that you have expertise in and you are interested in either writing or contributing to a book, see our author guide at `www.packtpub.com/authors`.

Customer support

Now that you are the proud owner of a Packt book, we have a number of things to help you to get the most from your purchase.

Downloading the example code

You can download the example code files for this book from your account at `http://www.packtpub.com`. If you purchased this book elsewhere, you can visit `http://www.packtpub.com/support` and register to have the files e-mailed directly to you.

You can download the code files by following these steps:

1. Log in or register to our website using your e-mail address and password.
2. Hover the mouse pointer on the **SUPPORT** tab at the top.
3. Click on **Code Downloads & Errata**.
4. Enter the name of the book in the **Search** box.
5. Select the book for which you're looking to download the code files.
6. Choose from the drop-down menu where you purchased this book from.
7. Click on **Code Download**.

You can also download the code files by clicking on the **Code Files** button on the book's webpage at the Packt Publishing website. This page can be accessed by entering the book's name in the **Search** box. Please note that you need to be logged in to your Packt account.

Once the file is downloaded, please make sure that you unzip or extract the folder using the latest version of:

▶ WinRAR / 7-Zip for Windows
▶ Zipeg / iZip / UnRarX for Mac
▶ 7-Zip / PeaZip for Linux

The code bundle for the book is also hosted on GitHub at `https://github.com/PacktPublishing/Service-Worker-Development-Cookbook`. We also have other code bundles from our rich catalog of books and videos available at `https://github.com/PacktPublishing/`. Check them out!

Errata

Although we have taken every care to ensure the accuracy of our content, mistakes do happen. If you find a mistake in one of our books—maybe a mistake in the text or the code—we would be grateful if you could report this to us. By doing so, you can save other readers from frustration and help us improve subsequent versions of this book. If you find any errata, please report them by visiting `http://www.packtpub.com/submit-errata`, selecting your book, clicking on the **Errata Submission Form** link, and entering the details of your errata. Once your errata are verified, your submission will be accepted and the errata will be uploaded to our website or added to any list of existing errata under the Errata section of that title.

To view the previously submitted errata, go to `https://www.packtpub.com/books/content/support` and enter the name of the book in the search field. The required information will appear under the **Errata** section.

Piracy

Piracy of copyrighted material on the Internet is an ongoing problem across all media. At Packt, we take the protection of our copyright and licenses very seriously. If you come across any illegal copies of our works in any form on the Internet, please provide us with the location address or website name immediately so that we can pursue a remedy.

Please contact us at `copyright@packtpub.com` with a link to the suspected pirated material.

We appreciate your help in protecting our authors and our ability to bring you valuable content.

Questions

If you have a problem with any aspect of this book, you can contact us at `questions@packtpub.com`, and we will do our best to address the problem.

1

Learning Service Worker Basics

In this chapter, we will cover the following topics:

- ▶ Setting up service workers
- ▶ Setting up SSL for Windows
- ▶ Setting up SSL for Mac
- ▶ Setting up GitHub pages for SSL
- ▶ Registering a service worker
- ▶ Registering a service worker in detail
- ▶ Debugging
- ▶ Providing stale version on error
- ▶ Creating mock responses
- ▶ Handling request timeouts

Introduction

If you travel a bit, chances are you have probably found yourself stuck with **zero network connectivity** way too often. This is frustrating, especially if you just wanted to continue reading some news articles, blog posts, or you wanted to get some work done.

Unfortunately, with your browser, attempting to make requests for something from the network while being offline doesn't quite work out so well.

Even though on planes, the subway, in hotels, and at conferences, Wi-Fi may provide you with opportunities to restore your connection, in general you will have to wait for the network to return online in order to request the pages you want to view.

Previous attempts to solve this issue include `AppCache`. It seems to work, to some extent, but the issue with `AppCache` is that it makes a lot of assumptions about user interactions. When those assumptions are not met, the application will fail to function as expected. It is also designed to work well with single page apps, not the traditional multi-page websites.

Also, one of the most challenging problems with providing a seamless user experience with web apps is making them functional while offline. This is an important issue to resolve, given that most users today access web apps on the move. Enter service workers, a script running in the background of our browser.

Being able to use a web app, regardless of the connectivity, means users can operate uninterrupted when they are on board a plane, the subway, or in places where connectivity is limited or not available. This technology will help boost client productivity and will increase the availability of the application.

With service workers, we are able to pre-cache some assets of a website. What we are referencing as assets are JavaScript files, CSS files, images, and some fonts. This will help us to speed up the loading time, instead of having to fetch information from the web servers every time we visit the same website. And of course, most importantly, those assets will be available for us when we are offline.

Service workers

A service worker is a script that stands between your browser and the network, giving you, among other things, the ability to intercept network requests, and respond to them in different ways.

In order for your website or app to work, the browser fetches its assets, such as HTML pages, JavaScript, CSS, images, and fonts. In the past, managing these resources was mainly the browser's responsibility. If the browser couldn't access the network, you would probably see its **Unable to connect to the Internet** message. There were techniques you could use to encourage the local caching of assets, but the browser often had the last say.

One feature service worker uses heavily is promises. So it is important to have a good understanding of promises.

Promises

Promises are a great mechanism for running async operations with success dependent on one another. This is central to the way service workers work.

Promises can do a great many things, but for now, all you need to know is that if something returns a promise, you can attach .then() to the end and include callbacks inside it for success, failure, and so on, or you can insert .catch(), the end if you want to include a failure callback.

Let's compare a traditional synchronous callback structure to its asynchronous promise equivalent:

sync

```
try {
  var value = Fn();
  console.log(value);
} catch(err) {
  console.log(err);
}
```

async

```
Fn().then(function(value) {
  console.log(value);
  }).catch(function(err) {
  console.log(err);
});
```

In the sync example, we have to wait for Fn() to run and return a value before any more of the code can execute. In the async example, Fn() returns a promise for the value, then the rest of the code can carry on running. When the promise resolves, the code inside then will be run asynchronously.

Promise.resolve(value)

This method returns an object of `Promise.then`, which is resolved with the value passed into the `resolve` method, as in `Promise.resolve(value)`. If this value has a `then` method, the returned method will follow it; otherwise, it will be fulfilled with the value.

Promise.reject(reason)

This method takes `reason` as an argument and returns a promise object that is rejected.

Setting up service workers

In order to get service workers running, we need to serve our code via **Hyper Text Transfer Protocol Secure** (**HTTPS**). Service workers are designed to run only across HTTPS for security reasons. Source code repositories such as GitHub support HTTPS, where you can host your files.

Getting ready

If you are using a newer version of a browser, the chances are that service workers are already enabled on it. But, if that is not the case, we will have to change few things in the browser settings. In the following section, we are going to cover how to enable service worker features in Chrome and Firefox.

How to do it...

Follow the steps below to enable service worker in Chrome and Firefox.

Chrome

To experiment in Chrome, you need to download Chrome Canary:

1. Go to `https://www.google.com/chrome/browser/canary.html` and download the latest version.
2. Open Chrome Canary and type `chrome://flags`.
3. Turn on `experimental-web-platform-features`.
4. Restart the browser.
5. The following image shows experimental features on the Chrome browser, where you enable the **Experimental Web Platform** feature by clicking on the **Enable** link underneath:

Firefox

To experiment in Firefox, you need to download Firefox Nightly:

1. Go to `https://nightly.mozilla.org/` and download the latest version.
2. Open Firefox Nightly, and go to `about:config`.

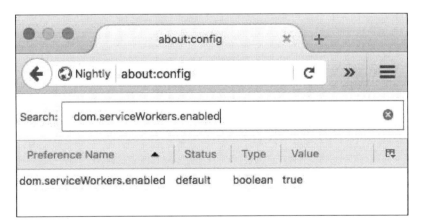

3. Set `experimental-web-platform-features` to `true`.
4. Restart the browser.

At the time of writing, Opera offers partial support for service workers, including basic support, as well as installing and uninstalling events. Internet Explorer and Safari do not support service workers.

Service workers are currently an experimental technology, meaning the syntax and the behavior are subject to change in future versions as the specification changes.

Setting up SSL for Windows

Service workers are designed to run only across HTTPS, so in order for us to test our code, we need our web pages to be delivered across HTTPS. In this recipe, we will cover getting your site setup with SSL support for Windows.

Getting ready

This recipe assumes you run Windows 7 or higher with **Internet Information Service** (**IIS**) enabled.

How to do it...

Follow these instructions to enable SSL:

1. First, open IIS; you can do this by running the following command inside the command line:

   ```
   Inetmgr
   ```

2. Select the server node in the tree view and double-click the **Server Certificates** feature in the list view, as shown:

3. Click on the **Create Self-Signed Certificate...** link in the **Actions** pane.

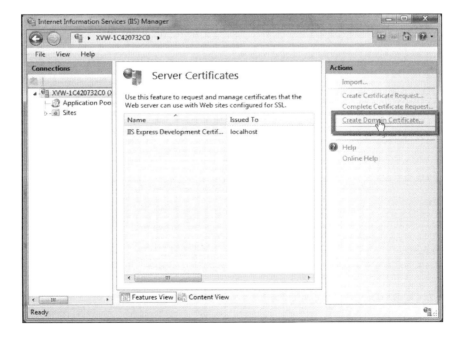

4. Enter a meaningful name for the new certificate and click **OK**.

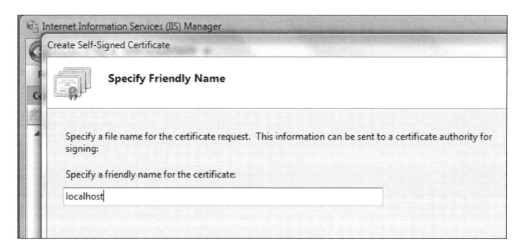

This will generate a self-signed certificate, which is marked for **Server Authentication** use, meaning it uses a server-side certificate for authenticating the identity of the server and also for HTTP SSL encryption.

In order to create an SSL binding, we have to select a site in the tree view and then, in the **Actions** pane, click **Bindings...**. This will bring up the bindings editor that manages bindings for your website, which include create, edit, and delete. Now, to add your new SSL binding to the site, click **Add...**.

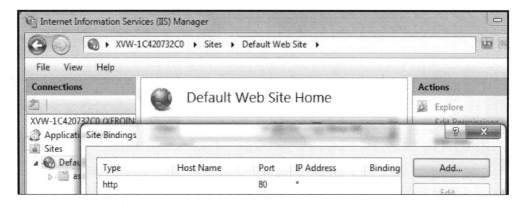

5. Port 80 is the default setting for a new binding for HTTP. We can select **https** in the **Type** drop-down list. Select the self-signed certificate we created in the previous section from the **SSL Certificate** drop-down list, and then click **OK**.

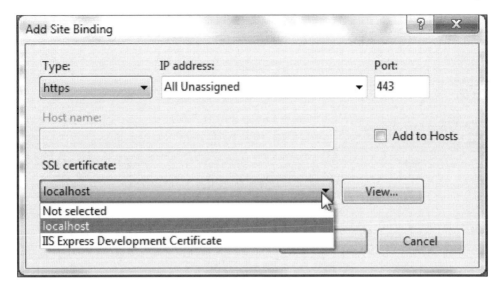

6. Now we have a new SSL binding on our site and all that remains is to make sure that it works.

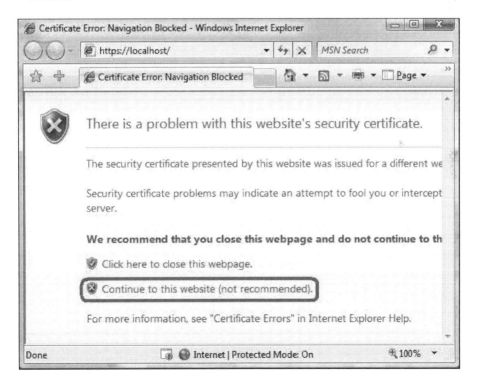

7. Click **Continue to this website** to proceed.

Setting up SSL for Mac

As mentioned in the previous recipe, service workers are designed to run only across HTTPS. So, in order for us to test our code, we need our web pages to be delivered across HTTPS. In this recipe, we will cover getting your site set up with SSL support for Mac.

Getting ready

This recipe assumes that you are running OS X 10.11, El Capitan, or higher. We are going to use a command-line utility called Vim for editing files, which already comes with Mac. Make sure not to use the number pad with Vim. Please be aware that this process is lengthy.

How to do it...

Follow these instructions to enable SSL:

1. First, we need to make sure Apache is running (you may get a prompt for a password):

    ```
    $ sudo apachectl start
    ```

2. The next step is to make some modifications to your `httpd.conf`. Because it's a system file, you will need to use `sudo` again:

    ```
    $ sudo vim /etc/apache2/httpd.conf
    ```

3. In this file, you should uncomment both `socache_shmcb_module` and `ssl_module`, and also the include the `httpd-ssl.conf` file by removing the leading # symbol on those lines (you can use / to search on the Vim editor):

    ```
    LoadModule socache_shmcb_module
    libexec/apache2/mod_socache_shmcb.so
    ...
    LoadModule ssl_module libexec/apache2/mod_ssl.so
    ...
    Include /private/etc/apache2/extra/httpd-ssl.conf
    ```

4. After saving the preceding file (press `:wq`), you should then open up your `/etc/apache2/extra/httpd-vhosts.conf` file:

    ```
    $ sudo vim /etc/apache2/extra/httpd-vhosts.conf
    ```

5. Here, you can create a VirtualHost entry for each virtual host that you wish to provide SSL support for:

    ```
    <VirtualHost *:80>
          DocumentRoot "/Library/WebServer/Documents"
        ServerName localhost
        SSLEngine on
    ```

```
SSLCertificateFile "/private/etc/apache2/localhost.crt"
SSLCertificateKeyFile
"/private/etc/apache2/localhost.key"
</VirtualHost>
```

Make sure you copy your development folder to the `DocumentRoot` directory as you did earlier: `/Library/WebServer/Documents`.

To get this all to work with Apache, we need to create a self-signed certificate that we have already referenced in the `VirtualHost` definition.

6. Generate a key:

   ```
   $ cd /etc/apache2
   ```

7. Press *Enter* with no input after the following command:

   ```
   $ sudo openssl genrsa -out localhost-key.pem 1024
   ```

8. Next, we have to generate a certificate signing request:

   ```
   $ sudo openssl req -new -key localhost-key.pem -out localhost.csr
   ```

9. Using this **certificate signing request** (**CSR**), generate the certificate:

   ```
   $ sudo openssl x509 -req -days 365 -in localhost.csr -signkey
   localhost-key.pem -out localhost.crt
   ```

10. Then we have to convert the key to a no-phrase key:

    ```
    $ sudo openssl rsa -in localhost-key.pem -out localhost.key
    ```

11. Now change `server.crt` to `localhost.crt` as well as `server.key` to `localhost.key`:

    ```
    $ sudo vim /etc/apache2/extra/httpd-ssl.conf
    ```

12. All you need to do now is double check your Apache configuration syntax:

    ```
    $ sudo apachectl configtest
    ```

13. If all goes well, restart Apache:

    ```
    $ sudo apachectl -k restart
    ```

14. Now, simply point your browser at `https://localhost`. If you are prompted for a self-signed certificate in Chrome you can hit the **Advanced** option on that page and proceed, while in Firefox, you need to expand the **I understand the risks** options and add an exception. This is owing to the fact that the self-signed certificates are not signed by any authority, and for this reason the browsers add warnings about them. Although, since you are the one who created the certificate, you understand it's safe to accept it.

15. To fix this, you need to add the certificate as a trusted root authority.

16. Open the **Keychain Access** utility in OS X. Select the **System** option on the left. Click the lock icon in the upper-left corner to enable changes.

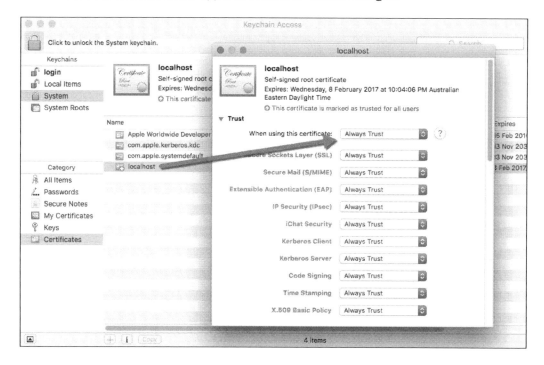

17. Click the plus button at the bottom and select the `/etc/apache2/localhost.cer` file you copied to the desktop. In the dialog that comes up, click **Always Trust**. After the localhost gets added to the system keychain, double-click it to open it again. Expand the **Trust** section and for the first option, pick **Always Trust**.

18. At this point, everything has been configured. Quit Chrome and all other browsers (this is required), fire up the web server, and try to navigate to the local HTTPS site again.

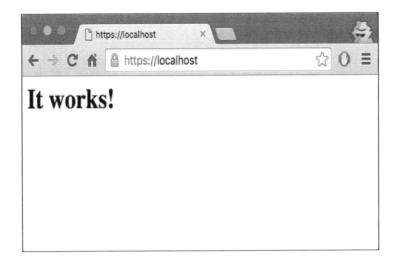

Detailed steps to download the code bundle are mentioned in the Preface of this book. Please have a look.

The code bundle for the book is also hosted on GitHub at `https://github.com/PacktPublishing/Service-Worker-Development-Cookbook`. We also have other code bundles from our rich catalog of books and videos available at `https://github.com/PacktPublishing/`. Check them out!

Setting up GitHub pages for SSL

Service workers are designed to run only across HTTPS. So, in order for us to test our code, we need our web pages to be delivered across HTTPS. GitHub pages are served across HTTPS and it's free to use. So let's get on with it.

Getting ready

Before registering for a GitHub account, please make sure you have a valid e-mail address.

How to do it...

Follow these instructions to set up GitHub pages:

1. Head over to GitHub (`https://github.com`) and register yourself to obtain an account, if you don't have one already.

2. Once you have done that, log in and create a new repository with the following format: `username.github.io`, where `username` is your username.

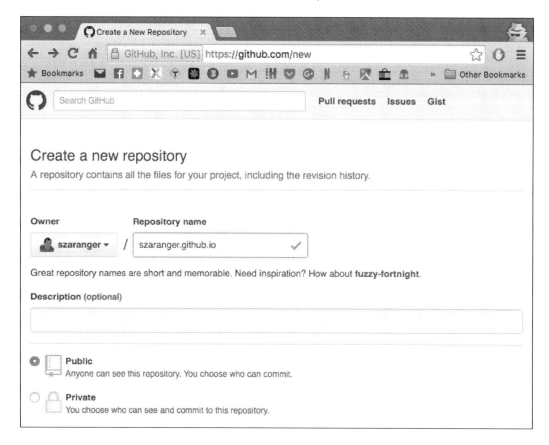

If the first part of the repository doesn't match your username exactly, it won't work.

3. Open your command-line window and clone your repository.

   ```
   $ git  clone https://github.com/username/username.github.io
   ```

4. Change the directory to `username.github.io`:

   ```
   $ cd username.github.io
   ```

5. Create a directory called `service-workers`:

   ```
   $ mkdir service-workers
   ```

6. Create an `index.html` file with some text:

   ```
   $ echo "Service Workers" > index.html
   ```

7. Now let's commit and push our changes to the repository:

   ```
   $ git add --all
   $ git commit -m "initial commit"
   $ git push -u origin master
   ```

8. Open up a browser and go to `http://username.github.io/service-workers/`.

Registering a service worker

Registering your service worker is the first step to getting a service worker up and running. By registering a service worker, we tell our website to use the service worker. And this registering process happens outside of the service worker, in our case inside the `index.html` file. You can do that inside a JavaScript file and then reference it within the `index.html` file, but not in the service worker script file.

In this basic registration demo, we will test to see if our service worker gets registered successfully.

Getting ready

To get started, with service workers, you will need to have the service worker experiment feature turned on in your browser settings. If you have not done this yet, refer to the first recipe: *Setting up service workers*. Service workers only run across HTTPS. To find out how to set up a development environment to support this feature, refer to the following recipes: *Setting up GitHub pages for SSL*, *Setting up SSL for Windows*, and *Setting up SSL for Mac*.

How to do it...

Follow these instructions to set up your file structure:

1. First, we need to create the `index.html` file as follows:

   ```html
   <!DOCTYPE html>
     <html lang="en">
      <head></head>
         <body>
   ```

```
<p>Registration status: <strong
id="status"></strong></p>
<script>
    if ('serviceWorker' in navigator) {
      navigator.serviceWorker.register(
        'service-worker.js',
        { scope: './' }
      ).then( function(serviceWorker) {
        document.getElementById('status').innerHTML =
            'successful';
      }).catch(function(error) {
          document.getElementById('status').
          innerHTML = error;
      });
    } else {
        document.getElementById('status').
        innerHTML =
    'unavailable';
    }
</script>
</body>
</html>
```

2. Create an empty JavaScript file called `service-worker.js` in the same folder as the `index.html` file.

3. With your two files in place, you can navigate to the GitHub page, `https://username.github.io/service-workers/01/01/index.html`, and you will see the success message in your browser.

How it works...

We started off by making sure that the service worker feature is available with the line `if ('serviceWorker' in navigator)`. If that's not the case, then we set the message to unavailable. If your browser does not support service workers, you will get this message.

Now we register the service worker with the empty JavaScript file and the scope. To ensure the registration is only applicable to the current directory and those underneath it, we override the default scope of `'/'` with `'./'` in the line `{ scope: './' }` as the scope has to be of the same origin.

If you decide that your script files should sit elsewhere, you will need a special header, such as `Service-Worker-allowed: true` or a specific content-type, such as `text/javascript`.

If the registration was successful, we print the message `successful` to the status message.

Otherwise, we print the error message as the status. The reason for the error could be something going wrong during the registration, for example, the `service-worker.js` file may not available or it may contain a syntax error.

There's more...

We can unregister the service worker by calling the following `unregister()` function:

```
serviceWorker.unregister().then(function() {
    document.getElementById('status').innerHTML = 'unregistered';
})
```

Known issues

There are a couple of issues with the Chrome browser when working with service workers, which might confuse you.

The ERR_FILE_EXISTS error message

Reloading pages with service workers will always show an `ERR_FILE_EXISTS` error message, even if there's nothing wrong with your code.

This seems to occur when we are trying to access an already registered service worker.

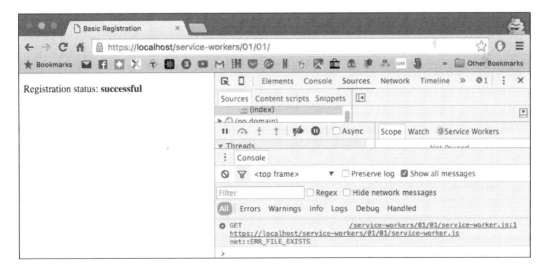

Stale console messages

Logging messages from the service worker scripts such as the `console.log` may not clear from the console, which seems like the events are being fired too many times on subsequent page loads.

Registering a service worker in detail

Understanding events involved in service worker registration and state transitions will give you greater control over your application by using this feature. In this detailed registration demo, we will take a look at the state transitions of service worker registration.

Getting ready

To get started with service workers, you will need to have the service worker experiment feature turned on in your browser settings. If you have not done this yet, refer to the previous recipe: *Setting up service workers*. Service workers only run across HTTPS. To find out how to set up a development environment to support this feature, refer to the following recipes: *Setting up GitHub pages for SSL*, *Setting up SSL for Windows*, and *Setting up SSL for Mac*.

How to do it...

Follow these instructions to set up your file structure:

1. First, we need to create an `index.html` file as follows:

```
<!DOCTYPE html>
<html lang="en">
<head>
  <meta charset="UTF-8">
  <title>Detailed Registration</title>
</head>
<body>
  <p>Registration status: <strong id="status"></strong></p>
  <p>State: <strong id="state"></strong></p>

  <script>
    function printState(state) {
      document.getElementById('state').innerHTML = state;
    }

    if ('serviceWorker' in navigator) {

      navigator.serviceWorker.register(
        'service-worker.js',
        { scope: './' }
      ).then( function(registration) {
```

```
            var serviceWorker;

            document.getElementById('status').innerHTML =
            'successful';

            if (registration.installing) {
              serviceWorker = registration.installing;
              printState('installing');
            } else if (registration.waiting) {
              serviceWorker = registration.waiting;
              printState('waiting');
            } else if (registration.active) {
              serviceWorker = registration.active;
              printState('active');
            }

            if (serviceWorker) {
              printState(serviceWorker.state);

              serviceWorker.addEventListener('statechange',
              function(e) {
                printState(e.target.state);
              });
            }
          }).catch(function(error) {
            document.getElementById('status').innerHTML =
            error;
          });
        } else {
            document.getElementById('status').innerHTML =
            'unavailable';
        }
    </script>
  </body>
</html>
```

2. Create a JavaScript file called `service-worker.js` in the same folder as the `index.html` file with the following code:

```
self.addEventListener('install', function(e) {
  console.log('Install Event:', e);
});

self.addEventListener('activate', function(e) {
  console.log('Activate Event:', e);
});
```

3. With your two files in place, you can navigate to the GitHub page, `https://username.github.io/service-workers/01/02/index.html`, and you will see the success message in your browser.

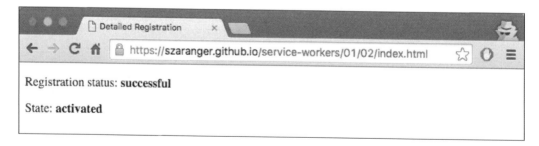

How it works...

When the registration is successful, we inspect the state of the registration and print it to the browser. In this case it is installing, waiting, or active:

```
if (registration.installing) {
    serviceWorker = registration.installing;
    printState('installing');
} else if (registration.waiting) {
    serviceWorker = registration.waiting;
    printState('waiting');
} else if (registration.active) {
    serviceWorker = registration.active;
    printState('active');
}
```

The `printState(state)` helper function will print out the state to the browser.

At the end we attach an event listener to the service worker called `statechange`. The callback of this event listener will print the state changes to the browser:

```
if (serviceWorker) {
    printState(serviceWorker.state);

    serviceWorker.addEventListener('statechange',
    function(e) {
      printState(e.target.state);
    });
}
```

When the registered service worker is in the activated state, we can refresh the page to see the service worker taking control.

To demonstrate a page loading, without the service worker taking control, press *Shift* and refresh the page. You will see the activate event logged in the web console.

We are subscribing to two event listeners in the `service-worker.js` file, `install` and `activate`:

```
self.addEventListener('install', function(e) {
  console.log('Install Event:', e);
});

self.addEventListener('activate', function(e) {
  console.log('Activate Event:', e);
});
```

These events get fired when this version of the script first gets registered for the given scope.

The install event is a good place to prefetch data and initialize caches, and the `activate` event works well for cleaning up data from the old version of the script.

There's more...

When the service worker is successfully registered, it will go through the following stages.

Install

In the life cycle of service workers, at the point when the service worker has registered without errors, but is not yet active, any service workers previously activated will still be in control. The service worker is considered new if there is any change in the service worker file between page reloads. It will therefore go through the installation step. At this stage, the service workers are not intercepting any requests.

Activate

The service worker is said to be at the activate stage when it becomes active for the first time. The service worker is now able to intercept requests. This will happen when we close the tab and reopen it, or the page is refreshed by a hard refresh using *Shift* + reload. It will not occur immediately after the install event.

Fetch

The fetch happens when there is a request being made within the current service worker scope.

Terminate

This can happen at any time, even outside of a request. But the termination happens mostly when the browser needs to reclaim memory. When a new request is made, the service worker will be restarted as needed, or a message will be received, but it will not go back through the activate step.

The service worker will intercept a request it is registered to catch all the time, even if it needs to be restarted in order to do so. But, having said that, we cannot guarantee it will be around for any length of time. Because of this, the global state will not be preserved, so we have to make sure to avoid using any global variables within the service worker file. Instead, we can use indexed or `localStorage` for persistence.

See also

▸   The previous recipe, *Registering a service worker*

Debugging

Service workers run in a separate thread in the browser from the pages they control. There are ways to communicate between workers and pages, but they execute in a separate scope. That means you will not have access to the DOM of those web pages from the service worker script, for example. Because of this, we cannot use the DevTools on the same web page to debug service worker scripts. We need to open a separate inspector to debug the service worker thread.

Service workers do most of their work by listening for relevant events and responding to them in a productive way. In the life cycle of service workers, different events are triggered at different points in a service worker's life cycle. So, if we want to cache assets, it is a good time to do that during the install state by listening to the `install` event. In the same way, we can debug service workers by adding breakpoints to the relevant event handlers.

Getting ready

To get started with service workers, you will need to have the service worker experiment feature turned on in your browser settings. If you have not done this yet, refer to the previous recipe: *Setting up service workers*. Service workers only run across HTTPS. To find out how to set up a development environment to support this feature, refer to the following recipes: *Setting up GitHub pages for SSL*, *Setting up SSL for Windows*, and *Setting up SSL for Mac*.

How to do it...

Follow these instructions to set up debugging for service workers:

1. To find out your currently running service workers, type the following into your browser: `chrome://inspect/#service-workers`:

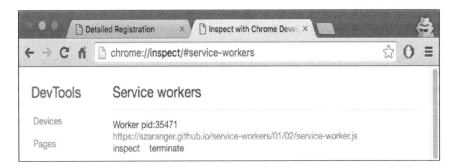

2. Otherwise, type the following into your browser: `chrome://serviceworker-internals` to find out the registered workers. If there aren't any listed, then there are no currently running service workers.

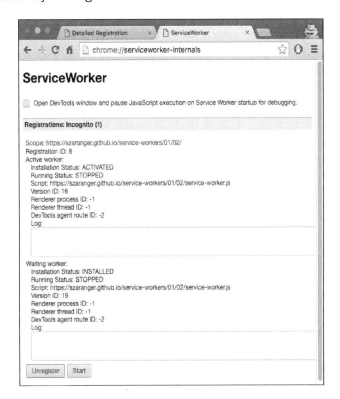

3. To debug your service worker with Chrome DevTools, navigate to the service worker page and open DevTools. (*Cmd + Alt + I* in Mac or *F12* in Windows)

4. You can add a breakpoint to inspect your code.

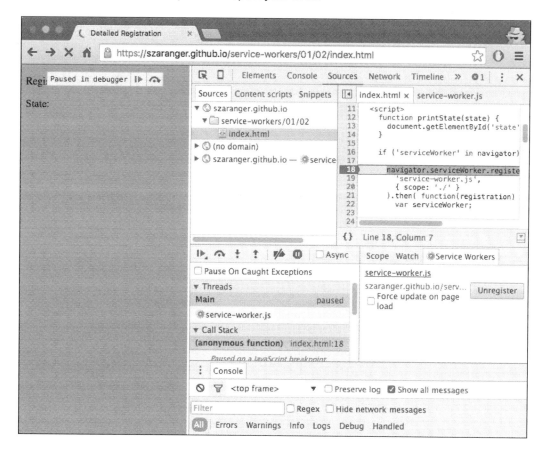

The service worker will be displayed in the **Threads** list, and the **Service Workers** tab lists all the **Active Running** service workers this page belongs to.

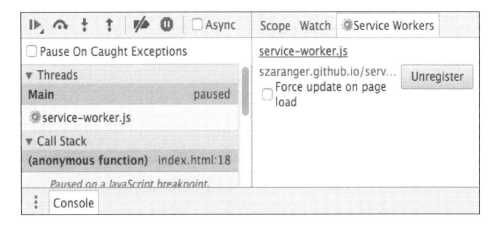

We can use the console for debugging as well. Any errors during the installation process will be printed on the console page. The console is useful for inspecting the service worker context.

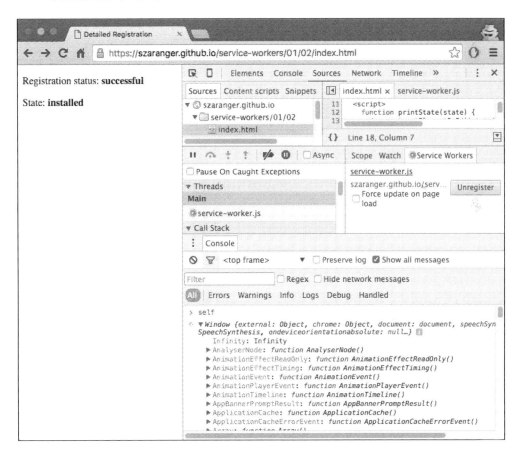

5. You will also find the debugging panel in the **Resources** tab of the DevTools useful. In order to view network activity of the worker, click the `inspect` link on the **Resources** tab to launch a dedicated DevTools window for the worker.

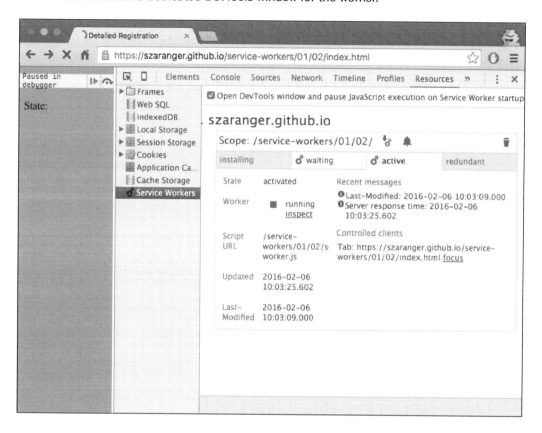

The resulting page `chrome://serviceworker-internals` shows the registered service workers. It also shows basic action buttons, which are explained in detail as follows:

- **Terminated**: Unregisters the worker.
- **Start/Stop**: Starts/stops the worker. This will happen automatically when you navigate to a page in the worker's scope.
- **Sync**: Dispatches a sync event to the worker. If you don't handle this event, nothing will happen.
- **Push**: Dispatches a push event to the worker. If you don't handle this event, nothing will happen.
- **Inspect**: Opens the worker in the inspector.

There's more...

When you are working with DevTools open, you might want to check to make sure that the **Disable cache** is not checked in the **Network** tab. If that option is checked, the requests will go to the network instead of the service worker.

Providing a stale version on error

If you travel a lot, chances are you have often experienced a lot of zero network connectivity. This is frustrating, especially if you want to view previously viewed pages. In this recipe, we will look at how we can address this issue by providing the user with the stale version from the cache.

Getting ready

To get started with service workers, you will need to have the service worker experiment feature turned on in your browser settings. If you have not done this yet, refer to the previous recipe: *Setting up service workers*. Service workers only run across HTTPS. To find out how to set up a development environment to support this feature, refer to the following recipes: *Setting up GitHub pages for SSL*, *Setting up SSL for Windows*, and *Setting up SSL for Mac*.

How to do it...

Follow these instructions to set up your file structure (or you can find the files in the provided directory, 01/05):

1. First, we need to create an `index.html` file as follows:

```html
<!DOCTYPE html>
<html lang="en">
<head>
  <meta charset="UTF-8">
  <title>Stale on Error</title>
</head>
<body>
  <p>Registration status: <strong id="status"></strong></p>
  <script>
    if ('serviceWorker' in navigator) {
      navigator.serviceWorker.register(
        'service-worker.js',
        { scope: './' }
      ).then( function(serviceWorker) {
```

```
            document.getElementById('status').innerHTML =
            'successful';
        }).catch(function(error) {
            document.getElementById('status').innerHTML =
            error;
        });

    } else {
        document.getElementById('status').innerHTML =
        'unavailable';
    }
  </script>
</body>
</html>
```

2. Create a JavaScript file called `service-worker.js` in the same folder as the `index.html` file with the following code:

```
var version = 1;
var cacheName = 'stale- ' + version;

self.addEventListener('install', function(event) {
    self.skipWaiting();
});

self.addEventListener('activate', function(event) {
    if (self.clients && clients.claim) {
        clients.claim();
    }
});

self.addEventListener('fetch', function(event) {

    event.respondWith(
        fetch(event.request).then(function(response) {
            caches.open(cacheName).then(function(cache) {

                if(response.status >= 500) {
                    cache.match(event.request).
                    then(function(response) {

                        return response;
                    }).catch(function() {

                        return response;
```

```
                });
            } else {
                    cache.put(event.request,
                    response.clone());
                return response;
            }
        });
    })
  );
});
```

3. With your two files in place, navigate to index.html.

How it works...

When the registration is successful, we inspect the state of the registration and print it to the browser.

In the service-worker.js file, we always fetch the response from the network:

```
event.respondWith(
        fetch(event.request).then(function(response) {
```

If we received an error response, we return the stale version from the cache:

```
if(response.status >= 500) {
                    cache.match(event.request).
                    then(function(response) {
                // Return stale version from cache
                return response;
    })
```

If we can't find the stale version, we return the network response, which is the error:

```
}).catch(function() {

return response;
});
```

If the response was successful (response code 200), we update the cached version:

```
} else {
cache.put(event.request, response.clone());
    return response;
}
```

The put() method of the cache interface allows key/value pairs to be added to the current cache object. The put() method also overrides any key/value pair previously stored in the cache that matches the request:

```
fetch(url).then(function (response) {
  return cache.put(url, response);
});
```

Creating mock responses

In order to mock API responses from your server to your app, which is instead of actual API responses for the API requests, we can make the service worker return mock responses that will be identical to an API response.

Getting ready

To get started with service workers, you will need to have the service worker experiment feature turned on in your browser settings. If you have not done this yet, refer to the previous recipe: *Setting up service workers*. Service workers only run across HTTPS. To find out how to set up a development environment to support this feature, refer to the following recipes: *Setting up GitHub pages for SSL*, *Setting up SSL for Windows*, and *Setting up SSL for Mac*.

How to do it...

Follow these instructions to set up your file structure (these can also be found in the provided directory, 01/03):

1. First, we need to create an index.html file as follows:

```
<!DOCTYPE html>
<html lang="en">
<head>
  <meta charset="UTF-8">
  <title>Detailed Registration</title>
</head>
<body>
  <p>Network status: <strong id="status"></strong></p>
  <div id="request" style="display: none">
    <input id="long-url" value="https://www.packtpub.com/"
    size="50">
      <input type="button" id="url-shorten-btn"
      value="Shorten URL" />
```

```
        </div>
        <div>
          <input type="checkbox" id="mock-checkbox"
          checked>Mock Response</input>
        </div>
        <div>
          <br />
          <a href="" id="short-url"></a>
        </div>
      </div>

<script>
  function printStatus(status) {
    document.getElementById('status').innerHTML = status;
  }

  function showRequest() {
    document.getElementById('url-shorten-btn')
    .addEventListener('click', sendRequest);
    document.getElementById('request').style.display =
    'block';
  }

  function sendRequest() {
    var xhr = new XMLHttpRequest(),
      request;

          xhr.open('POST',
          'https://www.googleapis.com/urlshortener/
          v1/url?' +
          'key=[Your API Key]');
      xhr.setRequestHeader('Content-Type',
      'application/json');

      if (document.getElementById('mock-checkbox').checked)
      {
              xhr.setRequestHeader('X-Mock-Response',
              'yes');
      }

      xhr.addEventListener('load', function() {
        var response = JSON.parse(xhr.response);
        var el = document.getElementById('short-url');
```

```
        el.href = response.id;
        el.innerHTML = response.id;
      });

      request = {
        longUrl: document.getElementById('long-url').value
      };

      xhr.send(JSON.stringify(request));
    }

    if ('serviceWorker' in navigator) {

      navigator.serviceWorker.register(
        'service-worker.js',
        { scope: './' }
      ).then( function(registration) {
        if (navigator.serviceWorker.controller) {
          printStatus('The service worker is currently
          handling ' +
          'network operations.');
          showRequest();
        } else {
          printStatus('Please reload this page to allow
          the ' + 'service worker to handle network
          operations.');
            }

      }).catch(function(error) {
        document.getElementById('status').innerHTML =
        error;
      });
    } else {
            document.getElementById('status').
            innerHTML = 'unavailable';
        }
  </script>
</body>
</html>
```

2. Create a JavaScript file called `service-worker.js` in the same folder as the `index.html` file with the following code:

```javascript
self.addEventListener('fetch', function(event) {
  console.log('Handling fetch event for',
  event.request.url);
  var requestUrl = new URL(event.request.url);

  if (requestUrl.pathname === '/urlshortener/v1/url' &&
      event.request.headers.has('X-Mock-Response')) {

    var response = {
      body: {
        kind: 'urlshortener#url',
        id: 'http://goo.gl/IKyjuU',
        longUrl: 'https://slightlyoff.github.io/
        ServiceWorker/spec/service_worker/index.html'
      },
      init: {
        status: 200,
        statusText: 'OK',
        headers: {
          'Content-Type': 'application/json',
          'X-Mock-Response': 'yes'
        }
      }
    };

    var mockResponse = new
    Response(JSON.stringify(response.body),
        response.init);

    console.log('Responding with a mock response body:',
        response.body);
    event.respondWith(mockResponse);
  }
});
```

3. With your two files in place, you can navigate to the GitHub page, `https://username.github.io/service-workers/01/03/index.html`, and you will see the success message in your browser.

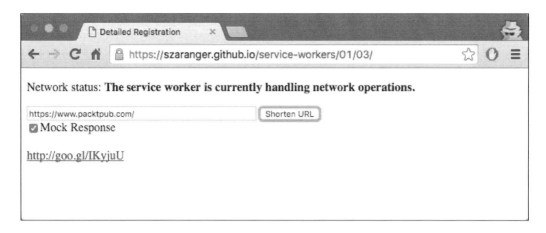

How it works...

After the service worker registers itself successfully, we check to make sure that it is currently handling the network operations:

```
if (navigator.serviceWorker.controller) {
printStatus('The service worker is currently handling
network operations.');
...
}
```

In this case, we are calling the `showRequest()` function to add an event listener to the URL shorten button, and show the `request` block. Otherwise, the whole `request` block will be hidden:

```
function showRequest() {
    document.getElementById('url-shorten-btn')
.addEventListener('click', sendRequest);
    document.getElementById('request').style.display = 'block';
}
```

The `sendRequest()` function builds the HTTP request. It creates a `POST` request with a URL of the Google API for URL shortening:

```
xhr.open('POST',
        'https://www.googleapis.com/urlshortener/v1/url?' +
    'key=[Your API Key]');
```

You will have to obtain an API key for this service to be used. For this, follow these instructions:

1. Visit the Google Developers Console page at `https://console.developers.google.com`.

2. You can either select an existing project or create a new one.

3. Expand **APIs & auth**, in the sidebar on the left.

4. Click **APIs**. Now, in the list of APIs provided, make sure the status is **ON** for the Google URL Shortener API.

5. Finally, in the sidebar on the left-hand side, select **Credentials**.

If the **Mock Response** is checked, set the request header `X-Mock-Response` to `yes`:

```
if (document.getElementById('mock-checkbox').checked) {
    xhr.setRequestHeader('X-Mock-Response', 'yes');
  }
```

Now add an event listener to the load event and pass in a callback to assign the response data to the link displaying the result:

```
xhr.addEventListener('load', function() {
var response = JSON.parse(xhr.response);
var el = document.getElementById('short-url');

   el.href = response.id;
   el.innerHTML = response.id;
});
```

At the end of the `sendRequest` function, we are sending the original URL as well as the `request` object we built as a request:

```
request = {
        longUrl: document.getElementById('long-url').value
      };
xhr.send(JSON.stringify(request));
```

In the `service-worker.js` file, we are adding an event listener for the fetch event. We check that the request URL path has the `urlshortner` in it and the request header has `X-Mock-Response`:

```
if (requestUrl.pathname === '/urlshortener/v1/url' &&
   event.request.headers.has('X-Mock-Response')) {
...
   }
```

We build a mock response object with a body, status, and the headers:

```
var response = {
    body: {
      kind: 'urlshortener#url',
      id: 'https://goo.gl/KqR3lJ',
      longUrl: 'https://www.packtpub.com/books/info/packt/about'
    },
    init: {
      status: 200,
      statusText: 'OK',
      headers: {
        'Content-Type': 'application/json',
        'X-Mock-Response': 'yes'
      }
    }
};
```

Finally, we create a response with the mock response:

```
var mockResponse = new Response(
JSON.stringify(response.body), response.init);

console.log('Mock Response: ', response.body);
event.respondWith(mockResponse);
```

Handling request timeouts

Long-running requests can be the result of connectivity issues. Service workers are an ideal solution for overcoming these problems. Let's look at how we can implement a solution with service workers to handle request timeouts.

Getting ready

To get started with service workers, you will need to have the service worker experiment feature turned on in your browser settings. If you have not done this yet, refer to the previous recipe: *Setting up service workers*. Service workers only run across HTTPS. To find out how to set up a development environment to support this feature, refer to the following recipes: *Setting up GitHub pages for SSL*, *Setting up SSL for Windows*, and *Setting up SSL for Mac*.

How to do it...

Follow these instructions to set up your file structure:

1. First, we need to create an `index.html` file as follows:

```html
<!DOCTYPE html>
<html lang="en">
<head>
  <meta charset="UTF-8">
  <title>Request Timeouts</title>
</head>
<body>
  <p>Registration status: <strong id="status"></strong></p>

  <script>
    if ('serviceWorker' in navigator) {
      navigator.serviceWorker.register(
        'service-worker.js',
        { scope: './' }

      ).then(function(serviceWorker) {
        document.getElementById('status').innerHTML =
        'successful';
});
    } else {
      document.getElementById('status').innerHTML =
      'unavailable';
    }
  </script>
  <script src="https://code.jquery.com/jquery-
  2.2.0.js"></script>
</body>
</html>
```

2. Create a JavaScript file called `service-worker.js` in the same folder as the `index.html` file with the following code:

```javascript
function timeout(delay) {
    return new Promise(function(resolve, reject) {
        setTimeout(function() {
            resolve(new Response('', {
                status: 408,
                statusText: 'Request timed out.'
            }));
```

```
        }, delay);
    });
}

self.addEventListener('install', function(event) {
    self.skipWaiting();
});

self.addEventListener('activate', function(event) {
    if (self.clients && clients.claim) {
        clients.claim();
    }
});

self.addEventListener('fetch', function(event) {
    if (/\.js$/.test(event.request.url)) {
        event.respondWith(Promise.race([timeout(400),
        fetch(event.request.url)]));
    } else {
        event.respondWith(fetch(event.request));
    }
});
```

3. With your two files in place, navigate to `index.html` and open the DevTools. You will see the time out error logged on the console.

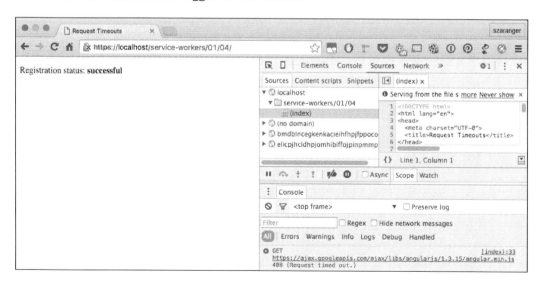

How it works...

In our `index.html` file, we're fetching a large uncompressed jQuery library:

```
<script src="https://code.jquery.com/jquery-2.2.0.js"></script>
```

In our `service-worker.js` file, the event listener of the install event is calling the `skipWaiting()` method, which forces the waiting service worker to become the active service worker:

```
self.addEventListener('install', function(event) {
    self.skipWaiting();
});
```

The `skipWaiting()` method is used inside the active event handler, which in turn uses `Clients.claim()` to ensure that updates to the underlying service worker take effect immediately, for both the current client and all other active clients:

```
self.addEventListener('activate', function(event) {
    if (self.clients && clients.claim) {
        clients.claim();
    }
});
```

In event listener for fetch, we pass in a `Promise.race()` function where the first iterable, which is `timeout(400)`, gets resolved first:

```
self.addEventListener('fetch', function(event) {
  if (/\.js$/.test(event.request.url)) {
    event.respondWith(Promise.race([timeout(400),
    fetch(event.request.url)]));
  } else {
    event.respondWith(fetch(event.request));
  }
});
```

We will elaborate on the `Promise.race()` function soon. The `timeout()` function returns a promise with 408, which is the code for the request timed out status.

There's more...

The `Promise.race()` method returns a promise that resolves, or rejects, as soon as one of the promises in the iterable resolves or rejects, with the value or reason from that promise:

```
var p1 = new Promise(function(resolve, reject) {
    setTimeout(resolve, 400, "one");
});
var p2 = new Promise(function(resolve, reject) {
    setTimeout(reject, 100, "two");
});

Promise.race([p1, p2]).then(function(value) {
  // Not called
}, function(reason) {
  console.log(reason); // "two"
  // p2 is faster, so it rejects
});
```

As you can see, `two` is faster, so the result is `reject`.

2
Working with Resource Files

In this chapter, we will cover the following topics:

- ▶ Displaying a custom offline page
- ▶ Loading images offline
- ▶ Loading CSS offline
- ▶ Loading fonts offline
- ▶ Implementing multiple fetch handlers
- ▶ Fetching remote resources

Introduction

You might have encountered, from time to time, having broken images appear on certain websites. This could be because of a number of reasons: the image might not have existed, it might not have been named properly, or the file path in the code might have been incorrect. Whatever the reason it might be, it could impact your website, and could lead the user to think that your website is broken.

Images are not the only resources that are essential to your website. **Cascading style sheets** (**CSS**), JavaScript files, and font files are also necessary to make your website appear functional. In this chapter, we are going to look at how to load these resources offline.

Before we start working on loading resources offline, let's find out how we can notify the user that the network is unavailable.

Displaying a custom offline page

Let's revisit the scenario from the first chapter where you are on a train, traveling home from work, and you are reading an important news article on the web using your mobile device. At the same moment that you click on a link to view more details, the train suddenly disappears into a tunnel. You've just lost connectivity, and are presented with the **Unable to connect to the Internet** message. Well, you will not doubt be less annoyed if you can still play the dinosaur game by hitting the spacebar on your desktop/laptop, or by tapping on your phone, but this can be an area where you can significantly enhance a client's user experience by using a service worker. One of the great features of service workers is that they allow you to intercept network requests and decide how you want to respond:

In this recipe, we are going to use a service worker to check whether a user has connectivity, and respond with a really simple offline page if they aren't connected.

Getting ready

To get started with service workers, you will need to have the service worker experiment feature turned on in your browser settings. If you have not done this yet, refer to the *Setting up service workers* recipe of *Chapter 1, Learning Service Worker Basics*. Service workers only run across HTTPS. To find out how to set up a development environment to support this feature, refer to the following recipes of *Chapter 1, Learning Service Worker Basics*: *Setting up GitHub pages for SSL*, *Setting up SSL for Windows*, and *Setting up SSL for Mac*.

How to do it...

Follow these instructions to set up your file structure:

1. First, we must create an `index.html` file as follows:

```html
<!DOCTYPE html>
<html lang="en">
<head>
  <meta charset="UTF-8">
  <title>Custom Offline Page</title>
</head>
<body>
  <p>Registration status: <strong id="status"></strong></p>

  <script>
    var scope = {
      scope: './'
    };

    if ('serviceWorker' in navigator) {
      navigator.serviceWorker.register('service-worker.js',
      scope)
      .then(
        function(serviceWorker) {
        document.getElementById('status').innerHTML =
        'successful';
      }).catch(function(error) {
        document.getElementById('status').innerHTML =
        error;
      });
    } else {
        document.getElementById('status').innerHTML =
        'unavailable';
      }
  </script>
</body>
</html>
```

2. Create a JavaScript file called `service-worker.js` in the same folder as the `index.html` file, with the following code:

```javascript
'use strict';

var version = 1;
var currentCache = {
  offline: 'offline-cache' + version
};

var offlineUrl = 'offline.html';

self.addEventListener('install', function(event) {
  event.waitUntil(
    caches.open(currentCache.offline).then(function(cache)
    {
      return cache.addAll([
        offlineUrl
      ]);
    })
  );
});

self.addEventListener('fetch', function(event) {
  var request = event.request,
    isRequestMethodGET = request.method === 'GET';

  if (request.mode === 'navigate' || isRequestMethodGET) {
    event.respondWith(
      fetch(createRequestWithCacheBusting(request.url)).
      catch(function(error) {
        console.log('OFFLINE: Returning offline page.',
        error);
        return caches.match(offlineUrl);
      })
    );
  } else {
    event.respondWith(caches.match(request)
        .then(function (response) {
        return response || fetch(request);
      })
    );
  }
});
function createRequestWithCacheBusting(url) {
  var request,
    cacheBustingUrl;

  request = new Request(url,
    {cache: 'reload'}
```

```
  );

  if ('cache' in request) {
    return request;
  }

  cacheBustingUrl = new URL(url, self.location.href);
  cacheBustingUrl.search += (cacheBustingUrl.search ? '&' :
  '') + 'cachebust=' + Date.now();

  return new Request(cacheBustingUrl);
}
```

3. Create a second HTML file called `offline.html` file as follows:

```html
<!DOCTYPE html>
<html>
 <head>
  <meta charset="UTF-8">
  <title>Offline</title>
  <style>
    #container {
      text-align: center;
      margin-top: 40px;
    }
    #container img {
      width: 80px;
      height: 80px;
    }
  </style>
 </head>
 <body>
   <div id="container">
     <svg xmlns="http://www.w3.org/2000/svg" width="25"
     height="25" viewBox="0 0 25 25">
       <path d="M16 0l-3 9h9l-1.866 2h-14.4L16 0zm2.267
       13h-14.4L2 15h9l-3 9 10.267-11z" fill="#04b8b8"/>
     </svg>
     <p>Whoops, something went wrong...!</p>
     <p>Your internet connection is not working.</p>
     <p>Please check your internet connection and try
     again.</p>
   <div>
   </body>
</html>
```

4. Open up a browser and go to `index.html`. You will see the **Registration status: successful** message:

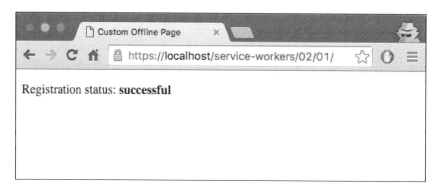

5. Now open up DevTools (*Cmd + Alt + I* or *F12*), go to the **Network** tab, click on the dropdown displaying **No throttling**, and select **Offline**:

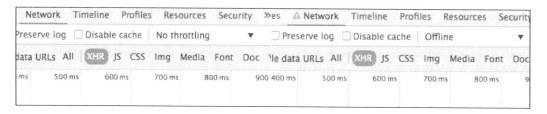

6. Now refresh your browser, and you will see the offline message and the following image:

How it works...

When the registration is successful, we are instructing the service worker to intercept a request and provide resources from the cached content using the fetch event, as illustrated in the following diagram:

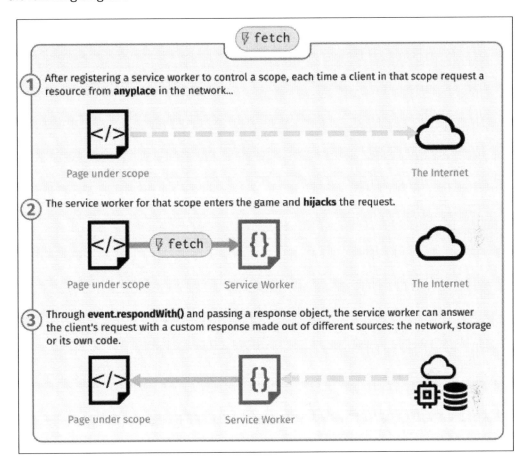

Inside the `index.html` file, when the registration is successful, we inspect the state of the registration and print it to the browser. Otherwise, we are printing the error message returned by the service worker:

```
navigator.serviceWorker.register(
    'service-worker.js',
    { scope: './' }
).then(function(serviceWorker) {
    document.getElementById('status').innerHTML =
        'successful';
```

```
      }).catch(function(error) {
         document.getElementById('status').innerHTML = error;
      });
```

The service worker script file will intercept network requests, check for connectivity, and provide the content to the user.

We start off by adding our offline page to the cache when we install the service worker. In the first few lines, we are specifying the cache version and the URL for the offline page. If we had different versions of our cache, you would simply update this version number, so a new version of the file will take effect. We call this **cache busting**:

```
var version = 1;
var currentCache = {
  offline: 'offline-cache' + version
};
```

We add an event listener to the install event and inside the callback, we make a request for this offline page and its resources; when we have a successful response, it gets added to the cache:

```
self.addEventListener('install', function(event) {
  event.waitUntil(
    caches.open(currentCache.offline)
    .then(function(cache) {
        return cache.addAll([
          offlineUrl
        ]);
    })
  );
});
```

Now that the offline page is stored in the cache, we can retrieve it whenever we need to. In the same service worker, we need to add the logic to return the offline page if we have no connectivity:

```
self.addEventListener('fetch', function(event) {
  var request = event.request,
    isRequestMethodGET = request.method === 'GET';

  if (request.mode === 'navigate' || isRequestMethodGET) {
    event.respondWith(
      fetch(createRequestWithCacheBusting(request.url)).
      catch(function(error) {
        console.log('OFFLINE: Returning offline page.', error);
```

```
      return caches.match(offlineUrl);
    })
  );
} else {
  event.respondWith(caches.match(request)
    .then(function (response) {
    return response || fetch(request);
  })
);
}
});
```

In the preceding listing, we are listening out for the fetch event, and if we detect that the user is trying to navigate to another page, and there is an error while doing so, we simply return the offline page from the cache. And there you go, we have our offline page working.

There's more...

The `waitUntil` event extends the lifetime of the install event, until all the caches are populated. In other words, it delays treating the installing worker as installed, until all the resources we specify are cached and the passed promise resolves successfully.

We saw an HTML and an image file get cached, and then being retrieved when our website is offline. We can cache other resources as well, including CSS and JavaScript files:

```
caches.open(currentCache.offline)
.then(function(cache) {
    return cache.addAll([
        'offline.html',
        '/assets/css/style.css',
        '/assets/js/index.js'
    ]);
  })
);
```

See also

- ▶ The *Registering a service worker in detail* recipe of *Chapter 1, Learning Service Worker Basics*
- ▶ The *Creating mock responses* recipe of *Chapter 1, Learning Service Worker Basics*

Loading images offline

Images are a resource that almost all websites in the world today use. Just like your HTML, CSS, and JavaScript, you can cache images to be viewed offline with service workers. In this chapter, we are going to look at how to load images offline, as well as handling responsive images.

Getting ready

To get started with service workers, you will need to have the service worker experiment feature turned on in your browser settings. If you have not done this yet, refer to the *Setting up service workers* recipe of *Chapter 1, Learning Service Worker Basics*. Service workers only run across HTTPS. To find out how to set up a development environment to support this feature, refer to the following recipes of *Chapter 1, Learning Service Worker Basics*: *Setting up GitHub pages for SSL*, *Setting up SSL for Windows*, and *Setting up SSL for Mac*.

How to do it...

Follow these instructions to set up your file structure:

1. First, we must create an `index.html` file as follows:

```html
<!DOCTYPE html>
<html lang="en">
<head>
  <meta charset="UTF-8">
  <title>Offline Images</title>
</head>
<body>
  <main>
    <p>Registration status: <strong
    id="status"></strong></p>
    <img src="packt-logo.png" alt="logo">
    <main>
    <script src="index.js"></script>
</body>
</html>
```

2. Now we have to create a JavaScript file `service-worker.js`, in the same folder as the `index.html` file, with the following code:

```javascript
'use strict';

var version = 1;
```

```
var cacheName = 'static-' + version;

self.addEventListener('install', installHandler);
self.addEventListener('fetch', fetchHandler);

function installHandler(event) {
    event.waitUntil(
        caches.open(cacheName).then(function(cache) {
            return cache.addAll([
                'index.html',
                'packt-logo.png'
            ]);
        })
    );
}

event.respondWith(
  fetch(event.request).catch(function() {
    return caches.match(event.request);
  })
);
```

3. Create a JavaScript file called `index.js`, in the same folder as the `index.html` file, with the following code:

```
'use strict';

var scope = {
  scope: './'
};

if ('serviceWorker' in navigator) {
  navigator.serviceWorker.register('service-worker.js',
  scope
  ).then( function(serviceWorker) {
    printStatus('successful');
  }).catch(function(error) {
    printStatus(error);
  });
} else {
  printStatus('unavailable');
}

function printStatus(status) {
  document.getElementById('status').innerHTML = status;
}
```

4. Download an image file and save it in the same folder as the `index.html` file. In this example, I am calling it `packt-logo.png`.

5. Open up a browser and go to the `index.html` file:

6. Open up Chrome Developer Tools (*Cmd + Alt + I* or *F12*), select the **Network** tab, and click **Offline**:

7. Refresh the page by pressing *Cmd + R* or *F5*, and you will see the image looks the same as it did online.

How it works...

In the `index.html` file, we are linking the image we have downloaded inside an `img` tag:

```
<body>
  <p>Registration status: <strong id="status"></strong></p>
  <img src="packt-logo.png" alt="logo">
  <script src="index.js"></script>
</body>
```

In the service worker script file, we add our offline page to the cache when we install the service worker. In the first few lines, we specify the cache version and the URL for the offline page:

```
var version = 1;
var cacheName = 'static-' + version;
```

The event listener for the install event calls the `waitUntil` function, where we cache `index.html` and the font file, in our case, `webfont-serif.woff`. The `cache.addAll` function takes an array of files to be cached:

```
self.addEventListener('install', function(event) {
    event.waitUntil(
        caches.open(cacheName).then(function(cache) {
            return cache.addAll([
                'index.html',
                'packt-logo.png'
            ]);
        })
    );
});
```

When we reload the page, after it is set to go offline, the fetch event gets fired, retrieves those two files from the cache, and sends them along with the response:

```
self.addEventListener('fetch', function(event) {
    event.respondWith(caches.match(event.request));
});
```

Now, the page will be displayed as it was online.

There's more...

If we were to develop our website following a mobile-first strategy, having responsive images would greatly benefit it. Let's look at how we can achieve this.

Handling responsive images

There are a number of ways to enable the responsive behavior for images. One of the older methods (not recommended) is by simply scripting, but this leads to a couple of problems. First, if a script determines which image to download, but the script itself is loaded after the images specified in the HTML have been downloaded, you may potentially end up with two downloaded images. Second, if you don't specify any image in HTML, and want to load only the image defined by the script, you'll end up with no image at all for browsers that have scripting disabled.

Hence, we need a better way to deal with responsive images. And thankfully, there is one! The recommended way is to use:

- `srcset`
- `sizes`
- `picture`

The srcset attribute

Before we explore how `srcset` is actually used, let's understand a few terms.

Device-pixel ratio

The device-pixel ratio is the number of device pixels per CSS pixel. Two key conditions contribute to the device-pixel ratio:

- **Pixel density of the device (number of physical pixels per inch)**: A high resolution device will have a higher pixel density and hence, for the same zoom level, it will have a high device-pixel ratio compared to a lower resolution device. For example: a high-end Lumia 950 phone will have a higher resolution than a budget Lumia 630 phone, and therefore it will have a higher device-pixel ratio for the same zoom level.

- **Zoom level of the browser**: For the same device, a higher zoom level means a higher number of device pixels per CSS pixel, and hence a higher device-pixel ratio. For example, consider this figure:

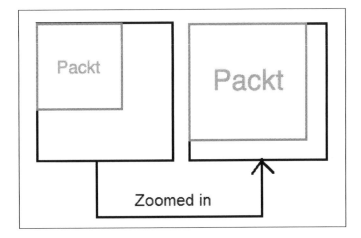

When you zoom in on your browser (*Ctrl* + +), the number of CSS pixels for your `div` remains the same, but the number of device pixels it occupies increases. So, you have a higher number of device pixels per CSS pixel.

When you want to display separate images (or usually, a separate asset of the same image) based on the device-pixel ratio, you'd go with a basic `srcset` implementation:

```
<img src="image-src.png" srcset="image-src.png 1x, image-2x.png 2x" />
```

The `x` descriptor in the `srcset` attribute is used to define the device-pixel ratio:

- For a device-pixel ratio of 1, the `image-src.png` image will be used.
- For a device-pixel ratio of 2, the `image-2x.png` image will be used.

The `src` attribute is used as a fallback for browsers that do not yet support `srcset` implementation.

This works well. Using the `x` descriptor, you'll always get the same image on devices with a similar device-pixel ratio—even if this means that you get the same image on a 13.5-inch laptop, and a 5-inch mobile phone, which both have the same device-pixel ratio.

The sizes attribute

The actual implementation where you'd want a different-sized image (different height and width) on different screen sizes is accomplished by using the `sizes` attribute along with the `w` descriptor of the `srcset` attribute.

Say you want the image to be viewed in half of the viewport width. You'll type:

```
<img src="image-src.png" sizes="50vw"
srcset="image-src.png 1x, image-2x.png 2x 400w">
```

The picture element

As we saw in the previous section, the `picture` element is used when you want to show a different image depending on the rendered size of the image. The `picture` element is a container, which contains other elements that control the image to be downloaded:

```
<picture>
  <img src="image-src.png" sizes="50vw"srcset="image-src.png 1x,
  image-2x.png 2x 400w">
</picture>
```

At runtime, the `srcset` attribute or the `<picture>` element selects the most appropriate image asset and performs a network request.

If you want to cache an image during the install step for the service worker, you have a few options:

▶ Installing a single low-resolution version of the image

▶ Installing a single high-resolution version of the image

It is ideal to limit the amount to two or three images in order to preserve memory.

To improve the load time, you may decide to go for the low resolution version at the time of installation, and you would try to retrieve higher resolution images from the network when the page is loaded; however, in the case that the high-resolution images fail, you would think you can easily fall back to the low resolution version, but there is one issue.

Let's assume we have two images:

Display density	Width	Height
1x	400	400
2x	800	800

Here is the markup for an `srcset` image:

```
<img src="image-src.png" srcset="image-src.png 1x, image-2x.png
2x" />
```

On a screen with a `2x` display, the browser could opt to download `image-2x.png`, if we are offline, then we could catch this request and return the `image-src.png` image instead if the image is cached, the browser may expect an image that considers the extra pixels on a `2x` screen, therefore the image will appear as 200 x 200 pixels instead of 400 x 400 pixels. The only fix is to set a fixed width and height on the image:

```
<img src="image-src.png" srcset="image-src.png 1x, image-2x.png
2x"
style="width:400px; height: 400px;" />
```

We can take the same approach to `srcset`.

No width or height set:

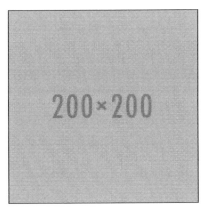

Height and width set:

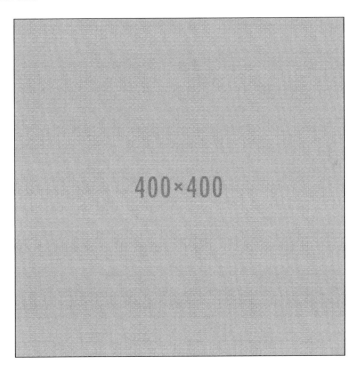

If you want to unregister the service worker, you can head to the Developer Toolbar in Chrome, and click the **Unregister** button in the **Service Workers** section, as shown in the following screenshot:

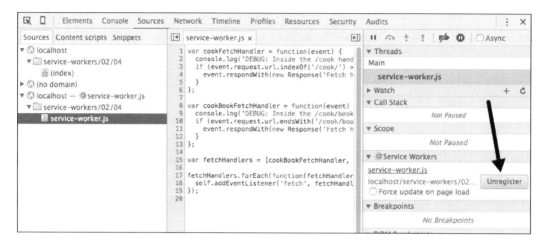

If you want to find out the resources stored in the caches, you can do so by opening Developer Tools and looking at the **Resources** tab:

If you are using Firefox Nightly, you can view the caches by opening up Developer Tools and looking at the Storage Inspector:

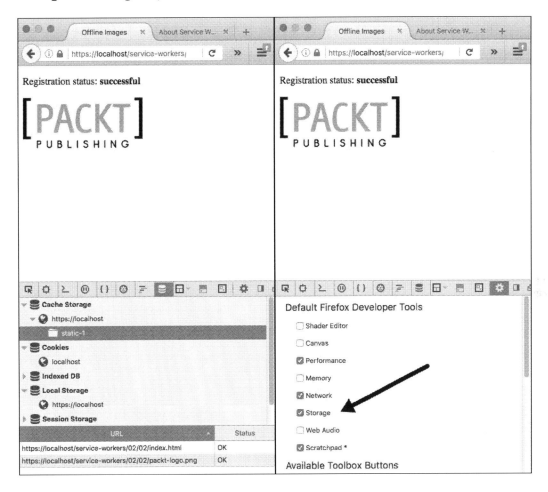

See also

▸ The *Registering a service worker in detail* recipe in *Chapter 1, Learning Service Worker Basics*

▸ The *Creating mock responses* recipe in *Chapter 1, Learning Service Worker Basics*

Loading CSS offline

CSS is essential in structuring your website and making it look functional. Because of this, if your website goes offline and the CSS is not available in the cache, your website will look broken. In order to achieve this, we cache CSS with service workers, and deliver those CSS files as external resources. In this recipe, we are going to look at how to load CSS offline.

Getting ready

To get started with service workers, you will need to have the service worker experiment feature turned on in your browser settings. If you have not done this yet, refer to the *Setting up service workers* recipe of *Chapter 1, Learning Service Worker Basics*. Service workers only run across HTTPS. To find out how to set up a development environment to support this feature, refer to the following recipes of *Chapter 1, Learning Service Worker Basics*: *Setting up GitHub pages for SSL, Setting up SSL for Windows*, and *Setting up SSL for Mac*.

How to do it...

Follow these instructions to set up your file structure:

1. First, we must create an `index.html` file as follows:

```
<!DOCTYPE html>
<html lang="en">
<head>
  <meta charset="UTF-8">
  <title>Offline CSS</title>
  <link rel="stylesheet" href="style-2.css">
  <link rel="stylesheet" href="style-1.css">
</head>
<body>
  <p>Registration status: <strong id="status"></strong></p>

  <script>
      var scope = {
      scope: './'
    };

    if ('serviceWorker' in navigator) {
      navigator.serviceWorker.register('service-worker.js',
      scope)
      .then(
        function(serviceWorker) {
        printStatus('successful');
```

```
        }).catch(function(error) {
            printStatus(error);
        });
    } else {
        printStatus('unavailable');
    }

    function printStatus(status) {
        document.getElementById('status').innerHTML = status;
    }   </script>
</body>
</html>
```

2. Create a JavaScript file called `service-worker.js`, in the same folder as the `index.html` file, with the following code:

```
var version = 1;
var cacheName = 'static-' + version;

self.addEventListener('install', installHandler);
self.addEventListener('fetch', fetchHandler);

function installHandler(event) {
    event.waitUntil(
        caches.open(cacheName).then(function(cache) {
            return cache.addAll([
                'index.html',
                'style-2.css'
            ]);
        })
    );
}

function fetchHandler(event) {
    if (/index/.test(event.request.url) || /style-
    2/.test(event.request.url)) {
        event.respondWith(caches.match(event.request));
    }
}
```

3. Create a CSS file called `style-1.css`, in the same folder as the `index.html` file, with the following code:

```
body {
    background-color: lightgreen;
}
```

4. Create another CSS file called `style-2.css`, in the same folder as the `index.html` file, with the following code:

```
body {
    background-color: red;
}
```

5. Open up a browser and go to the `index.html` file. You will see that the background color is green:

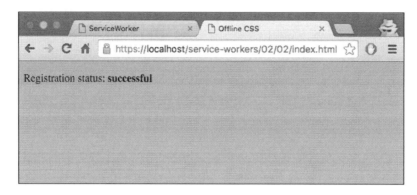

6. Now open up the Developer Tools (*Cmd + Shift + I* or *F12*) and change the **Network** tab to **Offline** as shown in the following screenshot:

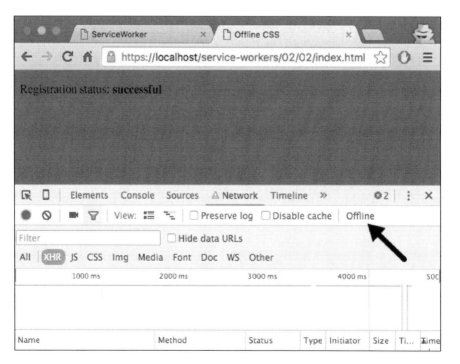

7. The color of the background is now red.

How it works...

In the header section of the `index.html` file, we are linking two CSS files:

```
<head>
  <meta charset="UTF-8">
  <title>Offline CSS</title>
  <link rel="stylesheet" href="style-2.css">
  <link rel="stylesheet" href="style-1.css">
</head>
```

In our styles sheets, we are referencing the same CSS property of body.

Because of the order we are calling the CSS files, the last selector takes effect on the online page, in our case, this is the `body` selector of `style-1.css`:

```
body {
    background-color: lightgreen;
}
```

In the `service-worker.js` file, we add `index.html` and the `style-2.css` file to the cache when we install the service worker. In the first few lines, we specify the cache version and the URL for the offline page:

```
var version = 1;
var cacheName = 'static-' + version;
```

The event listener for the install event calls the `waitUntil` function, where we cache `index.html`, and the CSS file. The `cache.addAll` function takes an array of files to be cached:

```
function installHandler(event) {
    event.waitUntil(
        caches.open(cacheName).then(function(cache) {
            return cache.addAll([
                'index.html',
                'style-2.css'
            ]);
        })
    );
}
```

When we reload the page, after it is set to go offline, the fetch event gets fired, retrieves those two files from the cache, and sends them along with the response:

```
self.addEventListener('fetch', function(event) {
    event.respondWith(caches.match(event.request));
});
```

Now, when we refresh the page, the background will change to red, as the CSS file we saved in the cache will be applied to the page this time.

Loading fonts offline

If your website uses external fonts, such as open source web fonts, you could cache them to be viewed offline with service workers. In this chapter, we are going to look at how to load fonts offline.

Getting ready

To get started with service workers, you will need to have the service worker experiment feature turned on in your browser settings. If you have not done this yet, refer to the *Setting up service workers* recipe of *Chapter 1, Learning Service Worker Basics*. Service workers only run across HTTPS. To find out how to set up a development environment to support this feature, refer to the following recipes of *Chapter 1, Learning Service Worker Basics*: *Setting up GitHub pages for SSL*, *Setting up SSL for Windows*, and *Setting up SSL for Mac*.

How to do it...

Follow these instructions to set up your file structure:

1. First, we must create an `index.html` file as follows:

    ```
    <!DOCTYPE html>
    <html lang="en">
    <head>
      <meta charset="UTF-8">
      <title>Offline Fonts</title>
      <style>
        @font-face{
          font-family: 'MyWebFont';
          src: url('webfont-serif.woff') format('woff');
        }
        p { font-family: 'MyWebFont', Arial, sans-serif; }
      </style>
    ```

```
</head>
<body>
   <p>Registration status: <strong id="status"></strong></p>

   <script>
      var scope = {
      scope: './'
   };

   if ('serviceWorker' in navigator) {
     navigator.serviceWorker.register('service-worker.js',
     scope)
     .then(
       function(serviceWorker) {
       printStatus('successful');
     }).catch(function(error) {
       printStatus(error);
     });
   } else {
     printStatus('unavailable');
   }

   function printStatus(status) {
     document.getElementById('status').innerHTML = status;
   }  </script>
</body>
</html>
```

2. Create a JavaScript file called `service-worker.js`, in the same folder as the `index.html` file, with the following code:

```
'use strict';

var version = 1;
var cacheName = 'static-' + version;

self.addEventListener('install', installHandler);
self.addEventListener('fetch', fetchHandler);

function installHandler(event) {
    event.waitUntil(
        caches.open(cacheName).then(function(cache) {
            return cache.addAll([
```

```
                  'index.html',
                  'webfont-serif.woff'
              ]);
          })
      );
  }


  function fetchHandler(event) {
      event.respondWith(caches.match(event.request));
  }
```

3. Download a web font from `https://www.google.com/fonts` and save it in the same folder as the `index.html` file. If you are not quite sure how to do this, please look at the following *There's more...* section.

4. Open up the browser and go to the `index.html` file:

5. Open up Chrome Developer Tools (*Cmd + Alt + I* or *Fb12*), select the **Network** tab, and click **Offline**:

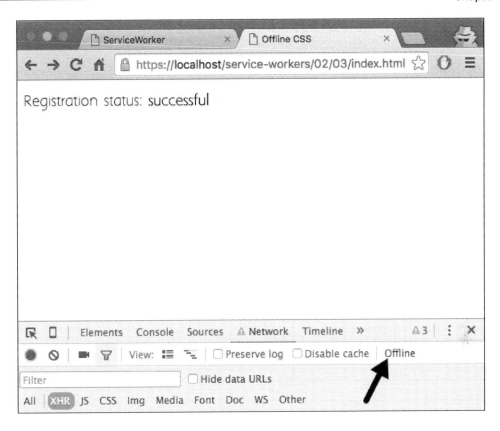

6. Refresh the page by pressing *Cmd + R* or *F5*, and you will see the font looks the same as it did online.

How it works...

In the header section of the `index.html` file, we link the font file we have downloaded inside a `style` tag:

```
<style>
  @font-face{
    font-family: 'MyWebFont';
    src: url('webfont-serif.woff') format('woff');
  }

  p { font-family: 'MyWebFont', Arial, sans-serif; }
</style>
```

The `@font-face` declaration will specify a font named `myWebFont` and specify the URL where it can be found. In our case, it is in the same directory as the `index.html` file. Then we reference the font inside the paragraph declaration as the `font-family` attribute:

```
p { font-family: 'MyWebFont', Arial, sans-serif; }
```

In the service worker script file, we add our offline page to the cache when we install the service worker. In the first few lines, we specify the cache version and the URL for the offline page:

```
var version = 1;
var cacheName = 'static-' + version;
```

The event listener for the install event calls the `waitUntil` function, where we cache the `index.html` file and the font file; in our case `webfont-serif.woff`. The `cache.addAll` function takes an array of files to be cached:

```
self.addEventListener('install', function(event) {
    event.waitUntil(
        caches.open(cacheName).then(function(cache) {
            return cache.addAll([
                'index.html',
                'webfont-serif.woff'
            ]);
        })
    );
});
```

When we reload the page, after it is set to go offline, the fetch event gets fired, retrieves those two files from the cache, and sends them along with the response:

```
self.addEventListener('fetch', function(event) {
    event.respondWith(caches.match(event.request));
});
```

Now, the page will be displayed as it was online.

There's more...

In order to find a free font family from Google and download it, please perform the following instructions:

1. Please navigate to `https://www.google.com/fonts`, and search, or browse, the desired font, then add the one you like to your collection by clicking on the blue **Add to Collection** button on the right side of the font:

2. Your collection will show at the bottom of your screen. Once it has, select the **Use this style** checkbox, towards the top-left side of the screen:

3. Now, when you click the arrow on the top right-hand side of the page, it will prompt you with a dialog. You can choose the first option, which downloads the file as a ZIP file:

4. Once you unzip the file, you will find the font you need inside the folder. If you want to unregister a service worker, you can go to `chrome://service-worker-internals` and click the **Unregister** button:

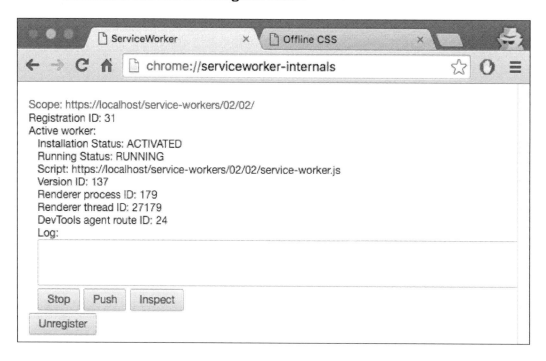

5. In Firefox Nightly, you can go to `about:serviceworkers` and click on the **Unregister** button:

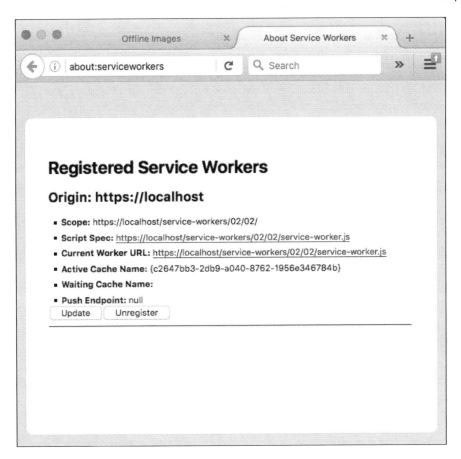

▶ The *Registering a service worker in detail* recipe in *Chapter 1, Learning Service Worker Basics*

▶ The *Creating mock responses* recipe in *Chapter 1, Learning Service Worker Basics*

Implementing multiple fetch handlers

Service workers can handle multiple fetch handlers, each of which intercepts a different type of request. This recipe explains, in detail, how different types of request can be handled by implementing separate fetch handlers.

Getting ready

To get started with service workers, you will need to have the service worker experiment feature turned on in your browser settings. If you have not done this yet, refer to the *Setting up service workers* recipe of *Chapter 1, Learning Service Worker Basics*. Service workers only run across HTTPS. To find out how to set up a development environment to support this feature, refer to the following recipes of *Chapter 1, Learning Service Worker Basics*: *Setting up GitHub pages for SSL, Setting up SSL for Windows*, and *Setting up SSL for Mac*.

How to do it...

Follow these instructions to set up your file structure:

1. First, we need to create an `index.html` file as follows:

```html
<!DOCTYPE html>
<html lang="en">
<head>
  <meta charset="UTF-8">
  <title>Multiple Fetch</title>
</head>
<body>
    <p>Registration status: <strong id="status"></strong></p>

    <script>
      if ('serviceWorker' in navigator) {
        navigator.serviceWorker.register(
          'service-worker.js',
          { scope: './' }
        ).then( function(serviceWorker) {
          document.getElementById('status').innerHTML =
          'successful';
        }).catch(function(error) {
          document.getElementById('status').innerHTML =
          error;
        });
      } else {
        document.getElementById('status').innerHTML =
        'unavailable';
      }
    </script>
</body>
</html>
```

2. Create a JavaScript file called `service-worker.js` in the same folder as the `index.html` file with the following code:

```
var cookFetchHandler = function(event) {
  console.log('DEBUG: Inside the /cook handler.');
  if (event.request.url.indexOf('/cook/') > 0) {
    event.respondWith(new Response('Fetch handler for
    /cook'));
  }
};

var cookBookFetchHandler = function(event) {
  console.log('DEBUG: Inside the /cook/book handler.');
  if (event.request.url.endsWith('/cook/book')) {
    event.respondWith(new Response('Fetch handler for
    /cook/book'));
  }
};

var fetchHandlers = [cookBookFetchHandler, cookFetchHandler];

fetchHandlers.forEach(function(fetchHandler) {
  self.addEventListener('fetch', fetchHandler);
});
```

3. Open up a browser and go to the `index.html` file. You will see the **Registration status: successful** message:

4. Change the URL by adding /cook/ in front as follows:

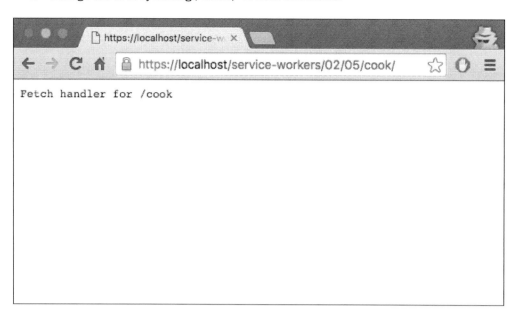

5. Change the URL again by adding /book in front as follows:

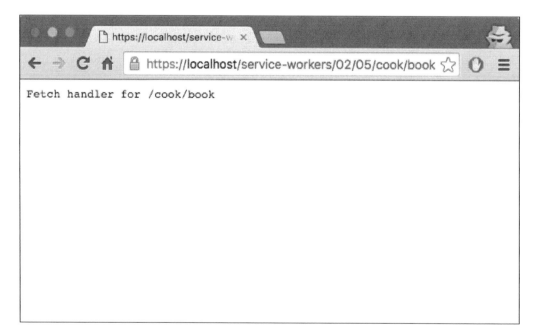

How it works...

When the registration is successful, we inspect the state of the registration, and print it to the browser. Now it's time to trigger the responses by the service worker. In the `service-worker.js` file, there are two registered fetch handlers, `cookFetchHandler` and `cookBookFetchHandler`:

```
var cookFetchHandler = function(event) {
  console.log('DEBUG: Inside the /cook handler.');
  if (event.request.url.indexOf('/cook/') > 0) {
    event.respondWith(new Response('Fetch handler for /cook'));
  }
};

var cookBookFetchHandler = function(event) {
  console.log('DEBUG: Inside the /cook/book handler.');
  if (event.request.url.endsWith('/cook/book')) {
    event.respondWith(new Response('Fetch handler for
    /cook/book'));
  }
};
```

The first handler, `cookFetchHandler`, intercepts requests ending with `/cook` anywhere in the URL, and returns a new response with the wording, `Fetch handler for /cook`.

The second handler, `cookBookFetchHandler`, intercepts requests ending with `/cook/book` anywhere in the URL, and returns a new response with the wording, `Fetch handler for /cook/book`.

Since `cookBookFetchHandler` is registered first, when it intercepts `/cook/book` requests, it will always first have the chance to return a response via `event.respondWith()`.The second handler gets its chance to handle `event.respondWith()` only if the first handler does not call it.

When the fetch event occurs, they are invoked one at a time, in the order they are registered. Any time a handler calls `event.respondWith()`, none of the other registered handlers will be run:

```
var fetchHandlers = [cookBookFetchHandler, cookFetchHandler];

fetchHandlers.forEach(function(fetchHandler) {
  self.addEventListener('fetch', fetchHandler);
});
```

If none of the registered fetch handlers call `event.respondWith()`, the browser takes control and makes a normal HTTP request. This is the normal procedure, when no service workers are involved.

Within each fetch handler, we have to make sure that the logic that determines whether or not to call `event.respondWith()`, is executed synchronously. Simple `if()` statements that check `event.request.url` are fine. Anything asynchronous, such as performing `caches.match()` and then deciding whether or not to call `event.respondWith()` based on the response, will trigger a race condition, and you're likely to see an `event already responded to` error in the console.

If you want to unregister the service worker, you can head to the Developer Toolbar in Chrome and click the **Unregister** button in the **Service Workers** section, as shown in the following screenshot:

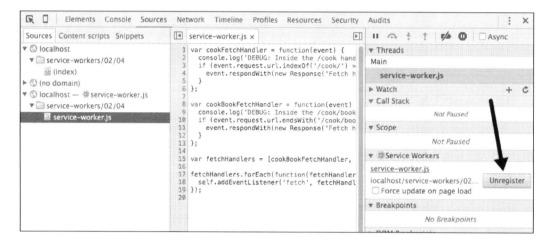

See also

▸ The *Registering a service worker in detail* recipe in *Chapter 1, Learning Service Worker Basics*

▸ The *Creating mock responses* recipe in *Chapter 1, Learning Service Worker Basics*

Fetching remote resources

Fetching remote resources can be done in a few different ways. In this recipe, we are going to look at two standard ways of fetching remote resources, as well as finding out how to use a service worker to act like a proxy middleware.

Getting ready

To get started with service workers, you will need to have the service worker experiment feature turned on in your browser settings. If you have not done this yet, refer to the *Setting up service workers* recipe of *Chapter 1, Learning Service Worker Basics*. Service workers only run across HTTPS. To find out how to set up a development environment to support this feature, refer to the *Setting up GitHub pages for SSL* recipe of *Chapter 1, Learning Service Worker Basics*.

How to do it...

Follow these instructions to set up your file structure:

1. First, we need to create an `index.html` file as follows:

```html
<!DOCTYPE html>
<html lang="en">
  <head>
    <meta charset="UTF-8">
    <title>Fetching Offline Resources</title>
    <style>
      .error {
        color: #FF0000;
      }
      .success {
        color: #00FF00;
      }
    </style>
  </head>
  <body>
    <section>
      <h1>Images</h1>
      <div id="https-acao-image"></div>
      <div id="https-image"></div>
      <div id="http-image"></div>
    </section>

    <section>
      <h1>HTTPS Fetch</h1>
      <div id="https-cors">
        <strong>https-cors</strong>
      </div>
      <div id="https-no-cors">
```

```html
      <strong>https-no-cors</strong>
    </div>
    <div id="https-acao-cors">
      <strong>https-acao-cors</strong>
    </div>
    <div id="https-acao-no-cors">
      <strong>https-acao-no-cors</strong>
    </div>
    <div id="service-https-cors">
      <strong>service-https-cors</strong>
    </div>
    <div id="service-http-cors">
      <strong>service-http-cors</strong>
    </div>
    <div id="service-http-no-cors">
      <strong>service-http-no-cors</strong>
    </div>
  </section>

  <section>
    <h1>HTTP Fetch</h1>
    <div id="http-cors">
      <strong>http-cors</strong>
    </div>
    <div id="http-no-cors">
      <strong>http-no-cors</strong>
    </div>
  </section>

  <script src="index.js"></script>
  </body>
</html>
```

2. Create a JavaScript file called `index.js`, in the same folder as the `index.html` file, with the following code:

```javascript
'use strict';

var protocols = {
'https':
'https://dz13w8afd47il.cloudfront.net/sites/all/themes/
packt_v4/images/packtlib-logo-dark.png',

  'https-acao':
```

```
'https://i942.photobucket.com/albums/ad261/szaranger/Packt/
packt-logo.png',

  'http':
'http://seanamarasinghe.com/
wp-content/uploads/2015/06/icon-128x128.jpg'
};

navigator.serviceWorker.getRegistration()
.then(function(registration) {
  var fetchModes = ['cors', 'no-cors'];

  if (!registration || !navigator.serviceWorker.controller)
  {
    navigator.serviceWorker.register(
    './service-worker.js').then(function() {
        console.log('Service worker registered,
        reloading the page');
        window.location.reload();
    });
  } else {
    console.log('Client is under service worker\s
    control');

    for (var protocol in protocols) {
      if (protocols.hasOwnProperty(protocol)) {
        buildImage(protocol, protocols[protocol]);

        for (var index = 0; index < fetchModes.length;
        index++) {
          var fetchMode = fetchModes[index],
            init = { method: 'GET',
                     mode: fetchMode,
                     cache: 'default' };

          fireRequest(fetchMode, protocol, init)();
        }
      }
    }
  }
});

function buildImage(protocol, url) {
  var element = protocol + '-image',
```

```javascript
      image = document.createElement('img');

    image.src = url;
    document.getElementById(element).appendChild(image);
  }


  function fireRequest(fetchMode, protocol, init) {
    return function() {
      var section = protocol + '-' + fetchMode,
        url = protocols[protocol];

      fetch(url, init).then(function(response) {
        printSuccess(response, url, section);
      }).catch(function(error) {
        printError(error, url, section);
      });

      fetch('./proxy/' + url, init).then(function(response) {
        url = './proxy/' + url;
        printSuccess(response, url, section);
      }).catch(function(error) {
        section = 'service-' + section;

        console.log(section, 'ERROR: ', url, error);
        log(section, 'ERROR: ' + error, 'error');
      });
    };
  }


  function printSuccess(response, url, section) {
    if (response.ok) {
      console.log(section, 'SUCCESS: ', url, response);
      log(section, 'SUCCESS');
    } else {
      console.log(section, 'FAIL:', url, response);
      log(section, 'FAIL: response type: ' + response.type +
                   ', response status: ' +
                   response.status, 'error');
    }
```

```
  }

  function printError(error, url, section) {
    console.log(section, 'ERROR: ', url, error);
    log(section, 'ERROR: ' + error, 'error');
  }

  function log(id, message, type) {
    var sectionElement = document.getElementById(id),
      logElement = document.createElement('p');

    if (type) {
      logElement.classList.add(type);
    }
    logElement.textContent = message;
    sectionElement.appendChild(logElement);
  }
```

3. Create a JavaScript file called `service-worker.js`, in the same folder as the `index.html` file, with the following code:

```
self.onfetch = function(event) {
  if (event.request.url.indexOf('proxy') > -1) {
    var init = { method: 'GET',
                 mode: event.request.mode,
                 cache: 'default' };
    var url = event.request.url.split('proxy/')[1];
    console.log('DEBUG: proxying', url);
    event.respondWith(fetch(url, init));
  } else {
    event.respondWith(fetch(event.request));
  }
};
```

4. Open up a browser and go to the `index.html` file:

How it works...

At the beginning of the `index.js` file, we are testing three different protocols for loading resources:

▸ `https`: HTTP with **Secure Socket Layer** (**SSL**) protocol

▸ `https-acao`: SSL protocol with the **Access-Control-Origin=*** header

▸ `http`: HTTP without SSL

We will use three different URLs, which will be loaded multiple times:

```
var protocols = {
  'https-acao':
    'https://i942.photobucket.com/albums/ad261/szaranger/
    Packt/packt-logo.png',
  'https':
    'https://dz13w8afd47il.cloudfront.net/sites/all/themes/
    packt_v4/images/packtlib-logo-dark.png',
  'http':
    'http://seanamarasinghe.com/wp-content/uploads/2015/06/
    icon-128x128.jpg'
};
```

We also use two different methods for fetching resources, with or without `cors`:

```
var fetchModes = ['cors', 'no-cors'];
```

Next, we check to see whether the service worker is registered:

```
navigator.serviceWorker.register(
'./service-worker.js').then(function() {
    console.log('Service worker registered, reloading the
    page');
    window.location.reload();
  });
```

If that is not the case, then we register it and reload the page to make sure the client is under the service worker's control:

```
for (var protocol in protocols) {
    if (protocols.hasOwnProperty(protocol)) {
      buildImage(protocol, protocols[protocol]);

      for (var i = 0; i < fetchModes.length; i++) {
        var fetchMode = fetchModes[i],
          init = {
            method: 'GET',
```

```
            mode: fetchMode,
            cache: 'default'
        };

        fireRequest(fetchMode, protocol, init)();
    }
  }
}
```

The `for` loops go through the provided `protocols` array, make requests for each protocol, build a DOM image element with each URL, and go through each mode of the `fetchModes` array.

The `init` object contains any custom settings that you want to apply to the request:

► `method`: The request method, for example, `GET` and `POST`

► `mode`: The mode you want to use for the request, for example, `cors`, `no-cors`, or `same-origin`

► `cache`: The cache mode you want to use for the request: `default`, `no-store`, `reload`, `no-cache`, `force-cache`, or `only-if-cached`

The `buildImage` function takes two arguments: `protocol` and `url`. It creates an image element on the fly and attaches the URL as the source of that image. Then it goes on to add that image to the DOM tree, where the ID is one of `https-acao-image`, `https-image`, or `http-image`. JavaScript has no control over the URL handling at this point; the browser handles the URLs:

```
function buildImage(protocol, url) {
    var element = protocol + '-image',
        image = document.createElement('img');

    image.src = url;
    document.getElementById(element).appendChild(image);
}
```

Images will be rendered for HTTPS requests only, as service workers only support connections over SSL:

The broken image is the one requested over standard HTTP, which fails to respond with the requested image.

Other requests over HTTP also fail to deliver, resulting in errors:

HTTP Fetch

http-cors

ERROR: TypeError: Failed to fetch

http-no-cors

ERROR: TypeError: Failed to fetch

The requests over SSL, with the **Access-Control-Origin=*** header (**Access Control Allow Origin**), will return results successfully:

---

https-acao-cors

SUCCESS

SUCCESS

By default, fetching a resource from a third-party URL will fail if it doesn't support CORS. You can add a non-CORS option to the request to overcome this, although this will cause an *opaque* response, which means you won't be able to tell whether the response was successful or not:

---

https-acao-no-cors

FAIL: response type: opaque, response status: 0

SUCCESS

The `fireRequest` function takes three arguments, `fetchMode`, `protocol`, and `init`. This function, in turn returns another function, which we can call a composition. We start with fetching the given resource directly from the remote resource:

```
fetch(url, init).then(function(response) {
    printSuccess(response, url, section);
}).catch(function(error) {
    printError(error, url, section);
});
```

If the fetch was successful, we print it to the console, as well as log it on the webpage. We do the same if the request fails, only we print `error`.

We also attempt to fetch the resource with the service worker's proxy, which the client recognizes as a local resource:

```
fetch('./proxy/' + url, init).then(function(response) {
    url = './proxy/' + url;
    printSuccess(response, url, section);
}).catch(function(error) {
    section = 'service-' + section;

    console.log(section, 'ERROR: ', url, error);
    log(section, 'ERROR: ' + error, 'error');
});
```

The printSuccess and printError functions log responses to the console, as well as the DOM of the web page:

```javascript
function printSuccess(response, url, section) {
  if (response.ok) {
    console.log(section, 'SUCCESS: ', url, response);
    log(section, 'SUCCESS');
  } else {
    console.log(section, 'FAIL:', url, response);
    log(section, 'FAIL: response type: ' + response.type +
                ', response status: ' + response.status,
                'error');
  }
}


function printError(error, url, section) {
  console.log(section, 'ERROR: ', url, error);
  log(section, 'ERROR: ' + error, 'error');
}
```

The helper function log finds the DOM element by the ID, and adds a paragraph element, as well as a class attribute, to depict the type of the message:

```javascript
function log(id, message, type) {
  var type = type || 'success',
    sectionElement = document.getElementById(id),
    logElement = document.createElement('p');

  if (type) {
    logElement.classList.add(type);
  }
  logElement.textContent = message;
  sectionElement.appendChild(logElement);
}
```

In the index.html file, we have style declarations in the head section:

```html
<style>
.error {
    color: #FF0000;
  }
  .success {
    color: #00FF00;
  }
</style>
```

In our `log()` function, we set the undefined type to success, so that it will display the color green when we add it to `classList`. The error type will display red as declared in the previous styles.

Let's move over to our `service-worker.js` file. There we have the `onfetch` event handler, which gets fired whenever a fetch event occurs. Here, we check to see whether the request has a `proxy/` parameter in it. If it does, then it responds with the remaining part of the URL:

```
var url = event.request.url.split('proxy/')[1];
console.log('DEBUG: proxying', url);
event.respondWith(fetch(url, init));
```

Otherwise, the response will perform the request with the full URL:

```
} else {
    event.respondWith(fetch(event.request));
}
```

There's more...

Let's examine the defaults of the `fetch()` function in more detail.

No credentials by default

When you use fetch, by default, requests won't contain credentials such as cookies. If you want credentials, you can call this instead:

```
fetch(url, {
  credentials: 'include'
});
```

This behavior is intentional, and is arguably better than XHR's more complex default behavior of sending credentials if the URL has the same origin, but omitting them otherwise.

Fetch's behavior is more like other CORS requests, such as `<img crossorigin>`, which never sends cookies unless you opt in with `<img crossorigin="use-credentials">`.

Non-CORS fail by default

By default, fetching a resource from a third-party URL will fail if it doesn't support CORS. You can add a non-CORS option to the **Request** function to overcome this, although this will cause an *opaque* response, which means you won't be able to tell whether the response was successful or not:

```
cache.addAll(urlsToPrefetch.map(function(urlToPrefetch) {
  return new Request(urlToPrefetch, { mode: 'no-cors' });
})).then(function() {
  console.log('All resources have been fetched and cached.');
});
```

If you want to unregister the service worker, you can head over to the `chrome://service-worker-internals` page in Chrome and click the **Unregister** button of the relevant service worker, as shown in the following screenshot:

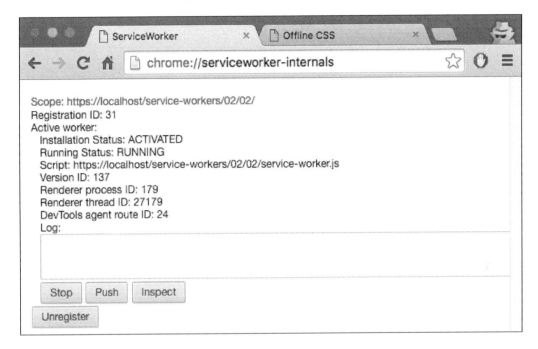

See also

▶ The *Registering a service worker in detail* recipe in *Chapter 1, Learning Service Worker Basics*

▶ The *Creating mock responses* recipe in *Chapter 1, Learning Service Worker Basics*

3

Accessing Offline Content

In this chapter, we will cover the following topics:

- ► Caching critical resources for offline use
- ► Showing cached content first
- ► Implementing a cache and network race
- ► Using window.caches
- ► Implementing stale-while-revalidate

Introduction

You don't need network access for your laptop or smartphone to be useful. Especially in areas where mobile data is expensive, with some proper planning, you can download certain apps that you can sync via free Wi-Fi, and then use them offline elsewhere.

Mobile apps such as Google Maps, FeedMe, and Wikipedia give us offline apps, which can be used anywhere regardless of the Internet. Making our own app offline-compatible is a great way of winning the hearts of our clients.

Let's start this chapter by looking at how to cache critical resources for use offline.

Caching critical resources for offline use

In this recipe, we look at how we can cache a set of critical resources to enable users to go offline and provide the user with the same experience. In the meantime, we will notify the user that they can go offline and continue to use the same features.

Getting ready

To get started with service workers, you will need to have the service worker experiment feature turned on in your browser settings. If you have not done this yet, refer to the first recipe of *Chapter 1, Learning Service Worker Basics*: *Setting up service workers*. Service workers only run across HTTPS. To find out how to set up a development environment to support this feature, refer to the following recipes of *Chapter 1, Learning Service Worker Basics*: *Setting up GitHub pages for SSL, Setting up SSL for Windows*, and *Setting up SSL for Mac*.

How to do it...

Follow these instructions to set up your file structure. Alternatively, you can download the files from the following location:

```
https://github.com/szaranger/szaranger.github.io/tree/master/service-
workers/03/01/
```

1. First, we must create an `index.html` file as follows:

```html
<!DOCTYPE html>
<html lang="en">
<head>
  <meta charset="UTF-8">
  <title>Caching Critical Resources</title>
  <link rel="stylesheet" href="style.css">
</head>
<body>
  <section id="registration-status">
    <p>Registration status: <strong
    id="status"></strong></p>
    <input type="button" id="resetButton" value="Reset" />
  </section>

  <main>
    <section>
    <h1>Brand Game</h1>
    <p>Attempts: <span id="attempts">0</span></p>
    <select id="choice">
```

```
    <option value="0">Apple</option>
    <option value="1">Google</option>
    <option value="2">Adobe</option>
    <option value="3">Facebook</option>
    <option value="4">Amazon</option>
  </select>
  <input type="button" id="tryButton" value="Try" />
  </section>
  <section>
    <img src="" id="logo" data-image="0" />
    <p id="result">
  </section>
  <div id="notification" class="hidden">
    <p>Ready to go offline!</p>
  </div>
</main>

<script src="index.js"></script>
<script src="game.js"></script>
</body>
</html>
```

2. Create a JavaScript file called `index.js`, in the same folder as the `index.html` file, with the following code:

```
'use strict';

var scope = {
  scope: './'
};

if ('serviceWorker' in navigator) {
  navigator.serviceWorker.register(
    'service-worker.js',
    scope
  ).then( function(serviceWorker) {
    printStatus('successful');
  }).catch(function(error) {
    printStatus(error);
  });
} else {
  printStatus('unavailable');
}
```

```
navigator.serviceWorker.addEventListener('controllerchange',
  function(event) {
    console.log('EVENT: controllerchange', event);

    navigator.serviceWorker.controller
      .addEventListener('statechange',
        function() {
          console.log('EVENT: statechange', this.state);
          if (this.state === 'activated') {
            document.querySelector('#notification').
            classList.remove('hidden');
          }
        }
      );
  }
);

function printStatus(status) {
  document.querySelector('#status').innerHTML = status;
}

document.querySelector('#resetButton').
addEventListener('click',
  function() {
    navigator.serviceWorker.getRegistration().then(function
    (registration) {
      registration.unregister();
      window.location.reload();
    });
  }
);
```

3. Create a JavaScript file called `game.js`, in the same folder as the `index.html` file, with the following code:

```
'use strict';

var attempts = 0,
  images = [

      'adobe',
      'apple',
      'google',
```

```
        'facebook',
        'amazon'
    ];

document.getElementById('tryButton').addEventListener
('click', function() {
  var imageElement = document.getElementById('logo'),
     choice = document.querySelector('#choice').value,
     attemptsEl = document.querySelector('#attempts'),
     result = document.querySelector('#result'),
     currentIndex = imageElement.getAttribute('data-image'),
     newIndex = getRandomIndex();

  do {
     newIndex = getRandomIndex();
  } while(newIndex === currentIndex);

  imageElement.src = images[newIndex] + '-logo.png';
  imageElement.setAttribute('data-image', newIndex);

  result.className = '';
  attempts++;

  if(newIndex == choice) {
     result.innerText = "Yay! Well done! You did it in " +
     attempts + " attempt(s)";
     result.classList.add('success');
     attemptsEl.innerText = attempts;
     attempts = 0;
  } else {
     result.innerText = "Boo! Try again..";
     result.classList.add('fail');
     attemptsEl.innerText = attempts;
  }

});

function getRandomIndex() {
  return Math.floor(Math.random() * 5);
}
```

4. Create a JavaScript file called `service-worker.js`, in the same folder as the `index.html` file, with the following code:

```javascript
'use strict';
var cacheName= 'dependencies-cache';

self.addEventListener('install', function(event) {
  event.waitUntil(
    caches.open(cacheName)
      .then(function(cache) {
        return cache.addAll([
          'apple',
    'google',
    'adobe',
    'facebook',
    'amazon'
        ]);
      })
      .then(function() {
        return self.skipWaiting();
      })
  );
});

self.addEventListener('fetch', function(event) {
  event.respondWith(
    caches.match(event.request)
      .then(function(response) {
        if (response) {
          console.log('Fetching from the cache: ',
          event.request.url);
          return response;
        } else {
          console.log('Fetching from server: ',
          event.request.url);
        }
        return fetch(event.request);
      }
    )
  );
});

self.addEventListener('activate', function(event) {
    console.log('Activating the service worker!');
    event.waitUntil(self.clients.claim());
});
```

5. Create a JavaScript file called `style.css`, in the same folder as the `index.html` file, with the following code:

```css
* {
    -webkit-box-sizing: border-box;
    -moz-box-sizing: border-box;
    box-sizing: border-box;
}

body {
    margin: 0 auto;
    text-align: center;
    font-family: sans-serif;
}

main {
    max-width: 350px;
    border: 1px solid #4CAF50;
    padding: 20px;
    border-radius: 5px;
    width: 350px;
    margin: 20px auto;
}

h1 {
    color: #4CAF50;
}

img {
    padding: 20px 0;
    max-width: 200px;
}

.success {
    color: #4CAF50;
    font-size: 2em;
}

.fail {
    color: #FF8401;
    font-size: 1.5em;
}
```

```
.hidden {
  display: none;
}

#registration-status {
  background-color: #FFE454;
  padding: 10px;
}

#notification {
  background-color: #4CAF50;
  padding: 3px;
  border-radius: 5px;
  max-width: 350px;
  color: #FFF;
}
```

6. Open up a browser and go to the `index.html` file:

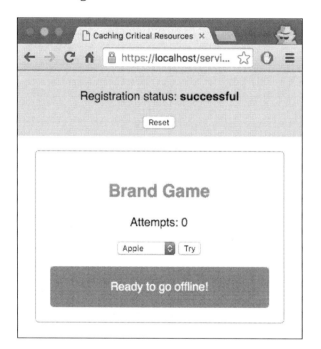

7. You will see the **Ready to go offline!** message. This means that we can play the game offline. Now open up DevTools (*Cmd + Alt + I* or *F12*), go to the **Network** tab, click on the dropdown displaying **No throttling**, and select **Offline**:

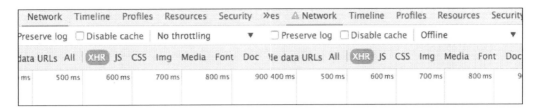

8. Now refresh your browser, and you will be able to continue playing the game.

9. You can select a company name from the dropdown and click the **Try** button:

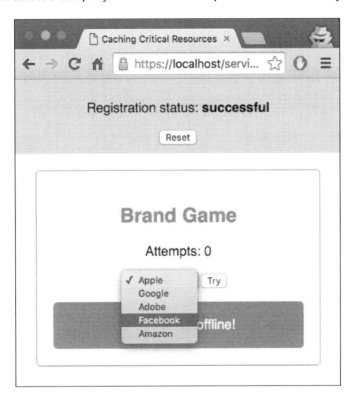

10. Every time the selection does not match the result, it will show a message saying **Boo! Try again..**, and you will see the attempts count:

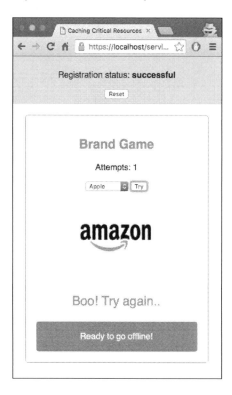

11. Once your selection matches you will get a success message with the attempt count, and you will see the attempts count:

How it works...

Our `index.html` file contains the structure for the dropdown, buttons, and image. The dropdown contains the options for the brand:

```
<select id="choice">
    <option value="0">Apple</option>
    <option value="1">Google</option>
    <option value="2">Adobe</option>
    <option value="3">Facebook</option>
    <option value="4">Amazon</option>
</select>
```

The values for the options are specified by numbers, which later match up with the images, so the order is important. As you can see, they start with 0, to adhere to the 0-based index of the array where we are going to store the names of the companies later on.

The `style.css` file contains all the styles we need for our page. The top two declarations are common styles for all the elements and the body element respectively:

```css
* {
    -webkit-box-sizing: border-box;
    -moz-box-sizing: border-box;
    box-sizing: border-box;
}

body {
    margin: 0 auto;
    text-align: center;
    font-family: sans-serif;
}
```

The styles for failed and successful messages contain orange and green colors:

```css
.success {
    color: #4CAF50;
    font-size: 2em;
}

.fail {
    color: #FF8401;
    font-size: 1.5em;
}
```

The notification message is initially hidden. This is done by assigning a class with `display:none`:

```css
.hidden {
    display: none;
}
```

The first of the three JavaScript files, `index.js`, performs service worker registration, and then listens to the `controllerchange` event. It also handles the event for the reset button.

The game engine for our little game is in the `game.js` file. So let's go through what's happening inside this file.

First, we declare two variables at the top, `attempts` and `images`, with initial values; `attempts` contains the initial value for tries, 0, and `images`, which is an array constant, has the brand names in order. The order of the brands is important so that it matches the dropdown in the `index.html` file:

```
var attempts = 0,
images = [
  'apple',
  'google',
  'adobe',
  'facebook',
  'amazon'
];
```

When the user clicks the `try` button, the game logic in the callback function is handled:

```
document.getElementById('tryButton').addEventListener('click',
function() {
  // callback
  ...
});
```

There is a lot going on in the declaration section in the callback handler. So let's look at each initialization:

1. First we grab the logo from the **Document Object Model** (**DOM**):

   ```
   var imageElement = document.getElementById('logo'),
   ```

2. We also capture the user `choice` and `attempts` element from the DOM, and the result element:

   ```
   choice = document.querySelector('#choice').value,
   attemptsEl = document.querySelector('#attempts'),
   result = document.querySelector('#result'),
   ```

3. Then we capture the data attribute from the logo element, and we generate a random number with `getRandomIndex()`:

   ```
   currentIndex = imageElement.getAttribute('data-image'),
   newIndex = getRandomIndex();
   ```

4. We generate a random number for the next index, as long as it is not the one we already have for the index:

   ```
   do {
       newIndex = getRandomIndex();
     } while(newIndex === currentIndex);
   ```

5. Next, we are set the brand images source to the image at the random index we created. Then we set the `data-image` attribute to the same index:

```
imageElement.src = images[newIndex] + '-logo.png';
imageElement.setAttribute('data-image', newIndex);
```

For example, this may create an HTML element like the following on our web page:

```
<img src="google-logo" data-image="1" />
```

6. We make sure the class name for the result element is cleared before adding a new one. Then we increase the attempts count:

```
result.className = '';
attempts++;
```

7. Next, we find out whether the new index is equal to the choice the user made. Note that we have used a double equation instead of triple deliberately, because the choice is a string and `newIndex` is an integer:

```
if (newIndex == choice) {
```

Let's move on to the `service-worker.js` file. There we handle three events: install, fetch, and activate. In the install event handler, we cache all the dependencies—the files we need to go offline:

```
return cache.addAll([
            'adobe-logo.png',
            'apple-logo.png',
            'google-logo.png',
            'style.css',
            'index.html',
            'index.js',
            'style.css'
        ]);
```

Inside the fetch handler, we check whether the resources are in the cache. If yes, then the response is provided by the cache:

```
caches.match(event.req uest)
        .then(function(response) {
        if (response) {
            console.log('Fetching from the cache: ',
            event.request.url);
            return response;
        }
```

Otherwise, return the result from the server itself:

```
else {
        console.log('Fetching from server: ',
        event.request.url);
    }
    return fetch(event.request);
```

Finally, we are forcing a `controllerchange` event on `navigator.serviceWorker` by calling `claim()`:

```
self.addEventListener('activate', function(event) {
    console.log('Activating the service worker!');
    event.waitUntil(self.clients.claim());
});
```

See also

▸ The *Registering a service worker in detail* recipe of *Chapter 1, Learning Service Worker Basics*

▸ The *Loading CSS offline* recipe of *Chapter 2, Working with Resource Files*

Showing cached content first

If you are a regular visitor to a certain website, chances are that you may be loading most of the resources, such as CSS and JavaScript files, from your cache, rather than from the server itself. This saves us necessary bandwidth for the server, as well as requests over the network. Having control over which content we deliver from the cache and server is a great advantage. Server workers provide us with this powerful feature by having programmatic control over the content. In this recipe, we are going to look at the methods that enable us to do so by creating a performance art event viewer web app.

Getting ready

To get started with service workers, you will need to have the service worker experiment feature turned on in your browser settings. If you have not done this yet, refer to the first recipe of *Chapter 1, Learning Service Worker Basics*: *Setting up service workers*. Service workers only run across HTTPS. To find out how to set up a development environment to support this feature, refer to the following recipes of *Chapter 1, Learning Service Worker Basics*: *Setting up GitHub pages for SSL*, *Setting up SSL for Windows*, and *Setting up SSL for Mac*.

How to do it...

Follow these instructions to set up your file structure. Alternatively, you can download the files from the following location:

```
https://github.com/szaranger/szaranger.github.io/tree/master/service-
workers/03/02/
```

1. First, we must create an `index.html` file as follows:

```html
<!DOCTYPE html>
<html lang="en">
<head>
  <meta charset="UTF-8">
  <title>Cache First, then Network</title>
  <link rel="stylesheet" href="style.css">
</head>
<body>
  <section id="events">
    <h1><span class="nyc">NYC</span> Events TONIGHT</h1>
    <aside>
      <img src="hypecal.png" />
      <h2>Source</h2>
      <section>
        <h3>Network</h3>
        <input type="checkbox" name="network" id="network-
        disabled-checkbox">
        <label for="network">Disabled</label><br />
        <h3>Cache</h3>
        <input type="checkbox" name="cache" id="cache-
        disabled-checkbox">
        <label for="cache">Disabled</label><br />
      </section>
      <h2>Delay</h2>
      <section>
        <h3>Network</h3>
        <input type="text" name="network-delay"
        id="network-delay" value="400" /> ms
        <h3>Cache</h3>
```

```
        <input type="text" name="cache-delay" id="cache-
        delay" value="1000" /> ms
      </section>
    <input type="button" id="fetch-btn" value="FETCH" />
  </aside>
  <section class="data connection">
    <table>
      <tr>
        <td><strong>Network</strong></td>
        <td><output id='network-status'></output></td>
      </tr>
      <tr>
        <td><strong>Cache</strong></td>
        <td><output id='cache-status'></output><td>
      </tr>
    </table>
  </section>
  <section class="data detail">
    <output id="data"></output>
  </section>
  <script src="index.js"></script>
</body>
</html>
```

2. Create a CSS file called `style.css` in the same folder as the `index.html` file. You can find the source code in the following location on GitHub:

   `https://github.com/szaranger/szaranger.github.io/blob/master/service-workers/03/02/style.css`

3. Create a JavaScript file called `index.js` in the same folder as the `index.html` file. You can find the source code in the following location on GitHub:

   `https://github.com/szaranger/szaranger.github.io/blob/master/service-workers/03/02/index.js`

4. Open up a browser and go to `index.html`:

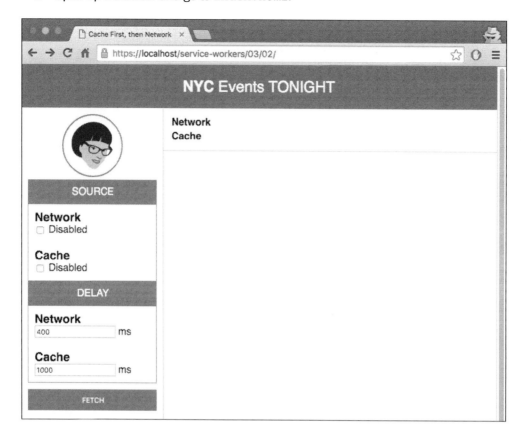

5. First, we are requesting data from the network with caching enabled. Click on the **Fetch** button:

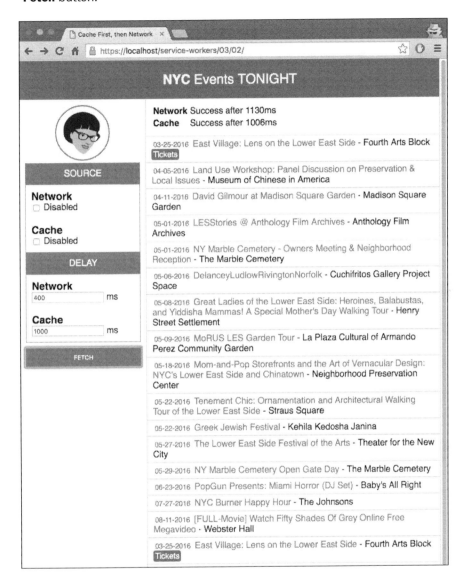

6. If you click **Fetch** again, the data has been retrieved first from cache, and then from the network, so you see duplicate data (see that the last line is the same as the first):

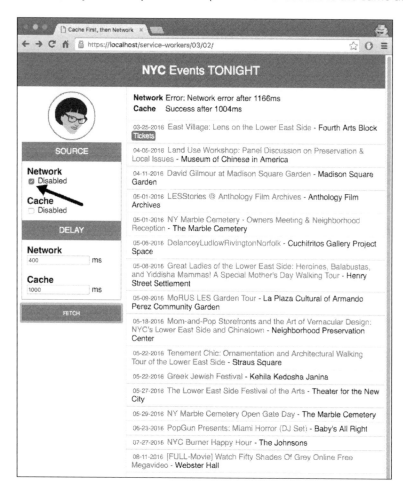

7. Now we are going to select the **Disabled** checkbox under the **Network** label, and click the **Fetch** button again, in order to fetch data only from the cache:

8. Select the **Disabled** checkbox under the **Network** label, as well as the **Cache** label, and click the **Fetch** button again:

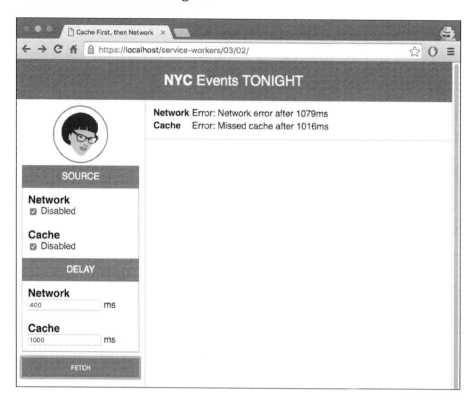

How it works...

In the `index.js` file, we are setting a page-specific name for the cache, as the caches are origin-based, and no other page should use the same cache name:

```
var CACHE_NAME = 'cache-and-then-network';
```

If you inspect the **Resources** tab of the development tools, you will find the cache inside the **Cache Storage** tab:

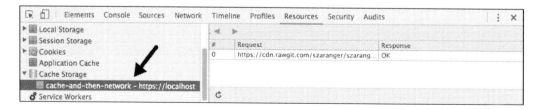

If we have already fetched network data, we don't want the cache fetch to complete and overwrite the data that we just got from the network. We use the `networkDataReceived` flag to let the cache fetch callbacks to know whether a network fetch has already completed:

```
var networkDataReceived = false;
```

We are storing elapsed time for the network and cache in two variables:

```
var networkFetchStartTime;
var cacheFetchStartTime;
```

The source URL, for example, is pointing to a file location in GitHub via RawGit:

```
var SOURCE_URL = 'https://cdn.rawgit.com/szaranger/
szaranger.github.io/master/service-workers/03/02/events';
```

If you want to set up your own source URL, you can easily do so by creating a gist or a repository on GitHub, and creating a file with your data in JSON format (you don't need the `.json` extension). Once you've done that, copy the URL of the file, head over to `https://rawgit.com`, and paste the link there to obtain another link with a content type header, as shown in the following screenshot:

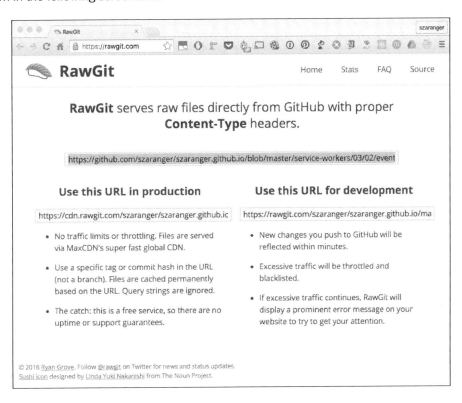

Between the time we press the **Fetch** button and when the data is received, we have to make sure the user doesn't change the search criteria, or press the **Fetch** button again. To handle this situation, we disable the controls:

```
function clear() {
  outlet.textContent = '';
  cacheStatus.textContent = '';
  networkStatus.textContent = '';
  networkDataReceived = false;
}

function disableEdit(enable) {
  fetchButton.disabled = enable;
  cacheDelayText.disabled = enable;
  cacheDisabledCheckbox.disabled = enable;
  networkDelayText.disabled = enable;
  networkDisabledCheckbox.disabled = enable;

  if(!enable) {
    clear();
  }
}
```

The returned data will be rendered to the screen in rows:

```
function displayEvents(events) {

  events.forEach(function(event) {
    var tickets = event.ticket ?
      '<a href="' + event.ticket + '" class="tickets">Tickets</a>'
      : '';

    outlet.innerHTML = outlet.innerHTML +
      '<article>' +
      '<span class="date">' + formatDate(event.date) + '</span>'
      +
      ' <span class="title">' + event.title + '</span>' +
      ' <span class="venue"> - ' + event.venue + '</span> ' +
      tickets +
      '</article>';
  });

}
```

Each item of the `events` array will be printed to the screen as rows:

03-25-2016 East Village: Lens on the Lower East Side - **Fourth Arts Block** `Tickets`	
04-05-2016 Land Use Workshop: Panel Discussion on Preservation & Local Issues - **Museum**	
04-11-2016 David Gilmour at Madison Square Garden - **Madison Square Garden**	

The function `handleFetchComplete` is the callback for both the cache and the network.

If the disabled checkbox is checked, we are simulating a network error by throwing an error:

```
var shouldNetworkError = networkDisabledCheckbox.checked,
    cloned;

  if (shouldNetworkError) {
    throw new Error('Network error');
  }
```

Because request bodies can only be read once, we have to clone the response:

```
cloned = response.clone();
```

We place the cloned response in the cache using `cache.put` as a key/value pair. This helps subsequent cache fetches to find this update data:

```
caches.open(CACHE_NAME).then(function(cache) {
    cache.put(SOURCE_URL, cloned); // cache.put(URL, response)
});
```

Now we read the response in JSON format. Also, we make sure that any in-flight cache requests will not be overwritten by the data we have just received, using the `networkDataReceived` flag:

```
response.json().then(function(data) {
    displayEvents(data);
    networkDataReceived = true;
});
```

To prevent overwriting the data we received from the network, we make sure only to update the page if the network request has not yet returned:

```
result.json().then(function(data) {
    if (!networkDataReceived) {
      displayEvents(data);
    }
});
```

When the user presses the **Fetch** button, they make nearly simultaneous requests of the network and the cache for data. This happens on a page load in a real-world application, instead of as a result of a user action:

```
fetchButton.addEventListener('click', function handleClick() {
...
}
```

We start by disabling any user input while the network fetch requests are initiated:

```
disableEdit(true);

networkStatus.textContent = 'Fetching events...';
networkFetchStartTime = Date.now();
```

We request data using the `fetch` API with a cache-busting URL, as well as the no-cache option in order to support Firefox, which hasn't implemented the caching options yet:

```
networkFetch = fetch(SOURCE_URL + '?cacheBuster=' + now, {
    mode: 'cors',
    cache: 'no-cache',
    headers: headers
})
```

In order to simulate network delays, we wait before calling the network fetch callback. In situations where the callback errors out, we have to make sure that we reject the promise we received from the original fetch:

```
return new Promise(function(resolve, reject) {
    setTimeout(function() {
      try {
        handleFetchComplete(response);
        resolve();
      } catch (err) {
        reject(err);
      }
    }, networkDelay);
  });
```

To simulate cache delays, we wait before calling the cache fetch callback. If the callback errors out, we make sure that we reject the promise we got from the original call to match:

```
return new Promise(function(resolve, reject) {
      setTimeout(function() {
        try {
          handleCacheFetchComplete(response);
          resolve();
```

```
        } catch (err) {
          reject(err);
        }
      }, cacheDelay);
    });
```

The `formatDate` function is a helper function for us to convert the date format we receive in the response into a much more readable format on the screen:

```
function formatDate(date) {
  var d = new Date(date),
      month = (d.getMonth() + 1).toString(),
      day = d.getDate().toString(),
      year = d.getFullYear();

  if (month.length < 2) month = '0' + month;
  if (day.length < 2) day = '0' + day;

  return [month, day, year].join('-');
}
```

If you use a different date format, you can shuffle the position of the array in the return statement to your preferred format.

Implementing a cache and network race

If your client is using older and slower hardware, including older hard drives, there is a chance that accessing resources from a hard drive could be slower than accessing the same resources on a faster Internet connection. But just because some of your users are using slower hardware, it doesn't justify accessing resources already in the hardware over the network all the time, because some users may have faster hardware that could be a waste of data. To resolve this issue, we can implement a solution that performs a race condition, and fetch data according to which resolves first.

Getting ready

To get started with service workers, you will need to have the service worker experiment feature turned on in your browser settings. If you have not done this yet, refer to the first recipe of *Chapter 1, Learning Service Worker Basics: Setting up service workers*. Service workers only run across HTTPS. To find out how to set up a development environment to support this feature, refer to the following recipes of *Chapter 1, Learning Service Worker Basics: Setting up GitHub pages for SSL, Setting up SSL for Windows*, and *Setting up SSL for Mac*.

How to do it...

Follow these instructions to set up your file structure. Alternatively, you can download the files from the following location:

```
https://github.com/szaranger/szaranger.github.io/tree/master/service-
workers/03/03/
```

1. First, we must create an `index.html` file as follows:

```
<!DOCTYPE html>
<html lang="en">
<head>
  <meta charset="UTF-8">
  <title>Cache &amp; Network Race</title>
  <link rel="stylesheet" href="style.css">
</head>
<body>
  <section id="registration-status">
    <p>Registration status: <strong
    id="status"></strong></p>
    <input type="button" id="resetButton" value="Reset" />
  </section>
  <script src="index.js"></script>
</body>
</html>
```

2. Create a JavaScript file called `style.css` in the same folder as the `index.html` file with the following code:

```
* {
  -webkit-box-sizing: border-box;
  -moz-box-sizing: border-box;
  box-sizing: border-box;
}

body {
  margin: 0 auto;
  text-align: center;
  font-family: sans-serif;
}

main {
  max-width: 350px;
  border: 1px solid #4CAF50;
  padding: 20px;
```

```css
  border-radius: 5px;
  width: 350px;
  margin: 20px auto;
}

h1 {
  color: #4CAF50;
}

img {
  padding: 20px 0;
  max-width: 200px;
}

.hidden {
  display: none;
}

#registration-status {
  background-color: #FFE454;
  padding: 10px;
}
```

3. Create a JavaScript file called `index.js`, in the same folder as the `index.html` file, with the following code:

```javascript
'use strict';

var scope = {
  scope: './'
};

if ('serviceWorker' in navigator) {
  navigator.serviceWorker.register(
    'service-worker.js',
    scope
  ).then( function(serviceWorker) {
    printStatus('successful');
  }).catch(function(error) {
    printStatus(error);
  });
} else {
  printStatus('unavailable');
}
```

```
        function printStatus(status) {
          document.querySelector('#status').innerHTML = status;
        }

        document.querySelector('#resetButton').addEventListener
        ('click',
          function() {
            navigator.serviceWorker.getRegistration().then(function
            (registration) {
              registration.unregister();
              window.location.reload();
            });
          }
        );
```

4. Create a JavaScript file called `service-worker.js`, in the same folder as the `index.html` file with the following code:

```
'use strict';

var cacheName = 'cache-network-race';

self.addEventListener('install', function(event) {
  event.waitUntil(
    caches.open(cacheName)
      .then(function(cache) {
        return cache.addAll([
          'index.html',
          'style.css',
          'index.js'
        ]);
      })
      .then(function() {
        return self.skipWaiting();
      })
  );
});

self.addEventListener('fetch', function(event) {
  event.respondWith(
    resolveAny([
      caches.match(event.request),
      fetch(event.request)
    ])
  );
```

```
});

function resolveAny(promises) {
  return new Promise(function(resolve, reject) {
    promises = promises.map(function(promise) {
      return Promise.resolve(promise);
    });

    promises.forEach(function(promise) {
      promise.then(resolve);
    });

    promises.reduce(function(a, b) {
      return a.catch(function() {
        return b;
      });
    }).catch(function() {
      return reject(Error("All have failed"));
    });
  });
}
```

5. Open up a browser and go to the `index.html` file:

6. Now open up DevTools (*Cmd + Alt + I* or *F12*), go to the **Network** tab, click on the dropdown, and select **GPRS(50 kb/s)** in order to simulate a slower network speed:

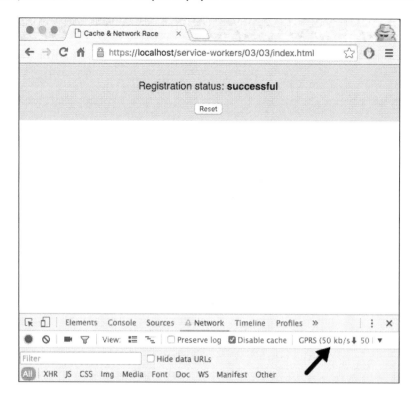

7. Refresh the page and you will see the same page. But if you view the network requests, you will be able to find out that the service worker kicked in:

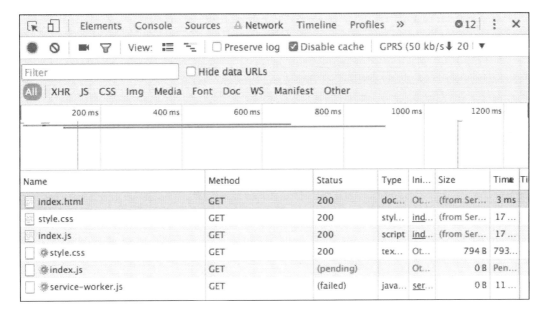

How it works...

In the `service-worker.js` file, we are caching the necessary resources for us to go offline and still use the application:

```
self.addEventListener('install', function(event) {
  event.waitUntil(
    caches.open(cacheName)
      .then(function(cache) {
        return cache.addAll([
          'index.html',
          'style.css',
          'index.js'
        ]);
      })
      .then(function() {
        return self.skipWaiting();
      })
  );
});
```

Then we create a function called `resolveAny`. The purpose of this function is to handle race conditions in a proper manner. The promise has a function called `race()`. This function is of no help to us, as it rejects if a promise has rejected before fulfilling.

The `resolveAny` function returns a new promise. Inside the promise, we make sure the array we pass in is an array of promises:

```
promises = promises.map(function(promise) {
    return Promise.resolve(promise);
});
```

Next, we make sure that we resolve the current promise as soon as another one in the array gets resolved:

```
promises.forEach(function(promise) {
    promise.then(resolve);
});
```

We also make sure to reject if all promises are rejected:

```
promises.reduce(function(a, b) {
    return a.catch(function() {
      return b;
    });
}
```

The callback function of the event listener for fetch calls the `resolveAny` function and passes in two functions, `caches.match(event.request)` and `fetch(event.request)`. Both these functions send the same request, resulting in a race condition.

Using window.caches

In this recipe, we look at how to prefetch specific resources during the installation of the service worker, as well as how to use the window.cache to make requests against the Cache Storage API, not within the scope of the service worker, but from the context of the HTML document.

Getting ready

To get started with service workers, you will need to have the service worker experiment feature turned on in your browser settings. If you have not done this yet, refer to the first recipe of *Chapter 1, Learning Service Worker Basics*: *Setting up service workers*. Service workers only run across HTTPS. To find out how to set up a development environment to support this feature, refer to the following recipes of *Chapter 1, Learning Service Worker Basics*: *Setting up GitHub pages for SSL, Setting up SSL for Windows*, and *Setting up SSL for Mac*.

How to do it...

Follow these instructions to set up your file structure. Alternatively, you can download the files from the following location:

```
https://github.com/szaranger/szaranger.github.io/tree/master/service-
workers/03/04/
```

1. First, we must create an `index.html` file as follows:

    ```html
    <!DOCTYPE html>
    <html lang="en">
    <head>
      <meta charset="UTF-8">
      <title>Using window.caches</title>
      <link rel="stylesheet" href="style.css">
    </head>
    <body>
      <section id="registration-status">
        <p>Registration status: <strong
        id="status"></strong></p>
        <input type="button" id="resetButton" value="Reset" />
      </section>
      <section id="article-area">
        <h1>Bookmark App</h1>
        <form action="#" method="post">
          <div>
            <label for="new-bookmark">+Add Bookmark</label>
            <input type="text" name="new-bookmark" id="new-
            bookmark" placeholder="new bookmark">
            <input type="submit" value="Add">
          </div>
        </form>
        <ul id="articles"></ul>
        <div id="bookmark-status"></div>
      </section>
      <script src="index.js"></script>
      <script src="app.js"></script>
    </body>
    </html>
    ```

2. Create a CSS file called `style.css` in the same folder as the `index.html` file. You can find the source code on GitHub at the following location:

   `https://github.com/szaranger/szaranger.github.io/blob/master/service-workers/03/04/style.css`

3. Create a JavaScript file called `index.js`, in the same folder as the `index.html` file, with the following code:

```javascript
'use strict';

var scope = {
  scope: './'
};

if ('serviceWorker' in navigator) {
  navigator.serviceWorker.register(
    'service-worker.js',
    scope
  ).then( function(serviceWorker) {
    printStatus('successful');
  }).catch(function(error) {
    printStatus(error);
  });
} else {
  printStatus('unavailable');
}

function printStatus(status) {
  document.querySelector('#status').innerHTML = status;
}

document.querySelector('#resetButton').addEventListener
('click',
  function() {
    navigator.serviceWorker.getRegistration().
    then(function(registration) {
      registration.unregister();
      window.location.reload();
    });
  }
);
```

4. Create a JavaScript file called `app.js` in the same folder as the `index.html` file. The source code for this file can be found on GitHub at the following location:

   ```
   https://github.com/szaranger/szaranger.github.io/blob/master/
   service-workers/03/04/app.js
   ```

5. Create an HTML file called `prefetched.html`:

   ```html
   <!DOCTYPE html>
   <html lang="en">
   <head>
     <meta charset="UTF-8">
     <title>Prefetched</title>
   </head>
   <body>
     <p>Prefetched Page</p>
   </body>
   </html>
   ```

6. Create a JavaScript file called `service-worker.js`, in the same folder as the `index.html` file, with the following code:

   ```javascript
   'use strict';

   var cacheVersion = 1;
   var currentCaches = {
     prefetch: 'window-cache-v' + cacheVersion
   };

   self.addEventListener('install', function(event) {
     var prefetchUrls = [

       './prefetched.html',

     ];

     console.log('EVENT: install. Prefetching resource:',
       prefetchUrls);

     event.waitUntil(
       caches.open(currentCaches.prefetch).
       then(function(cache) {
   ```

```
        return cache.addAll(prefetchUrls.map(function
        (prefetchUrl) {
          return new Request(prefetchUrl, {mode: 'no-cors'});
        })).then(function() {
          console.log('SUCCESS: All resources fetched and
          cached.');
        });
      }).catch(function(error) {
        console.error('FAIL: Prefetch:', error);
      })
    );
});


self.addEventListener('activate', function(event) {
  var expectedCacheNames = Object.keys(currentCaches).
  map(function(key) {
    return currentCaches[key];
  });

  event.waitUntil(
    caches.keys().then(function(cacheNames) {
      return Promise.all(
        cacheNames.map(function(cacheName) {
          if (expectedCacheNames.indexOf(cacheName) === -1)
          {
            console.log('DELETE: Out of date cache:',
            cacheName);
            return caches.delete(cacheName);
          }
        })
      );
    })
  );
});
```

7. Open up a browser and go to the index.html file. You will see one
    prefetched bookmark:

8. Add a bookmark by typing a URL and clicking on the **Add** button on the right:

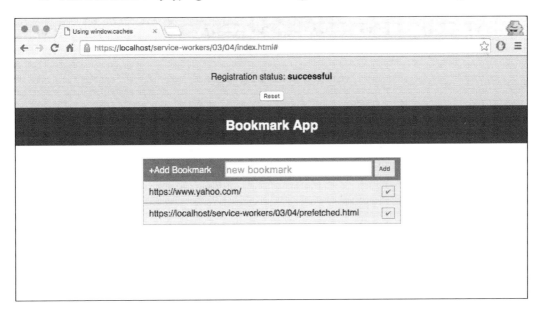

9. You can delete a bookmark by clicking on the tick icon on the right-hand side of the bookmark.

10. Add another bookmark and refresh the page. You will see the bookmarks are intact.

How it works...

In our `service-worker.js` file, we maintain a cache version in order to use a fresh cache by incrementing the `cacheVersion` value. When the updated service worker kicks in, the old caches will be removed as a part of the activate event handler:

```
var cacheVersion = 1;
var currentCaches = {
  prefetch: 'window-cache-v' + cacheVersion
};
```

The following resource will be displayed as a bookmarked URL when you load the page for the first time, and the event will be logged in your developer console:

```
var prefetchUrls = [
    './prefetched.html',
  ];
console.log('EVENT: install. Prefetching resource:',
    prefetchUrls);
```

If there is a possibility that the resources being fetched are served off a server that does not support CORS, it is important to use `{mode: 'no-cors'}`:

```
return new Request(prefetchUrl, {mode: 'no-cors'});
```

The `catch()` method handles any exceptions from the `caches.open()` and `cache.addAll()` steps:

```
}).catch(function(error) {
    console.error('FAIL: Prefetch:', error);
})
```

In the event handler for activate, we delete all caches that are not named in `currentCaches`. While in this example there is only one cache, the same logic handles cases where there are multiple versioned caches:

```
var expectedCacheNames =
Object.keys(currentCaches).map(function(key) {
    return currentCaches[key];
  });
```

If this cache name isn't present in the array of "expected" cache names, then delete it:

```
if (expectedCacheNames.indexOf(cacheName) === -1) {
console.log('DELETE: Out of date cache:', cacheName);
    return caches.delete(cacheName);
}
```

Let's move on to the `app.js` file, where most of the work is taking place. The `initializeBookmarks` function attaches an event listener to the form for the submit button. In the callback for submit, the value of the text field is extracted and then a list is generated with it. This list is then attached to the unordered list represented by the ID of the articles in the `index.html` file. We then call the `showBookmarks()` function:

```
function initializeBookmarks() {
    form.addEventListener('submit', function( event ) {
        var text = newBookmark.value;
        if (text !== '') {
            articles.innerHTML += '<li>' + text + '</li>';
            addUrlToCache(text);
            newBookmark.value = '';
            newBookmark.focus();
        }
        event.preventDefault();
    }, false);
    showBookmarks();
}
```

We also add an event listener to the unordered articles list for the click event. Inside the callback, we remove the item itself if it's a list (`li`) element. This is how we remove articles from the list:

```
articles.addEventListener( 'click', function( event ) {
    var target = event.target;
    if ( target.tagName === 'LI' ) {
        target.parentNode.removeChild( target );
    };

    event.preventDefault();
}, false);
```

In the `showBookmarks()` function, we clear out any of the previous URLs, in case this function was called after adding a new URL to the cache:

```
while (articles.firstChild) {
    articles.removeChild(articles.firstChild);
}
```

We then iterate over all the available caches, and for each of the caches, iterate over all of the URLs, adding each cache to the bookmark list:

```
window.caches.keys().then(function(cacheNames) {
    cacheNames.forEach(function(cacheName) {
        window.caches.open(cacheName).then(function(cache) {
```

```
            cache.keys().then(function(requests) {
              requests.forEach(function(request) {
                addRequestToBookmarks(cacheName, request);
              });
            });
          });
        });
      });
```

Now let's look at the function that actually uses `window.fetch()` to retrieve a response from the network and store it in the named cache. The important thing here is that the service worker controlling this page has no fetch event handler, therefore this request is made without the involvement of the service worker:

```
function addUrlToCache(url) {
  window.fetch(url, { mode: 'no-cors' }).then(function(response) {
    if (response.status < 400) {
      caches.open(cacheName).then(function(cache) {
        cache.put(url, response).then(showBookmarks);
      });
    }
  }).catch(function(error) {
    document.querySelector('#status').textContent = error;
  });
}
```

The `addRequestToBookmarks()` function is a helper function for adding a cached request to the list of the cached bookmarks. In this function, we're creating a span, a button, and a list item, and appending those to the unordered articles list:

```
function addRequestToBookmarks(cacheName, request) {
  var url = request.url,
    span = document.createElement('span'),
    button = document.createElement('button'),
    li = document.createElement('li');

  span.textContent = url;
  button.textContent = '✓';
  button.dataset.url = url;
  button.dataset.cacheName = cacheName;
  button.classList.add('done');
  button.addEventListener('click', function() {
    removeCachedBookmark(this.dataset.cacheName,
    this.dataset.url).then(function() {
      var parent = this.parentNode,
```

```
            grandParent = parent.parentNode;
            grandParent.removeChild(parent);
        }.bind(this));
    });
    li.appendChild(span);
    li.appendChild(button);
    articles.appendChild(li);
}
```

Next, the `removeCachedBookmark()` function removes the cache entry by a given a cache name and a URL:

```
function removeCachedBookmark(cacheName, url) {
    return window.caches.open(cacheName).then(function(cache) {
        return cache.delete(url);
    });
}
```

The `waitUntilInstalled()` helper function returns a promise which gets resolved once the service worker registration passes the `installing` state:

```
function waitUntilInstalled(registration) {
    return new Promise(function(resolve, reject) {
        if (registration.installing) {
```

If the current registration portrays the `installing` service worker, then we make sure to wait until the installation step, where the resources are pre-fetched, completes to display the bookmark list:

```
registration.installing.addEventListener('statechange',
function(event) {
    if (event.target.state === 'installed') {
    resolve();
    } else if(event.target.state === 'redundant') {
    reject();
    }
});
```

If that's not the case, and this isn't the `installing` service worker, then we can safely assume the installation must have been completed during a previous visit to the current page, and the resources have already been prefetched. Therefore we can now show the list of bookmarks right away:

```
    } else {
        resolve();
    }
```

Implementing stale-while-revalidate

Having the latest version of the cache is sometimes not absolutely necessary for resources such as certain images of a web page. We can use the cached version if available, and fetch an update next time.

Getting ready

To get started with service workers, you will need to have the service worker experiment feature turned on in your browser settings. If you have not done this yet, refer to the first recipe of *Chapter 1, Learning Service Worker Basics: Setting up service workers*. Service workers only run across HTTPS. To find out how to set up a development environment to support this feature, refer to the following recipes of *Chapter 1, Learning Service Worker Basics: Setting up GitHub pages for SSL, Setting up SSL for Windows*, and *Setting up SSL for Mac*.

How to do it...

Follow these instructions to set up your file structure. Alternatively, you can download the files from the following location:

```
https://github.com/szaranger/szaranger.github.io/tree/master/service-
workers/03/05/
```

1. First, we must create an `index.html` file as follows:

```html
<!DOCTYPE html>
<html lang="en">
<head>
  <meta charset="UTF-8">
  <title>Cache First, then Network</title>
  <link rel="stylesheet" href="style.css">
</head>
<body>
  <section id="registration-status">
    <p>Registration status: <strong
    id="status"></strong></p>
    <input type="button" id="resetButton" value="Reset" />
  </section>
  <section>
    <img src="adobe-logo" alt="adobe logo">
  </section>
  <script src="index.js"></script>
</body>
</html>
```

2. Create a JavaScript file called `index.js` in the same folder as the `index.html` file with the following code:

```javascript
'use strict';

var scope = {
  scope: './'
};

if ('serviceWorker' in navigator) {
  navigator.serviceWorker.register(
    'service-worker.js',
    scope
  ).then( function(serviceWorker) {
    printStatus('successful');
  }).catch(function(error) {
    printStatus(error);
  });
} else {
  printStatus('unavailable');
}

function printStatus(status) {
  document.querySelector('#status').innerHTML = status;
}

document.querySelector('#resetButton').addEventListener
('click',
  function() {
    navigator.serviceWorker.getRegistration().
    then(function(registration) {
      registration.unregister();
      window.location.reload();
    });
  }
);
```

3. Create a JavaScript file called `service-worker.js`, in the same folder as the `index.html` file, with the following code:

```javascript
'use strict';

var cacheName= 'stale-while-revalidate';

self.addEventListener('install', function(event) {
  event.waitUntil(
```

```
        caches.open(cacheName)
          .then(function(cache) {
            return cache.addAll([
              'adobe-logo.png',
              'style.css',
              'index.html',
              'index.js',
              'style.css'
            ]);
          })
          .then(function() {
            return self.skipWaiting();
          })
      );
    });

    self.addEventListener('fetch', function(event) {
      event.respondWith(
        caches.open('stale-while-revalidate')
          .then(function(cache) {
            return cache.match(event.request)
              .then(function(response) {
                var promise;

                if (response) {
                  console.log('Fetching from the cache: ',
                  event.request.url);
                } else {
                  console.log('Fetching from server: ',
                  event.request.url);
                }

                promise = fetch(event.request)
                  .then(function(networkResponse) {
                    var cloned = networkResponse.clone();
                    cache.put(event.request, cloned);
                    console.log('Fetching from the cache: ',
                    event.request.url);
                    return networkResponse;
                  }
                )
                console.log('Fetching from server: ',
                event.request.url);
```

```
                return response || promise;
              }
            )
          }
        )
      );
    });

    self.addEventListener('activate', function(event) {
        console.log('Activating the service worker!');
        event.waitUntil(self.clients.claim());
    });
```

4. Download the `adobe-log.png` image from the source code, or use your own image in the same folder as the `index.html` file.

5. Open up a browser and go to `index.html`. You will see the **Registration status: successful** message and the logo:

6. Now if you refresh the page and inspect the **Console** tab of the Developer Tools, you will be able to see that the `adobe-logo.png` file has been fetched from the cache.

How it works...

In our `service-worker.js` file, we make sure that if a cached version is available, we use it instead of a network request, but fetch an update the next time:

```
self.addEventListener('fetch', function(event) {
  event.respondWith(
    caches.open('stale-while-revalidate')
      .then(function(cache) {
        return cache.match(event.request)
          .then(function(response) {
            var promise;

            if (response) {
              console.log('Fetching from the cache: ',
              event.request.url);
            } else {
              console.log('Fetching from server: ',
              event.request.url);
            }
            promise = fetch(event.request)
              .then(function(networkResponse) {
                var cloned = networkResponse.clone();
                cache.put(event.request, cloned);
                console.log('Fetching from the cache: ',
                event.request.url);
                return networkResponse;
              }
            )
            console.log('Fetching from server: ',
            event.request.url);
            return response || promise;
          }
        )
      }
    )
  );
});
```

4

Accessing Offline Content with Advanced Techniques

In this chapter, we will cover the following topics:

- ► Templating
- ► Implementing read-through caching
- ► Allowing offline Google Analytics
- ► Allowing offline user interaction
- ► Implementing selective caching

Introduction

In this chapter, we will continue to improve on our experience working with offline content using the service worker.

We will look into advanced techniques, including how to use templating with a template engine, diving into Google Analytics, how to solve issues with offline user interaction, and implementing selective caching.

Let's start off this chapter by experimenting with templating for the service worker.

Templating

Traditional server-side page rendering has become a thing of the past with modern-day **single page applications** (**SPAs**). Even though server-side rendering is faster, state data will prove hard to implement with the service worker. Instead, we can request JSON data and a template, allow the service worker to take in the data and the template, and render a response page. JavaScript templating is a client-side data binding method, implemented with the use of the JavaScript language.

In order to learn more about templating, please refer the following link:

```
https://en.wikipedia.org/wiki/JavaScript_templating
```

Getting ready

To get started with service workers, you will need to have the service worker experiment feature turned on in your browser settings. If you have not done this yet, refer to the first recipe of *Chapter 1, Learning Service Worker Basics: Setting up service workers*. Service workers only run across HTTPS. To find out how to set up a development environment to support this feature, refer to the following recipes: *Setting up GitHub pages for SSL, Setting up SSL for Windows*, and *Setting up SSL for Mac*.

How to do it...

Follow these instructions to set up your file structure. Alternatively, you can download the files from the following location:

```
https://github.com/szaranger/szaranger.github.io/tree/master/service-
workers/04/01/
```

1. First, we must create an `index.html` file as follows:

```
<!DOCTYPE html>
<html lang="en">
<head>
  <meta charset="UTF-8">
  <title>Templating</title>
  <style>
  * {
    -webkit-box-sizing: border-box;
    -moz-box-sizing: border-box;
    box-sizing: border-box;
  }
```

```
body {
  margin: 0 auto;
  text-align: center;
  font-family: sans-serif;
}

main {
  max-width: 350px;
  border: 1px solid #4CAF50;
  padding: 20px;
  border-radius: 5px;
  width: 350px;
  margin: 20px auto;
}

h1 {
  color: #4CAF50;
}

img {
  padding: 20px 0;
  max-width: 200px;
}

.hidden {
  display: none;
}

.frameworks {
  margin: 20px auto;
}

table, th, td {
  border: 1px solid black;
  border-collapse: collapse;
}

.frameworks th {
  background-color: #000;
  color: #FFF;
  padding: 3px 10px;
}
```

```
     .frameworks tr {
       text-align: left;
     }

     .frameworks td {
       background-color: #FFF;
       padding: 3px 10px;
     }

     #registration-status {
       background-color: #FFE454;
       padding: 10px;
     }
   </style>
 </head>
 <body>
   <section id="registration-status">
     <p>Registration status: <strong
     id="status"></strong></p>
     <input type="button" id="resetButton" value="Reset" />
   </section>
   <section>
       <h2>JS Frameworks & Creators</h2>
       <table class="frameworks">
         <tr>
           <th>Framework</th>
           <th>Name</th>
           <th>Twitter</th>
         </tr>
         {{#users}}
           <tr>
               <td>{{framework}}</td>
               <td>{{person.firstName}}
               {{person.lastName}}</td>
               <td><a href="https://twitter.com/
               {{twitter}}">@{{twitter}}</a></td>
           </tr>
         {{/users}}
       </table>
   </section>

   <script>
   'use strict';
```

```
      var scope = {
        scope: './'
      };

      if ('serviceWorker' in navigator) {
        navigator.serviceWorker.register(
          'service-worker.js',
          scope
        ).then( function(serviceWorker) {
          printStatus('successful');
        }).catch(function(error) {
          printStatus(error);
        });
      } else {
        printStatus('unavailable');
      }

      function printStatus(status) {
        document.querySelector('#status').innerHTML = status;
      }

      document.querySelector('#resetButton').
      addEventListener('click',
        function() {
          navigator.serviceWorker.getRegistration().
          then(function(registration) {
            registration.unregister();
            window.location.reload();
          });
        }
      );
    </script>
  </body>
</html>
```

2. Create a JavaScript file called `service-worker.js`, in the same folder as the `index.html` file, with the following code:

```
'use strict';

importScripts('handlebars.js');

var cacheName= 'template-cache';
```

```
self.addEventListener('install', function(event) {
  event.waitUntil(
    caches.open(cacheName)
      .then(function(cache) {
        return cache.addAll([
          'index.html',
          'service-worker.js',
          'people.json'
        ]);
      })
      .then(function() {
        return self.skipWaiting();
      })
  );
});

self.addEventListener('fetch', function(event) {
  var requestURL = new URL(event.request.url);

  event.respondWith(
    Promise.all([
      caches.match('index.html').then(function(res) {
        if(res) {
          return res.text();
        }
      }),
      caches.match('people.json').then(function(res) {
        return res.json();
      })
    ]).then(function(resps) {
      var template = resps[0],
        data = resps[1],
        renderTemplate = Handlebars.compile(template);

      return new Response(renderTemplate(data), {
        headers: {
          'Content-Type': 'text/html'
        }
      });
    })
  );
});
```

3. Create a JSON file called `people.js`, in the same folder as the `index.html` file, with the following code:

```
{
  "users":[
    {
      "framework": "Ember",
      "person":{
        "firstName": "Yehuda",
        "lastName": "Katz"
      },
      "twitter": "wycats"
    },
    {
      "framework": "React",
      "person":{
        "firstName": "Jordan",
        "lastName": "Walke"
      },
      "twitter": "jordwalke"
    },
    {
      "framework": "Angular",
      "person":{
        "firstName": "Miško",
        "lastName": "Hevery"
      },
      "twitter": "mhevery"
    }
  ]
}
```

4. Download the handlebars library from `http://handlebarsjs.com/installation.html` and save as `handlebars.js` in the same directory as the `index.html` file, as shown in the following screenshot:

5. Open up a browser and go to the `index.html` file:

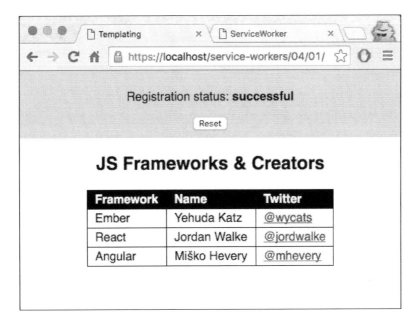

How it works...

We are using handlebars as our choice of templating engine for this example.

The template for the service worker is the `index.html` file itself. We are using double curly braces, the `Handlebars` syntax, inside a table:

```
<table class="frameworks">
    <tr>
    <th>Framework</th>
        <th>Name</th>
        <th>Twitter</th>
    </tr>
    {{#users}}
        <tr>
            <td>{{framework}}</td>
            <td>{{person.firstName}} {{person.lastName}}</td>
            <td><a href="https://twitter.com/{{twitter}}">
            @{{twitter}}</a></td>
            </tr>
        {{/users}}
</table>
```

The values are read from the JSON file that we feed into the template. The {{#users}} tag is an array, and it works like a loop, printing out the content inside the users property to the screen by replacing the placeholder, such as {{twitter}}, with the relevant value.

The people.json file contains data we need for our template. The users property contains an array of the users:

```json
{
  "users":[
    {
      "framework": "Ember",
      "person":{
        "firstName": "Yehuda",
        "lastName": "Katz"
      },
      "twitter": "wycats"
    },
    {
      "framework": "React",
      "person":{
        "firstName": "Jordan",
        "lastName": "Walke"
      },
      "twitter": "jordwalke"
    },
    {
      "framework": "Angular",
      "person":{
        "firstName": "Miško",
        "lastName": "Hevery"
      },
      "twitter": "mhevery"
    }
  ]
}
```

Let's move on to the service-worker.js file. There we handle two events: install and fetch. In the install event handler, we are caching all the dependencies:

```js
return cache.addAll([
        'index.html',
        'style.css',
```

```
        'service-worker.js',
        'people.json'
    ]);
```

Inside the fetch handler, we check to see whether the fetch request is the template, in our case the `index.html` file, and we send the response in text format:

```
caches.match('index.html').then(function(response) {
        if(response) {
            return response.text();
        }
    }),
```

If the fetch request is the JSON file, we return the result in JSON format:

```
caches.match('people.json').then(function(response) {
        return response.json();
    })
```

Finally, we render the template with the JSON data and then send the response back with a header:

```
]).then(function(resps) {
        var template = resps[0],
            data = resps[1],
            renderTemplate = Handlebars.compile(template);

        return new Response(renderTemplate(data), {
            headers: {
                'Content-Type': 'text/html'
            }
        });
    })
```

The `Handlebars.compile()` function takes in a template and returns a function, which can in turn take in data and render an output.

See also

▸ The *Registering a service worker in detail* recipe in *Chapter 1, Learning Service Worker Basics*

Implementing read-through caching

Read-through caching is an assertive approach to all-out caching for types of static content you visit regularly. This is not very suitable for dynamic content, such as news or sports. A selective caching approach would be better suited for such instances. Read-through caching saves us the necessary bandwidth for the server, as well as requests over the network. The way read-through caching works is that after the service worker takes control of your page, when the first `fetch()` request is called, the response will be cached, and subsequent requests to the same URL will be served from the cache.

Getting ready

To get started with service workers, you will need to have the service worker experiment feature turned on in your browser settings. If you have not done this yet, refer to the first recipe of *Chapter 1, Learning Service Worker Basics*: *Setting up service workers*. Service workers only run across HTTPS. To find out how to set up a development environment to support this feature, refer to the following recipes of *Chapter 1, Learning Service Worker Basics*: *Setting up GitHub pages for SSL*, *Setting up SSL for Windows*, and *Setting up SSL for Mac*.

How to do it...

Follow the instructions to set up your file structure. Alternatively, you can download the files from the following location:

```
https://github.com/szaranger/szaranger.github.io/tree/master/service-
workers/04/02/
```

1. First, we must create an `index.html` file as follows:

```html
<!DOCTYPE html>
<html lang="en">
<head>
  <meta charset="UTF-8">
  <title>Read-through Caching</title>
  <link rel="stylesheet" href="style.css">
</head>
<body>
  <section id="registration-status">
    <p>Registration status: <strong
    id="status"></strong></p>
    <input type="button" id="resetButton" value="Reset" />
  </section>
```

```
    <section></section>
    <script src="index.js"></script>
</body>
</html>
```

2. Create a CSS file called `style.css` in the same folder as the `index.html` file:

```css
* {
  -webkit-box-sizing: border-box;
  -moz-box-sizing: border-box;
  box-sizing: border-box;
}

body {
  margin: 0 auto;
  text-align: center;
  font-family: sans-serif;
}

main {
  max-width: 350px;
  border: 1px solid #4CAF50;
  padding: 20px;
  border-radius: 5px;
  width: 350px;
  margin: 20px auto;
}

h1 {
  color: #4CAF50;
}

img {
  padding: 20px 0;
  max-width: 200px;
}

.hidden {
  display: none;
}

#registration-status {
  background-color: #FFE454;
  padding: 10px;
}
```

3. Create a JavaScript file called `index.js` in the same folder as the `index.html` file:

```javascript
'use strict';

var scope = {
  scope: './'
};

if ('serviceWorker' in navigator) {
  navigator.serviceWorker.register(
    'service-worker.js',
    scope
  ).then( function(serviceWorker) {
    printStatus('successful');
  }).catch(function(error) {
    printStatus(error);
  });
} else {
  printStatus('unavailable');
}

function printStatus(status) {
  document.querySelector('#status').innerHTML = status;
}

document.querySelector('#resetButton').
addEventListener('click',
  function() {
    navigator.serviceWorker.getRegistration().
    then(function(registration) {
      registration.unregister();
      window.location.reload();
    });
  }
);
```

4. Create a JavaScript file called `service-worker.js` in the same folder as the `index.html` file:

```javascript
'use strict';

var version = 1,
  currentCaches= { readThrough : 'version-' + version },
  NOT_FOUND = -1,
```

```
    ERROR_RESPONSE = 400;

self.addEventListener('activate', function(event) {
  var expectingCacheNames =
  Object.keys(currentCaches).map(function(key) {
    return currentCaches[key];
  });

  event.waitUntil(
    caches.keys().then(function(cacheNames) {
      return Promise.all(
        cacheNames.map(function(cacheName) {
          if (expectingCacheNames.indexOf(cacheName) ===
          NOT_FOUND) {
            console.log(
              '%c DELETE: Out of date cache: %s',
              'color: #ff0000',
              cacheName
            );
            return caches.delete(cacheName);
          }
        })
      );
    })
  );
});

self.addEventListener('fetch', function(event) {
  var request = event.request,
    requestUrl = request.url;

  console.log(
    '%c ⚡ EVENT: %c Handling fetch event for %s',
    'color: #F57F20',
    'color: #000',
    requestUrl
  );

  event.respondWith(
    caches.open(currentCaches['readThrough']).
    then(function(cache) {
      return cache.match(request).then(function(response) {
```

```
      if (response) {
        console.log(
          '%c ✓ RESPONSE: %c Found in cache: %s',
          'color: #5EBD00',
          'color: #000000',
          response
        );

        return response;
      }
      console.log(
        '%c ✗ RESPONSE: %c For %s not found in cache. ' +
        'fetching from network...',
        'color: #F05266',
        'color: #000',
        requestUrl
      );

      return fetch(request.clone()).
      then(function(response) {
        console.log(
          '%c RESPONSE: %c For %s from network is: %O',
          'color: #F05266',
          'color: #000',
          requestUrl,
          response
        );

        if (response.status < ERROR_RESPONSE) {
          cache.put(request, response.clone());
        }

        return response;
      });
    }).catch(function(err) {
      console.error('FAIL: Read-through cache:', err);
      throw error;
    });
  })
 );
});
```

5. Open up a browser and go to `index.html`:

6. Open up Developer Tools (*Cmd + Alt + I* or *F12*). You will see messages logged on the console, saying most resources were not found in the cache, so were fetched from the network:

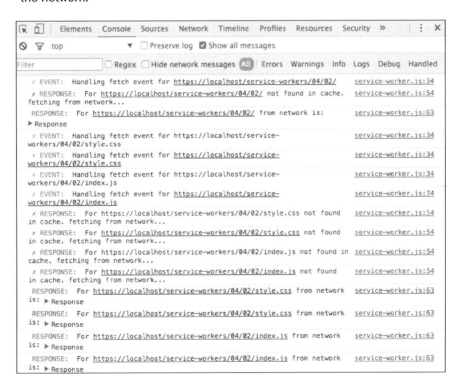

7. If you refresh the page, you will see different messages appearing in the console. This time, the resources are fetched from the cache:

```
⨯ EVENT:   Handling fetch event for https://localhost/service-        /service-workers/04/02/service-worker.js:34
workers/04/02/
✓ RESPONSE:  Found in cache: Response                                  /service-workers/04/02/service-worker.js:45
⨯ EVENT:   Handling fetch event for https://localhost/service-workers/04/02/style.css    service-worker.js:34
⨯ EVENT:   Handling fetch event for https://localhost/service-        /service-workers/04/02/service-worker.js:34
workers/04/02/style.css
⨯ EVENT:   Handling fetch event for https://localhost/service-workers/04/02/index.js     service-worker.js:34
⨯ EVENT:   Handling fetch event for https://localhost/service-        /service-workers/04/02/service-worker.js:34
workers/04/02/index.js
✓ RESPONSE:  Found in cache: Response                                                    service-worker.js:45
✓ RESPONSE:  Found in cache: Response                                  /service-workers/04/02/service-worker.js:45
✓ RESPONSE:  Found in cache: Response                                                    service-worker.js:45
✓ RESPONSE:  Found in cache: Response                                  /service-workers/04/02/service-worker.js:45
```

How it works...

In the `service-worker.js` file, we are setting a page-specific name for the cache, as the caches are origin-based, and no other page should use the same cache name. We are also versioning the cache, in order to address a scenario where you would want a fresh cache; in this instance, we can update the version:

```
var version = 1,
    currentCaches= { readThrough : 'version-' + version },
```

We also make sure that the old caches are purged at the time the service worker is activated. So, we delete all the caches that do not match the name we previously specified for our cache name:

```
self.addEventListener('activate', function(event) {
  var expectingCacheNames =
  Object.keys(currentCaches).map(function(key) {
    return currentCaches[key];
  });

  event.waitUntil(
    caches.keys().then(function(cacheNames) {
      return Promise.all(
        cacheNames.map(function(cacheName) {
          if (expectingCacheNames.indexOf(cacheName) ===
          NOT_FOUND) {
            console.log('%c DELETE: Out of date cache: %s',
              'color: #ff0000', cacheName);
            return caches.delete(cacheName);
          }
        })
      );
```

```
    })
  );
});
```

The fetch event listener looks into the cache to find whether our requested resource is in the cache; if it is found, it will respond with the entry:

```
event.respondWith(
    caches.open(currentCaches['readThrough']).then(function(cache)
    {
        return cache.match(request).then(function(response) {
            if (response) {
                console.log(
                    '%c ✓ RESPONSE: %c Found in cache: %s',
                    'color: #5EBD00','color: #000000',response
                );

                return response;
            }
```

Otherwise, if there is no entry for `event.request` in the cache, the response is going to be undefined, so we have to fetch the resource using `fetch()`:

```
return fetch(request.clone()).then(function(response) {
        console.log(
            '%c RESPONSE: %c For %s from network is: %O',
            'color: #F05266',
            'color: #000',
            requestUrl,
            response
        );
```

Here, the `clone()` call is useful if we use `cache.put()` later.

Making a copy is necessary because both `cache.put()` and `fetch()` will consume the request.

We also make sure not to cache error responses by checking the `response.status` parameter is not 400 or above:

```
if (response.status < ERROR_RESPONSE) {
```

Lastly, we call the `clone()` method on the response, in order to save a copy in the cache, and then return the response to the browser:

```
...
cache.put(request, response.clone());
}

return response;
```

Allowing offline Google Analytics

We discussed read-through caching in the previous recipe. Let's quickly recap what read-through caching is. After a service worker gains control of the page, the first time a new resource has been requested, the response will be stored in the service worker cache.

In this recipe, we are utilizing this feature to store any failed Google Analytics/collect pings in an IndexedDb database. IndexedDb is a client-side, user-specific storage specification that allows us to store data in an indexed manner, and is backed by an API that provides search capabilities. So any time the service worker starts up, any saved Google Analytics pings will be replayed.

To learn more about IndexedDb you can follow these links:

▸ https://developer.mozilla.org/en-US/docs/Web/API/IndexedDB_API/Using_IndexedDB

▸ http://seanamarasinghe.com/developer/indexeddb/

This will give you a great platform to perform transactions offline, regardless of connectivity and availability.

Getting ready

To get started with service workers, you will need to have the service worker experiment feature turned on in your browser settings. If you have not done this yet, refer to the first recipe of *Chapter 1, Learning Service Worker Basics: Setting up service workers*. Service workers only run across HTTPS. To find out how to set up a development environment to support this feature, refer to the following recipes: *Setting up GitHub pages for SSL, Setting up SSL for Windows*, and *Setting up SSL for Mac*.

How to do it...

Follow the instructions to set up your file structure. Alternatively, you can download the files from the following location:

```
https://github.com/szaranger/szaranger.github.io/tree/master/service-
workers/04/03/
```

1. First, we must create an `index.html` file as follows:

```html
<!DOCTYPE html>
<html lang="en">
<head>
  <meta charset="UTF-8">
  <title>Offline Google Analytics</title>
  <link rel="stylesheet" href="style.css">
</head>
<body>
  <section id="registration-status">
    <p>Registration status: <strong
    id="status"></strong></p>
    <input type="button" id="resetButton" value="Reset" />
  </section>
  <section id="outlet">
    <p id="message"></p>
    <div id="images" style="display: none">
      <img src="https://raw.githubusercontent.com/
      szaranger/szaranger.github.io/master/service-
      workers/04/03/serice-worker.jpg">
    </div>
  </section>
  <script src="index.js"></script>
  <script>
    /* jshint ignore:start */
    (function(i,s,o,g,r,a,m){i
    ['GoogleAnalyticsObject']=r;i[r]=i[r]||function(){
      (i[r].q=i[r].q||[]).push(arguments)},i[r].l=1*new
      Date();a=s.createElement(o),
      m=s.getElementsByTagName(o)[0];a.async=1;
      a.src=g;m.parentNode.insertBefore(a,m)
    })(window,document,'script','//www.google-
    analytics.com/analytics.js','ga');
    ga('create', 'UA-12345678-1', 'auto');
```

```
        ga('send', 'pageview');
        /* jshint ignore:end */
    </script>
</body>
</html>
```

2. Create a CSS file called `style.css`, in the same folder as the `index.html` file, with the following code:

```css
* {
  -webkit-box-sizing: border-box;
  -moz-box-sizing: border-box;
  box-sizing: border-box;
}

body {
  margin: 0 auto;
  text-align: center;
  font-family: sans-serif;
}

main {
  max-width: 350px;
  border: 1px solid #4CAF50;
  padding: 20px;
  border-radius: 5px;
  width: 350px;
  margin: 20px auto;
}

h1 {
  color: #4CAF50;
}

img {
  padding: 20px 0;
  max-width: 400px;
}

.hidden {
  display: none;
}
```

```css
#registration-status {
  background-color: #FFE454;
  padding: 10px;
}
```

3. Create a JavaScript file called `index.js`, in the same folder as the `index.html` file, with the following code:

```javascript
'use strict';

var scope = {
  scope: './'
};

if ('serviceWorker' in navigator) {
  navigator.serviceWorker.register(

    'service-worker.js',

    scope
  ).then( function(serviceWorker) {
    printStatus('successful');
    if (navigator.serviceWorker.controller) {
      showImages();
    } else {
      document.querySelector('#message').textContent =
      'Reload the page for images to be loaded from the
      service worker cache';
    }
  }).catch(function(error) {
    printStatus(error);
  });
} else {
  printStatus('unavailable');
}

function printStatus(status) {
  document.querySelector('#status').innerHTML = status;
}

document.querySelector('#resetButton').
addEventListener('click',
  function() {
```

```
    navigator.serviceWorker.getRegistration().
    then(function(registration) {
      registration.unregister();
      window.location.reload();
    });
  }
);

function showImages() {
  document.querySelector('#images').style.display =
  'block';
}
```

4. Create a JavaScript file called `analytics.js`, in the same folder as the `index.html` file, with the following code:

```
'use strict';

var RW = 'readwrite';

function checkForAnalyticsRequest(requestUrl) {
  var url = new URL(requestUrl),
    regex = /^(w{3}|ssl)\.google-analytics.com$/;

  if (url.hostname.match(regex) && url.pathname ===
  '/collect') {
    console.log('INDEXEDDB: Store request(Google analytics)
    for replaying later.');
    saveGoogleAnalyticsRequest(requestUrl);
  }
}

function saveGoogleAnalyticsRequest(requestUrl) {
  getIDBObjectStore(idbInstance, idbStore, RW).add({
    url: requestUrl,
    timestamp: Date.now()
  });
}

function replayGoogleAnalyticsRequests(idbInstance,
idbStore, throttle) {
  var savedGoogleAnalyticsRequests = [];
```

```
getIDBObjectStore(idbInstance,
idbStore).openCursor().onsuccess = function(event) {
  var cursor = event.target.result;

  if (cursor) {
    savedGoogleAnalyticsRequests.push(cursor.value);
    cursor.continue();
  } else {
    console.log('REPLAY: Starting %d Google Analytics
    requests',
      savedGoogleAnalyticsRequests.length);

    savedGoogleAnalyticsRequests.forEach
    (function(savedRequest) {
      var queueTime = Date.now() -
      savedRequest.timestamp;
      if (queueTime > throttle) {
        getIDBObjectStore(idbInstance,
        idbStore, RW).delete(savedRequest.url);
        console.log('REQUEST: Queued for %dms ' +
          'STOPPED: Replay attempt', queueTime);
      } else {
        var requestUrl = savedRequest.url +
        '&qt=' + queueTime;

        console.log('%c ♪ REPLAY: %s %s', 'color:
        #1C99D8', 'in progress...', requestUrl);

        fetch(requestUrl).then(function(response) {
          if (response.status < 400) {
            getIDBObjectStore(idbInstance, idbStore,
            RW).delete(savedRequest.url);
            console.log('%c ♪ REPLAY: %s', 'color:
            #1C99D8', 'success');
          } else {
            console.error('♪ REPLAY: fail -', response);
          }
        }).catch(function(err) {
          console.error('♪ REPLAY: fail - ', err);
        });
      }
    });
  }
};
}
```

5. Open up a browser and go to the `index.html` file:

6. Now open up DevTools (*Cmd + Alt + I* or *F12*) and go to the **Network** tab. You will see the /`collect` requests have a state of **200**, which means successful:

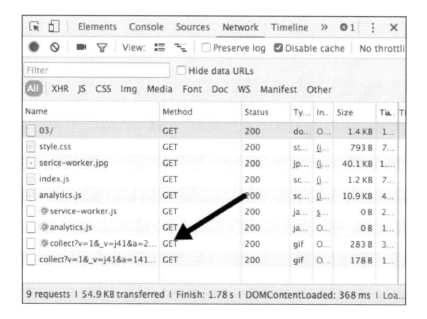

7. Refresh the page. You will see an image as shown in the following screenshot:

8. Go to the **Console** tab of DevTools:

9. Now, go to the **Network** tab of DevTools and select **Offline**:

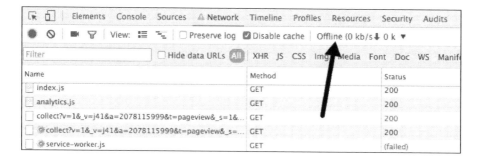

10. Refresh the page and you will still see the same page, but if you view the network requests, you will be able to find out that the service worker has saved the analytics requests in IndexedDb:

```
INDEXEDDB: Store request(Google analytics) for replaying later.
INDEXEDDB: Store request(Google analytics) for replaying later.
```

11. Now change the **Offline** option to **No throttling** in DevTools:

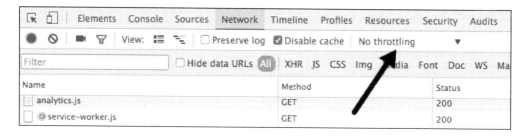

12. Click on the **Reset** button on this page to refresh the service worker, and monitor the console in DevTools. You will see that the replay message extracted from IndexedDb has been sent:

```
REPLAY: Starting 1 Google Analytics requests
  ♪ REPLAY: in progress... https://www.google-analytics.com/collect?v=1&_v=j41&a=542896784&t=pageview&...
I~&jid=&cid=1955052445.1460464514&tid=UA-12345678-1&z=1513801897&qt=312805
  ♪ REPLAY: success
>
```

How it works...

In the `service-worker.js` file, we are accessing IndexedDb by getting a reference to it. Then we go on attaching event handlers for the `error`, `upgradeneed`, and `onsuccess` events of the database instance:

```
var db = openIDBDatabase('offline-google-analytics', idbVersion);
db.onerror = function(err) {
  console.error('%c ✖ ERROR: IndexedDB - %s', 'color: #ff0000',
  err);
};

db.onupgradeneeded = function() {
  this.result.createObjectStore(idbStore, {keyPath: 'url'});
};

db.onsuccess = function() {
  idbInstance = this.result;
  replayGoogleAnalyticsRequests(idbInstance, idbStore, throttle);
};
```

Because of the read-through, caching will cache the initial requests; the subsequent requests to the same resource will be handled by the `fetch()` event handler of the service worker. The fetch event handler queries the cache for requests in the `currentCaches` cache, and sends the response back to the browser:

```
event.respondWith(
    caches.open(currentCaches['offline-google-
    analytics']).then(function(cache) {
      return cache.match(event.request).then(function(res) {
        if (res) {
          console.log(
            '%c ✓ RESPONSE: %c Found in cache: %s',
            'color: #5EBD00', 'color: #000000', res
          );

          return res;
        }
```

If the response was not found, it will send a fetch request to the network:

```
return fetch(event.request.clone()).then(function(res) {
        console.log('%c ✓ RESPONSE: %c For %s from network: %O',
            'color: #5EBD00', 'color: #000000',
            event.request.url, res);

        if (res.status < 400) {
            cache.put(event.request, res.clone());
        }
```

If the response for the preceding request was successful, the response will be cloned and added to the cache, with the request as the key and the response as the value:

```
promises = promises.map(function(promise) {
        return Promise.resolve(promise);
    });
```

Next, we make sure that we resolve the current promise as soon as another one in the array gets resolved:

```
if (res.status < 400) {
        cache.put(event.request, res.clone());
    }
```

If the response is not a server error, and is likely to be a timeout, we pass the request URL to `checkForAnalyticsRequest()`:

```
} else if (res.status >= 500) {
        checkForAnalyticsRequest(event.request.url);
    }
```

The `checkForAnalyticsRequest()` function is in the `analytics.js` file. Let's examine this method. The passed-in URL is first checked to make sure whether it's a call to `google-analytics.com`, regardless of whether the subdomain is www or ssl, and the path name has `/collect` in it. This is to make sure this is an analytics ping:

```
function checkForAnalyticsRequest(requestUrl) {
    var url = new URL(requestUrl),
        regex = /^(w{3}|ssl)\.google-analytics.com$/;

    if (url.hostname.match(regex) && url.pathname === '/collect') {
        console.log('INDEXEDDB: Store request(Google analytics) for
        replaying later.');
        saveGoogleAnalyticsRequest(requestUrl);
    }
}
```

The `saveGoogleAnalyticsRequest()` method will add the URL and the timestamp to the store, which in turn saves the entry.

The `onsuccess()` method, back in the `service-worker.js` file, calls the `replayGoogleAnalyticsRequests()` method. Inside this method, the analytics requests will be saved in a queue called `savedGoogleAnalyticsRequests`:

```
function replayGoogleAnalyticsRequests(idbInstance, idbStore,
throttle) {
  var savedGoogleAnalyticsRequests = [];

  getIDBObjectStore(idbInstance, idbStore).openCursor().onsuccess
= function(event) {
    var cursor = event.target.result;
```

The `openCursor()` function is a pointer to the database where you can traverse records.

The callback of the `onsuccess` event handler will pass in the value of `event.target.result` into the `savedGoogleAnalyticsRequests` array:

```
getIDBObjectStore(idbInstance, idbStore).openCursor().onsuccess =
function(event) {
    var cursor = event.target.result;

    if (cursor) {
      savedGoogleAnalyticsRequests.push(cursor.value);
      cursor.continue();
    }
```

Otherwise, each saved Google Analytics request will be replayed:

```
    } else {
        console.log('REPLAY: Starting %d Google Analytics requests',
          savedGoogleAnalyticsRequests.length);

        savedGoogleAnalyticsRequests.forEach(function(savedRequest) {
          var queueTime = Date.now() - savedRequest.timestamp;
          if (queueTime > throttle) {
            getIDBObjectStore(idbInstance, idbStore,
            RW).delete(savedRequest.url);
            console.log('REQUEST: Queued for %dms ' +
              'STOPPED: Replay attempt', queueTime);
          } else {
            var requestUrl = savedRequest.url + '&qt=' + queueTime;
```

```
console.log('%c ♫ REPLAY: %s %s', 'color: #1C99D8', 'in
progress...', requestUrl);

fetch(requestUrl).then(function(response) {
  if (response.status < 400) {
    getIDBObjectStore(idbInstance, idbStore,
    RW).delete(savedRequest.url);
    console.log('%c ♫ REPLAY: %s', 'color: #1C99D8',
    'success');
  } else {
    console.error('♫ REPLAY: fail -', response);
  }
}).catch(function(err) {
  console.error('♫ REPLAY: fail - ', err);
});
  }
});
}
```

See also

▸   The *Implementing read-through caching* recipe

Allowing offline user interaction

Most websites out there, including news articles, sports videos, or music, are not quite able to be taken offline completely, given their amount of content. There is no real reason for having everything in your cache if you don't access them. But giving the user the option of saving the content in the cache to read later is the ideal solution. In this recipe, we are going to investigate how we can achieve this.

Getting ready

To get started with service workers, you will need to have the service worker experiment feature turned on in your browser settings. If you have not done this yet, refer to the first recipe of *Chapter 1, Learning Service Worker Basics: Setting up service workers*. Service workers only run across HTTPS. To find out how to set up a development environment to support this feature, refer to the following recipes: *Setting up GitHub pages for SSL, Setting up SSL for Windows*, and *Setting up SSL for Mac*.

How to do it...

Follow the instructions to set up your file structure. Alternatively, you can download the files from the following location:

`https://github.com/szaranger/szaranger.github.io/tree/master/service-workers/04/04/`

1. First, we must create an `index.html` file as follows:

```html
<!DOCTYPE html>
<html lang="en">
<head>
  <meta charset="UTF-8">
  <title>Offline User Interaction</title>
  <link rel="stylesheet" href="style.css">
</head>
<body>
  <section id="registration-status">
    <p>Registration status: <strong
    id="status"></strong></p>
    <input type="button" id="resetButton" value="Reset" />
  </section>
  <section>
    <video width="320" height="240" id="video-01" controls>
      <source src="video.mp4" type="video/mp4">
      Your browser does not support the video tag.
    </video>
    <input type="button" id="watch-later" value="Watch
    Later" />
  </section>
  <script src="index.js"></script>
</body>
</html>
```

2. Create a JavaScript file called `index.js`, in the same folder as the `index.html` file, with the following code:

```javascript
'use strict';

var scope = {
  scope: './'
};
```

```
if ('serviceWorker' in navigator) {
  navigator.serviceWorker.register(
    'service-worker.js',
    scope
  ).then( function(serviceWorker) {
    printStatus('successful');
  }).catch(function(error) {
    printStatus(error);
  });
} else {
  printStatus('unavailable');
}

document.querySelector('#resetButton').
addEventListener('click',
  function() {
    navigator.serviceWorker.getRegistration().
    then(function(registration) {
      registration.unregister();
      window.location.reload();
    });
  }
);

function printStatus(status) {
  document.querySelector('#status').innerHTML = status;
}

document.getElementById('watch-later').
addEventListener('click', function(event) {
  event.preventDefault();

  caches.open('video').then(function(cache) {
    fetch('video.mp4').then(function(response) {
      return response.url;
    }).then(function(url) {
      cache.add(url);
    });
  });
});
```

3. Create a JavaScript file called `service-worker.js`, in the same folder as the `index.html` file, with the following code:

```javascript
'use strict';

var cacheName= 'user-interaction-cache';

self.addEventListener('install', function(event) {
  event.waitUntil(
    caches.open(cacheName)
      .then(function(cache) {
        return cache.addAll([
          'index.html'
        ]);
      })
      .then(function() {
        return self.skipWaiting();
      })
  );
});

self.addEventListener('fetch', function(event) {
  event.respondWith(
    caches.match(event.request)
      .then(function(response) {
        if (response) {
          console.log('Fetching from the cache: ',
          event.request.url);
          return response;
        } else {
          console.log('Fetching from server: ',
          event.request.url);
        }
        return fetch(event.request);
      }
    )
  );
});

self.addEventListener('activate', function(event) {
  console.log('Activating the service worker!');
  event.waitUntil(self.clients.claim());
});
```

4. Create a CSS file called `style.css`, in the same folder as the `index.html` file, with the following code:

```css
* {
  -webkit-box-sizing: border-box;
  -moz-box-sizing: border-box;
  box-sizing: border-box;
}

body {
  margin: 0 auto;
  text-align: center;
  font-family: sans-serif;
}

main {
  max-width: 350px;
  border: 1px solid #4CAF50;
  padding: 20px;
  border-radius: 5px;
  width: 350px;
  margin: 20px auto;
}

h1 {
  color: #4CAF50;
}

img {
  padding: 20px 0;
  max-width: 200px;
}

.hidden {
  display: none;
}

#registration-status {
  background-color: #FFE454;
  padding: 10px;
}
```

```
input#watch-later {
    display: block;
    margin: 10px auto;
    padding: 50px;
}
```

5. Open up a browser and go to the `index.html` file. You will see one prefetched bookmark:

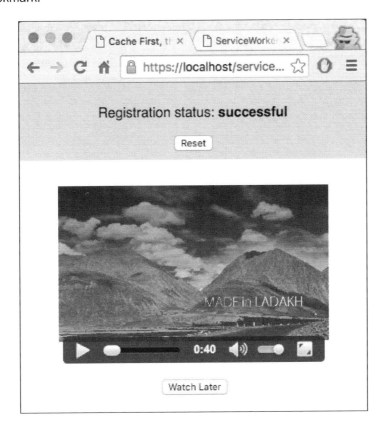

6. Add the video to the cache by clicking on the **Watch Later** button:

7. Now, change the **Offline** option to **No throttling** in DevTools:

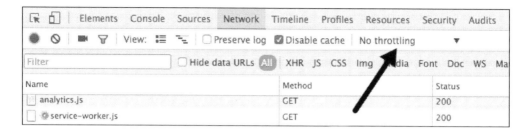

8. Now refresh the page. You will see that styles aren't loaded, but the video is still accessible:

How it works...

In our `service-worker.js` file, we are only caching the `index.html` file in order to load the page:

```
caches.open(cacheName)
    .then(function(cache) {
```

```
        return cache.addAll([
          'index.html'
        ]);
      })
```

In the `index.html` file, we have a video tag with its source pointing to a video file. If the `.mp4` extension is not supported by the browser, it will show the `Your browser does not support the video tag` message:

```
<section>
    <video width="320" height="240" id="video-01" controls>
        <source src="video.mp4" type="video/mp4">
        Your browser does not support the video tag.
    </video>
    <input type="button" id="watch-later" value="Watch Later" />
</section>
```

When you click the **Watch Later** button, the event handler gets fired, which is in turn is handled inside the `index.js` file:

```
document.getElementById('watch-later').addEventListener('click',
function(event) {
  event.preventDefault();

  caches.open('video').then(function(cache) {
    fetch('video.mp4').then(function(response) {
      return response.url;
    }).then(function(url) {
      cache.add(url);
    });
  });
});
```

The `cache.add()` function adds the response URL to the cache. Back in `service-worker.js`, the event listener for fetch retrieves this saved response when we refresh the page in offline mode:

```
self.addEventListener('fetch', function(event) {
  event.respondWith(
    caches.match(event.request)
      .then(function(response) {
        if (response) {
          console.log('Fetching from the cache: ',
          event.request.url);
          return response;
```

```
      } else {
        console.log('Fetching from server: ',
        event.request.url);
      }
      return fetch(event.request);
    }
  )
 );
});
```

Implementing selective caching

In the second recipe of this chapter, *Implementing read-through caching*, we discussed caching all resources at the time of the first request, and we talked about how it does not suit some scenarios, such as news or sports, where most articles will become outdated and you will never access them again. The solution we pointed out at the time was selective caching. So let's look at a working example.

Getting ready

To get started with service workers, you will need to have the service worker experiment feature turned on in your browser settings. If you have not done this yet, refer to the first recipe of *Chapter 1, Learning Service Worker Basics*: *Setting up service workers*. Service workers only run across HTTPS. To find out how to set up a development environment to support this feature, refer to the following recipes: *Setting up GitHub pages for SSL, Setting up SSL for Windows*, and *Setting up SSL for Mac*.

How to do it...

Follow these instructions to set up your file structure:

1. First, we must create an `index.html` file as follows:

```html
<!DOCTYPE html>
<html lang="en">
<head>
  <meta charset="UTF-8">
  <title>Cache First, then Network</title>
  <link rel="stylesheet" href="style.css">
</head>
<body>
```

```
    <section id="registration-status">
      <p>Registration status: <strong
      id="status"></strong></p>
      <input type="button" id="resetButton" value="Reset" />
    </section>
    <section id="outlet">
      <p></p>
    </section>
    <script src="index.js"></script>
  </body>
</html>
```

2. Create a JavaScript file called `index.js`, in the same folder as the `index.html` file, with the following code:

```
'use strict';

var scope = {
  scope: './'
};

if ('serviceWorker' in navigator) {
  navigator.serviceWorker.register(
    'service-worker.js',
    scope
  ).then( function(serviceWorker) {
    printStatus('successful');
    document.querySelector('#outlet p').textContent =
    'The service worker controlling this page has cached
    this funky font.';
  }).catch(function(error) {
    printStatus(error);
  });
} else {
  printStatus('unavailable');
}

function printStatus(status) {
  document.querySelector('#status').innerHTML = status;
}

document.querySelector('#resetButton').addEventListener
('click',
```

```
      function() {
        navigator.serviceWorker.getRegistration().
        then(function(registration) {
          registration.unregister();
          window.location.reload();
        });
      }
    );
```

3. Download the `webfont-serif.woff` file from the source code, or use your own font file, in the same folder as the `index.html` file.

4. Create a JavaScript file called `service-worker.js`, in the same folder as the `index.html` file, with the following code:

```
'use strict';

var cacheVersion = 1,
  currentCaches = {
  font: 'selective-caching-v' + cacheVersion
};

self.addEventListener('activate', function(event) {
  var cacheNamesExpected =
  Object.keys(currentCaches).map(function(key) {
    return currentCaches[key];
  });

  event.waitUntil(
    caches.keys().then(function(cacheNames) {
      return Promise.all(
        cacheNames.map(function(cacheName) {
          if (cacheNamesExpected.indexOf(cacheName) === -1)
          {
            console.log('DELETE: out of date cache:',
            cacheName);
            return caches.delete(cacheName);
          }
        })
      );
    })
  );
});
```

```
self.addEventListener('fetch', function(event) {
  console.log('%c ⚡ EVENT: %c Handling fetch event for
  %s','color: #F57F20',
  'color: #000',
  event.request.url);

  event.respondWith(
    caches.open(currentCaches.font).then(function(cache) {
      return cache.match(event.request).then(function(res)
      {
        if (res) {
          console.log(
            '%c ✓ RESPONSE: %c Found in cache: %s',
            'color: #5EBD00', 'color: #000000', res
          );
          return res;
        }

        console.log('%c ✗ RESPONSE: %c Not found for %s in
        cache. ' +
          'Attempt to fetch from network', 'color:
          #EB4A4B', 'color: #000000',
          event.request.url);

        return fetch(event.request.clone()).
        then(function(res) {
          console.log('%c ✓ RESPONSE: %c For %s from
          network: %O',
            'color: #5EBD00', 'color: #000000',
            event.request.url, res);

          if (res.status < 400 &&
              res.headers.has('content-type') &&
              res.headers.get('content-
              type').match(/^font\//i)) {
            console.log('%c ✓ RESPONSE: %c Caching to %s ',
              'color: #5EBD00', 'color: #000000',
              event.request.url);
            cache.put(event.request, res.clone());
          } else {
            console.log('%c ✓ RESPONSE: %c Not caching to %s ',
```

```
                       'color: #5EBD00', 'color: #000000',
                       event.request.url);
                 }

                 return res;
             });
         }).catch(function(err) {
             throw error;
         });
       })
     );
   });
```

5. Create a CSS file called `style.css`, in the same folder as the `index.html` file, with the following code:

```css
* {
  -webkit-box-sizing: border-box;
  -moz-box-sizing: border-box;
  box-sizing: border-box;
}

body {
  margin: 0 auto;
  text-align: center;
  font-family: sans-serif;
}

main {
  max-width: 350px;
  border: 1px solid #4CAF50;
  padding: 20px;
  border-radius: 5px;
  width: 350px;
  margin: 20px auto;
}

h1 {
  color: #4CAF50;
}

img {
```

```
  padding: 20px 0;
  max-width: 200px;
}

.hidden {
  display: none;
}

#registration-status {
  background-color: #FFE454;
  padding: 10px;
}

@font-face{
  font-family: 'MyWebFont';
  src: url('webfont-serif.woff') format('woff');
}

#outlet p {
  font-family: 'MyWebFont', Arial, sans-serif;
}
```

6. Open up a browser and go to `index.html`. You will see the **Registration status: successful** message and the logo:

7. Now, if you refresh the page and inspect the **Console** tab of the Developer Tools, you will be able to see that the `webfont-serif.woff` file has been fetched from the cache.

How it works...

In our `index.html` file, we add a placeholder section for our message to be displayed:

```html
<section id="outlet">
  <p></p>
</section>
```

In the `style.css` file, we declare the font family we are going to use, and then assign it to the paragraph we are targeting:

```css
@font-face{
font-family: 'MyWebFont';
src: url('webfont-serif.woff') format('woff');
}


#outlet p {
    font-family: 'MyWebFont', Arial, sans-serif;
}
```

In our `service-worker.js` file, we make sure that if a cached version is available, we use it instead of a network request, but fetch an update the next time:

```javascript
if (res.status < 400 &&
            res.headers.has('content-type') &&
            res.headers.get('content-type').match(/^font\//i)) {
        console.log('%c ✓ RESPONSE: %c Caching to %s ',
            'color: #5EBD00', 'color: #000000',
            event.request.url);
        cache.put(event.request, res.clone());
    } else {
        console.log('%c ✓ RESPONSE: %c Not caching to %s ',
            'color: #5EBD00', 'color: #000000',
            event.request.url);
    }
```

See also

▸   The *Implementing read-through caching* recipe

5

Reaching Beyond the Offline Cache

In this chapter, we will cover the following topics:

- Getting network responses offline
- Caching content from ZIP
- Selecting the best content provider (load balancer)
- Redirecting a request
- Setting request headers
- Making a service worker act like a remote server (virtual server)
- Making a service worker act as a dependency injector
- Forcing immediate control
- Implementing fallback responses
- Deferring offline requests

Introduction

In this chapter, we will reach beyond the offline cache and look into advance techniques such as offline network responses; advanced request handling including redirecting, setting request headers, deferring offline requests, and implementing fallback requests; and using a service worker as a load balancer or dependency injector, forcing immediate control, and also caching content from ZIP files.

Let's start off this chapter by looking at how to get network responses offline.

Getting network responses offline

Read-through caching is an assertive approach of all-out caching for the type of static content that you visit regularly. This is not very suitable for dynamic content such as news and sports. A selective caching approach would be better suited for such instances. Read-through caching saves us bandwidth for the server as well as requests over the network. The way read-through caching works is that after the service worker takes control of your page when the first `fetch()` request is called, the response will be cached and subsequent requests to the same URL will be served from the cache.

Getting ready

To get started with service workers, you will need to have the service worker experiment feature turned on in your browser settings. If you have not done this yet, refer to the first recipe of *Chapter 1, Learning Service Worker Basics: Setting up service workers*. Service workers only run across HTTPS. To find out how to set up a development environment to support this feature, refer to the following recipes of *Chapter 1, Learning Service Worker Basics: Setting up GitHub pages for SSL, Setting up SSL for Windows*, and *Setting up SSL for Mac*.

How to do it...

Follow these instructions to set up your file structure:

1. Copy the `index.html`, `index.js`, `service-worker.js`, and `style.css` files from the following location:

    `https://github.com/szaranger/szaranger.github.io/blob/master/service-workers/05/01/`

2. Open up a browser and go to `index.html`.

3. Open up the Developer Toolbar (*Cmd + Alt + I* or *F12*). Now refresh the page and look at the message in the console. You will see the `style.css` file is served from the network, but the `index.js` file is served from the cache.

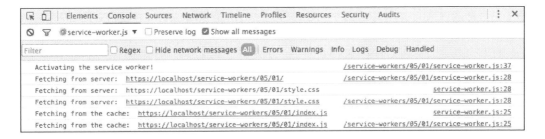

How it works...

When the service worker file is installing the service worker, it saves the `index.html` file and the `index.js` file in the cache. We are intentionally skipping the `style.css` file here, so when you refresh the page, the service worker first looks at the cached files, finds `index.html` and `index.js` files there, and serves them from the cache. The `style.css` file is not in the cache, however, so the service worker fetches it from the network.

```
self.addEventListener('install', function(event) {
  event.waitUntil(
    caches.open(cacheName)
      .then(function(cache) {
        return cache.addAll([
          'index.html',
          'index.js'
        ]);
      })
      .then(function() {
        return self.skipWaiting();
      })
  );
});
```

Caching content from ZIP

If you are concerned about the speed of loading your application over the Internet, one of the areas you might look into is reducing the number of requests made by your app to download resources. One way of reducing HTTP requests is sending your resource files, such as, images as a ZIP package to the client.

In this recipe, we will look at how we can cache resources from a ZIP file.

Getting ready

To get started with service workers, you will need to have the service worker experiment feature turned on in your browser settings. If you have not done this yet, refer to the first recipe of *Chapter 1, Learning Service Worker Basics*: *Setting up service workers*. Service workers only run across HTTPS. To find out how to set up a development environment to support this feature, refer to the following recipes of *Chapter 1, Learning Service Worker Basics*: *Setting up GitHub pages for SSL*, *Setting up SSL for Windows*, and *Setting up SSL for Mac*.

How to do it...

Follow these instructions to set up your file structure:

1. First, we must create an `index.html` file and copy the code from the following location:

   `https://github.com/szaranger/szaranger.github.io/blob/master/service-workers/05/02/index.html`

2. Create a JavaScript file called `service-worker.js` in the same folder as the `index.html` and copy the code from the following location:

   `https://github.com/szaranger/szaranger.github.io/blob/master/service-workers/05/02/index.html`

3. Copy the third-party code from the following location into a new folder called `vendor`:

   `https://github.com/szaranger/szaranger.github.io/blob/master/service-workers/05/02/vendor`

4. Add `archive.zip`, `cacheProvider.js`, `helper.js`, `index.js`, the `images` folder, and `style.css` into the same directory as the `index.html` file from the following location:

   `https://github.com/szaranger/szaranger.github.io/blob/master/service-workers/05/02/`

5. Open up a browser and go to the `index.html` file.

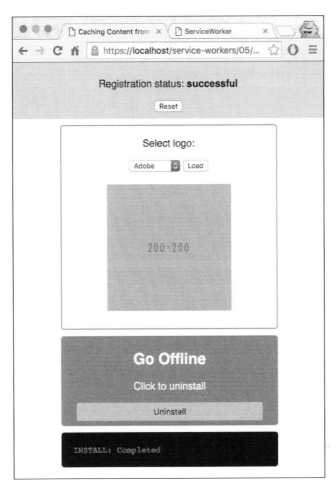

6. Select a brand from the drop-down menu and click **Load**.

7. Now click on the **Uninstall** button.

How it works...

In our `index.html` file, we check whether the service worker is controlling the page. If so, we display the images.

```
navigator.serviceWorker.getRegistration().then(function(reg) {
    if (reg && reg.active) {
        displayImages();
    }
});
```

When the service worker is active at the time of installation, we show the drop-down list:

```
navigator.serviceWorker.oncontrollerchange = function() {
    if (navigator.serviceWorker.controller) {
        printInstall('INSTALL: Completed');
        displayImages();
    }
};
```

Uninstalling the package does not remove the resources from the cache because the offline cache will not be erased by uninstalling the service worker:

```
document.querySelector('#uninstall').onclick = function() {
    ...
}
```

Let's move on to the `service-worker.js` file. There we import some third-party scripts from the vendor folder, and also some of our own:

```
importScripts('./vendor/zip.js');
importScripts('./vendor/ArrayBufferReader.js');
importScripts('./vendor/deflate.js');
importScripts('./vendor/inflate.js');
importScripts('./helper.js');
importScripts('./cacheProvider.js');
```

At the time of the installation, we are getting the content from the ZIP file, `responses-offline`, and storing it in the cache.

```
self.oninstall = function(event) {
  event.waitUntil(
    fetch(zipURL)
      .then(function(res) {
        return res.arrayBuffer();
      })
      .then(getZipFileReader)
      .then(cacheFileContents)
      .then(self.skipWaiting.bind(self))
  );
};
```

Gain control of the clients at the point of activation:

```
self.onactivate = function(evt) {
  evt.waitUntil(self.clients.claim());
};
```

Query the cache and, if the request doesn't match, send the request to the network:

```
self.onfetch = function(evt) {
  evt.respondWith(openCache().then(function(cache) {
    var request = evt.request;

    return cache.match(request).then(function(res) {
      return res || fetch(request);
    });
  }));
};
```

Now let's look at the `cacheProvider.js` file for the functions handling the cache.

We don't cache the folders, only the files inside them:

```
function cacheEntry(entry) {
  if (entry.directory) {
    return Promise.resolve();
  }
```

The blob writer is a supported format for the response object's constructor. The data will be read the way the writer wants it to be read:

```
return new Promise(function(fulfill, reject) {
    var blobWriter = new zip.BlobWriter();

    entry.getData(blobWriter, function(data) {
        return openCache().then(function(cache) {
            var fileLocation = getFileLocation(entry.filename),
            response = new Response(data, { headers: {
```

We identify the type of the file by looking at its extension:

```
response = new Response(data, { headers: {
        'Content-Type': getContentType(entry.filename)
    } });
```

We have to clone the `response` object because once it is being used, you cannot use it again:

```
if (entry.filename === ROOT) {
        cache.put(getFileLocation(), response.clone());
    }

    return cache.put(fileLocation, response);
}).then(fulfill, reject);
```

Let's look at the `helper.js` file as well. The `getZipFileReader(data)` function wraps the `zip.js` API in a promise:

```
function getZipFileReader(data) {
    return new Promise(function(fulfill, reject) {
      var arrayBufferReader = new zip.ArrayBufferReader(data);
      zip.createReader(arrayBufferReader, fulfill, reject);
    });
}
```

The `getContentType(filename)` method returns the content type of a file by the extension:

```
function getContentType(filename) {
    var tokens = filename.split('.');
    var extension = tokens[tokens.length - 1];
    return contentTypes[extension] || 'text/plain';
}
```

Selecting the best content provider (load balancer)

In this recipe, we are going to look at how we can use the service worker as a load balancer so we can decide which content provider is the best suited for us to get content from, depending on the load of the content provider.

Getting ready

To get started with service workers, you will need to have the service worker experiment feature turned on in your browser settings. If you have not done this yet, refer to the first recipe of *Chapter 1, Learning Service Worker Basics: Setting up service workers*. Service workers only run across HTTPS. To find out how to set up a development environment to support this feature, refer to the following recipes: *Setting up GitHub pages for SSL, Setting up SSL for Windows*, and *Setting up SSL for Mac*. You also need to make sure Node.js is available to you. You can read how to install Node.js at `https://nodejs.org/en/`.

How to do it...

Follow these instructions to set up your file structure:

1. Download all the files from the following location:

    `https://github.com/szaranger/szaranger.github.io/blob/master/service-workers/05/03/`

2. Run the following command in the command line (make sure you have Node.js installed or read how to do so on `https://nodejs.org/en/`):

    `npm install`

3. Open up a browser and go to `index.html`.

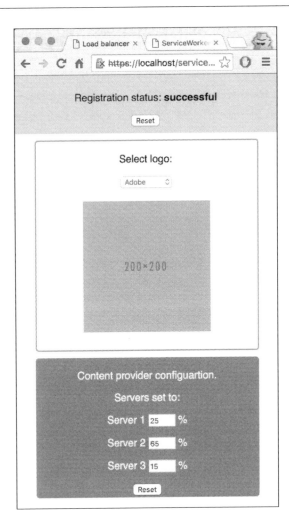

4. You can select the logo from the drop-down list and it will load the image from the best content provider, with less load. You can also manually set the server loads and click **Reset**.

How it works...

In the `service-worker.js` file, we are forcing the service worker to gain control of the clients straight away:

```
self.oninstall = function(evt) {
  evt.waitUntil(self.skipWaiting());
};

self.onactivate = function(evt) {
  evt.waitUntil(self.clients.claim());
};
```

We use a regex pattern to check whether the request contains images:

```
function isResource(req) {
  return req.url.match(/\/images\/.*$/) && req.method === 'GET';
}
```

The method for the best server returns the server with the lowest load and then returns the image from that server:

```
function fetchContentFromBestServer(req) {
  var session = req.url.match(/\?session=([^&]*)/)[1];
  return getContentServerLoads(session)
    .then(selectContentServer)
    .then(function(serverUrl) {
      var resourcePath = req.url.match(/\/images\/[^?]*/)[0],
        serverReq = new Request(serverUrl + resourcePath);

      return fetch(serverReq);
    });
}
```

The Express server will be queried to find the server loads:

```
function getContentServerLoads(session) {
  return fetch(baseURL + '/server-loads?session=' +
  session).then(function(res) {
    return res.json();
  });
}
```

In the `index.js` file, we are setting the handlers for image selection:

```
navigator.serviceWorker.ready.then(displayUI);

function displayUI() {
  getServerLoads().then(function(loads) {
    serverLoads.forEach(function(input, index) {
      input.value = loads[index];
      input.disabled = false;
    });
    document.querySelector('#image-selection').disabled = false;
  });
}
```

Also, when the user clicks on the **Reset** button, the manual load values will be sent to the Express server:

```
document.querySelector('#load-configuration').onsubmit =
function(event) {
  event.preventDefault();

  var loads = serverLoads.map(function(input) {
    return parseInt(input.value, 10);
  });

  fetch(setSession(baseURL + '/server-loads'), {
    method: 'PUT',
    headers: { 'Content-Type': 'application/json' },
    body: JSON.stringify(loads)
  }).then(function(res) {
    return res.json();
  }).then(function(result) {
    document.querySelector('#server-label').textContent = result;
  });
};
```

When changing the image selection, in order to prevent caching, we add a cache bust parameter:

```
document.querySelector('#image-selection').onchange = function() {
  var imgUrl = document.querySelector('select').value,
    img = document.querySelector('img');
  if (imgUrl) {
    img.src = setSession(imgUrl) + '&_b=' + Date.now();
```

We are setting the session values with a random string and store them in `localStorage`:

```
function getSession() {
  var session = localStorage.getItem('session');
  if (!session) {
    session = '' + Date.now() + '-' + Math.random();
    localStorage.setItem('session', session);
  }
  return session;
}
```

The `server.js` file is an Express server running on a specified port. The service worker requires the server to run over a SSL connection. To achieve this, we are using HTTP node module and we are setting the location of the key/value pairs we created in the following recipes of *Chapter 1, Learning Service Worker Basics*: *Setting up GitHub pages for SSL*, *Setting up SSL for Windows*, and *Setting up SSL for Mac*.

```
var https = require('https');
var fs = require('fs');

var privateKey = fs.readFileSync('/private/etc/apache2/localhost-
key.pem', 'utf8');
var certificate = fs.readFileSync('/private/etc/apache2/localhost-
cert.pem', 'utf8');
var credentials = { key: privateKey, cert: certificate };
var httpsServer = https.createServer(credentials, app);
```

We are also allowing cross-origin resource sharing for our web page to access this server.

```
app.use(function(req, res, next) {
  res.header("Access-Control-Allow-Origin", "*");
  res.header("Access-Control-Allow-Methods", "POST, GET, PUT,
DELETE, OPTIONS");
  res.header("Access-Control-Allow-Headers", "Origin, X-Requested-
With, Content-Type, Accept");
  next();
});
```

Redirecting a request

Relative URLs, such as `test/`, should redirect to `index.html` if there is one in the `test/` directory. Let's test this scenario with the service worker.

Getting ready

To get started with service workers, you will need to have the service worker experiment feature turned on in your browser settings. If you have not done this yet, refer to the first recipe of *Chapter 1, Learning Service Worker Basics*: *Setting up service workers*. Service workers only run across HTTPS. To find out how to set up a development environment to support this feature, refer to the following recipes: *Setting up GitHub pages for SSL, Setting up SSL for Windows*, and *Setting up SSL for Mac*.

How to do it...

Follow these instructions to set up your file structure:

1. First, we must create an `index.html` file as follows:

```
<!DOCTYPE html>
<html lang="en">
<head>
  <meta charset="UTF-8">
  <title>Redirect request</title>
  <link rel="stylesheet" href="style.css">
</head>
<body>
  <section id="registration-status">
    <p>Registration status: <strong
    id="status"></strong></p>
    <input type="button" id="resetButton" value="Reset" />
  </section>
  <section>
    <h1>Redirect</h1>
    <p>Relative URLs should redirect to
    <strong>index.html</strong> if it exists.</p>
    <p><a href="test">Click</a></p>
  </section>
  <script src="index.js"></script>
</body>
</html>
```

2. Create a CSS file called `style.css`, in the same folder as the `index.html` file, with the following code:

```
* {
  -webkit-box-sizing: border-box;
  -moz-box-sizing: border-box;
```

```
    box-sizing: border-box;
  }

  body {
    margin: 0 auto;
    text-align: center;
    font-family: sans-serif;
  }

  main {
    max-width: 350px;
    border: 1px solid #4CAF50;
    padding: 20px;
    border-radius: 5px;
    width: 350px;
    margin: 20px auto;
  }

  h1 {
    color: #4CAF50;
  }

  img {
    padding: 20px 0;
    max-width: 400px;
  }

  .hidden {
    display: none;
  }

  #registration-status {
    background-color: #FFE454;
    padding: 10px;
  }
```

3. Create a JavaScript file called `index.js`, in the same folder as the `index.html` file, with the following code:

```
'use strict';

var scope = {
  scope: './'
```

```
};

if ('serviceWorker' in navigator) {
  navigator.serviceWorker.register(
    'service-worker.js',
    scope
  ).then( function(serviceWorker) {
    printStatus('successful');
    if (navigator.serviceWorker.controller) {
      showImages();
    } else {
      document.querySelector('#message').textContent =
      'Reload the page for images to be loaded from the
      service worker cache';
    }
  }).catch(function(error) {
    printStatus(error);
  });
} else {
  printStatus('unavailable');
}

function printStatus(status) {
  document.querySelector('#status').innerHTML = status;
}

document.querySelector('#resetButton').addEventListener
('click',
  function() {
    navigator.serviceWorker.getRegistration().
    then(function(registration) {
      registration.unregister();
      window.location.reload();
    });
  }
);
```

4. Create a JavaScript file called `service-worker.js` in the same folder as the `index.html` file

5. :

```
'use strict';

var cacheName= 'redirect-request';
```

```
self.addEventListener('activate', function() {
  clients.claim();
});

self.addEventListener('fetch', function(evt) {
  console.log(evt.request);
  evt.respondWith(
    fetch(evt.request).catch(function() {
      return new Response("FETCH: failed");
    })
  );
});
```

6. Open up a browser and go to `index.html`.

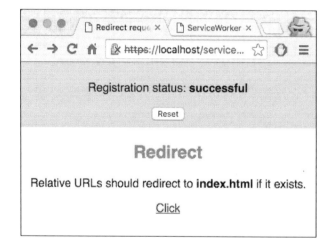

7. Now open up the DevTools (*Cmd* + *Alt* + *I* or *F12*) and make sure the **Preserve log** checkbox is clicked. Now click on the **Click** link. The page will be redirected to the index.html file of the test/ directory.

How it works...

In the `service-worker.js` file, we let all the fetch requests through to the network:

```
self.addEventListener('fetch', function(evt) {
  console.log(evt.request);
  evt.respondWith(
    fetch(evt.request).catch(function() {
      return new Response("FETCH: failed");
    })
  );
});
```

This way, the relative URL will redirect to the HTTP version of `test/`, if the `test/index.html` file exists.

Setting request headers

If we wanted to find out the request header details sent to the network, we can log the request header details to the console. In this recipe, we are going to find out how to do this.

Getting ready

To get started with service workers, you will need to have the service worker experiment feature turned on in your browser settings. If you have not done this yet, refer to the first recipe of *Chapter 1, Learning Service Worker Basics: Setting up service workers*. Service workers only run across HTTPS. To find out how to set up a development environment to support this feature, refer to the following recipes: *Setting up GitHub pages for SSL, Setting up SSL for Windows*, and *Setting up SSL for Mac*.

How to do it...

Follow these instructions to set up your file structure:

1. First, we must create an `index.html` file, as follows:

    ```
    <!DOCTYPE html>
    <html lang="en">
    <head>
      <meta charset="UTF-8">
      <title>Request headers</title>
      <link rel="stylesheet" href="style.css">
    </head>
    ```

```html
<body>
  <section id="registration-status">
    <p>Registration status: <strong
    id="status"></strong></p>
    <input type="button" id="resetButton" value="Reset" />
  </section>
  <script src="index.js"></script>
  <section>
    <img src="adobe-logo.png" alt="logo">
  </section>
</body>
</html>
```

2. Create a JavaScript file called `service-worker.js`, in the same folder as the `index.html` file, with the following code:

```javascript
'use strict';

self.addEventListener('fetch', function(evt) {
  var request = evt.request;

  console.log(
    "FETCH: ",
    evt.request.url,
    "HEADERS: ",
    new Set(request.headers)
  );

  evt.respondWith(fetch(request));
});
```

3. Create a CSS file called `style.css`, in the same folder as the `index.html` file, with the following code:

```css
* {
  -webkit-box-sizing: border-box;
  -moz-box-sizing: border-box;
  box-sizing: border-box;
}

body {
  margin: 0 auto;
  text-align: center;
  font-family: sans-serif;
}
```

```
main {
  max-width: 350px;
  border: 1px solid #4CAF50;
  padding: 20px;
  border-radius: 5px;
  width: 350px;
  margin: 20px auto;
}

h1 {
  color: #4CAF50;
}

img {
  padding: 20px 0;
  max-width: 200px;
}

.hidden {
  display: none;
}

#registration-status {
  background-color: #FFE454;
  padding: 10px;
}
```

4. Open up a browser and go to the `index.html` file. You will see one pre-fetched bookmark.

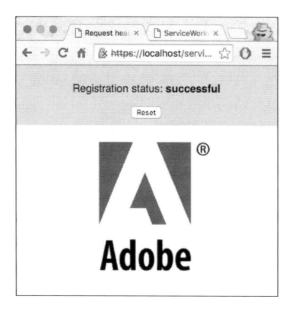

5. Now open up the DevTools (*Cmd + Alt + I* or *F12*), and refresh the page. Check out the log details on the console.

How it works...

In our `service-worker.js` file, the fetch event handler logs the request details, as well as the header details of any request:

```
caches.open(cacheName)
    .then(function(cache) {
      return cache.addAll([
        'index.html'
      ]);
    })
```

In the `index.html` file, we are loading an image which will be intercepted by the controlling service worker's fetch event.

```
<section >
    <img src="adobe-logo.png" alt="logo">
</section>
```

Making a service worker act like a remote server

Service workers not only act like load balancers, as we discussed in the *Selecting the best content provider (load balancer)* recipe of this chapter; they can also act like virtual servers. This allows us to decouple the UI from the typical server-side business logic.

In this recipe, we are going to learn how we can move the business logic portion to a service worker responding to traditional RESTful fetch requests. To demonstrate this feature, we are going to implement a to-do app.

Getting ready

To get started with service workers, you will need to have the service worker experiment feature turned on in your browser settings. If you have not done this yet, refer to the first recipe of *Chapter 1, Learning Service Worker Basics: Setting up service workers.* Service workers only run across HTTPS. To find out how to set up a development environment to support this feature, refer to the following recipes: *Setting up GitHub pages for SSL, Setting up SSL for Windows,* and *Setting up SSL for Mac.*

How to do it...

Follow these instructions to set up your file structure:

1. Download all the files from the following location:

    ```
    https://github.com/szaranger/szaranger.github.io/blob/master/
    service-workers/05/06/
    ```

2. Open up a browser and go to the `index.html` file. You will see the to-do app with pre-fetched to-dos.

3. Now open up DevTools (*Cmd + Alt + I* or *F12*) and refresh the page. Check out the log details on the console. You will see the endpoint has been accessed.

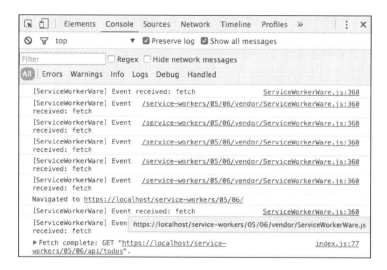

4. You can add to-do items and their priorities, and you can also remove them by clicking on the remove icon.

How it works...

We need to implement the endpoints to start with. In the `worker.js` file, we are
creating an instance of the `ServiceWorkerWare` module. We then declare the routes
for our to-do items.

We determine the root using `self.location`:

```
root = (function() {
    var tkns = (self.location + '').split('/');
    tkns[tkns.length - 1] = '';
    return tkns.join('/');
})();
```

Retrieve all to-do items:

```
worker.get(root + 'api/todos', function(request, response) {
    return new Response(JSON.stringify(todos.filter(function(item) {
        return item !== null;
    })));
});
```

Retrieve the 0-based position (`id`) for deleting a specific to-do item:

```
worker.delete(root + 'api/todos/:id', function(request, response) {
    var id = parseInt(request.parameters.id, 10) - 1;
    if (!todos[id].isSticky) {
        todos[id] = null;
    }
    return new Response({ status: 204 });
});
```

To add a new to-do item to the collection, use the following code:

```
worker.post(root + 'api/todos', function(request, response) {
    return request.json().then(function(quote) {
        quote.id = todos.length + 1;
        todos.push(quote);
        return new Response(JSON.stringify(quote), { status: 201 });
    });
});
```

In the `index.html` file, we are loading an image that will be intercepted by the controlling
service worker's fetch event:

```
<section >
    <img src="adobe-logo.png" alt="logo">
</section>
```

In our `service-worker.js` file, we are importing a third-party script called `ServiceWorkerWare.js` and our custom script, `worker.js`, and declaring a to-do list with pre-filled to-do items:

```
importScripts('./vendor/ServiceWorkerWare.js');
importScripts('./worker.js');

var todos = [
  {
    text: 'Buy Milk',
    priority: 'high'
  },
  {
    text: 'Refill Car',
    priority: 'medium'
  },
  {
    text: 'Return loaned book',
    priority: 'low'
  }
].map(function(todo, index) {
  todo.id = index + 1;
  todo.isSticky = true;

  return todo;
});
```

The `index.js` file is where most of our work is taking place. When the service worker gets hold of the control of the page, it shows the list of to-do items:

```
navigator.serviceWorker.oncontrollerchange = function() {
    this.controller.onstatechange = function() {
        if (this.state === 'activated') {
            loadTodos();
        }
    };
};
```

Clicking the **+** button will retrieve the to-do item and post it to the backend:

```
document.getElementById('add-form').onsubmit = function(event) {
```

Any to-do item with no priority provided will be left blank:

```
todoPriority = document.getElementById('priority').value.trim() ||
                        'Not specified';
```

Finally, send the to-do item to the backend via a post request:

```
fetch(endPoint, {
    method: 'POST',
    body: JSON.stringify(todo),
    headers: headers
})
```

Making a service worker act as a dependency injector

Dependency injection is a great pattern for avoiding hardcoded dependencies for components. In this recipe, we are going to examine how we can use a service worker to development and production environments by passing in two injectors to our components without hardcoding the dependencies.

Getting ready

To get started with service workers, you will need to have the service worker experiment feature turned on in your browser settings. If you have not done this yet, refer to the first recipe of *Chapter 1, Learning Service Worker Basics*: *Setting up service workers*. Service workers only run across HTTPS. To find out how to set up a development environment to support this feature, refer to the following recipes: *Setting up GitHub pages for SSL*, *Setting up SSL for Windows*, and *Setting up SSL for Mac*.

How to do it...

Follow these instructions to set up your file structure:

1. Download all the files from the following location:

    ```
    https://github.com/szaranger/szaranger.github.io/blob/master/
    service-workers/05/07/
    ```

2. Open up a browser and go to the `index.html` file:

3. Click on the **Production** link. You will see a hash added in front of the URL, `#production`.

4. Now click on the buttons. You will get the JavaScript alert messages as a result.

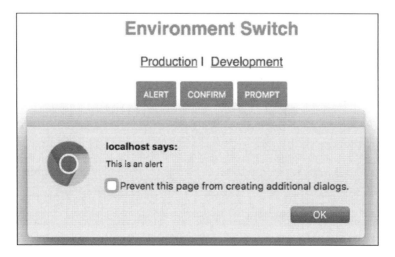

5. Open up DevTools (*Cmd + Alt + I* or *F12*).

6. Now click on the **Development** button and then click on the buttons. Check out the log details on the console. You will get the console messages as a result.

```
alert: This is an alert                                           dialogs:4
confirm: This is a dialog                                         dialogs:8
prompt: This is a prompt                                          dialogs:13
```

How it works...

We are adding a section to the `index.html` file with two links and three buttons; the links are for production and development, and the buttons are for prompts:

```html
<section id="actions">
    <h1>Environment Switch</h1>
    <p>
      <a href="#production">Production</a> | 
      <a href="#development">Development</a>
    </p>
    <p>
      <button id="alert">Alert</button>
      <button id="confirm">Confirm</button>
      <button id="prompt">Prompt</button>
    </p>
</section>
```

In the `index.js` file, the service worker registration handler is given the `development-sw.js` file that we are going to implement soon:

```js
if ('serviceWorker' in navigator) {
  navigator.serviceWorker.register(
    'development-sw.js',
    scope
  )
```

We create a bootstrap file for identifying location URL hash changes and performing a dependency injection when we click on development or production links.

This way, by checking the hash of the URL, we can switch between development and production environments:

```js
window.onhashchange = function() {
  var newInjector = window.location.hash.substr(1) ||
  'production',
```

```
        lastInjector = getLastInjector();

    if (newInjector !== lastInjector) {
      navigator.serviceWorker.oncontrollerchange = function() {
        this.controller.onstatechange = function() {
          if (this.state === 'activated') {
            window.location.reload();
          }
        };
      };
      registerNewInjector(newInjector);
    }
  };
```

Now we force an initial check:

```
    window.onhashchange();
```

Depending on the type of environment, register a service worker:

```
    function registerNewInjector(newInjector) {
      var newInjectorUrl = newInjector + '-sw.js';
      return navigator.serviceWorker.register(newInjectorUrl);
    }
```

If there are any registered service workers, get the current inspecting injector:

```
        function getLastInjector() {
            var newInjector,
            ctr = navigator.serviceWorker.controller;

            if (ctr) {
                newInjector = ctr.scriptURL.endsWith('production-
                sw.js')
                    ? 'production' : 'development';
            }
            return newInjector;
        }
```

Let's look at the `injector.js` file now. Let's make the service worker take control of the client straight away:

```
    function onInstall(evt) {
      evt.waitUntil(self.skipWaiting());
    }
```

```
function onActivate(evt) {
  evt.waitUntil(self.clients.claim());
}
```

The rest of the code is responsible for retrieving actual and abstract resources, and responding to the request accordingly:

```
function onFetch(evt) {
  var abstractRes = evt.request.url,
    actualRes = getActualRes(abstractRes);

  evt.respondWith(fetch(actualRes || abstractRes));
}

function getActualRes(abstractRes) {
  var actualRes,
    keys = Object.keys(mapping);

  for (var i = 0, len = keys.length; i < len; i++) {
    var key = keys[i];

    if (abstractRes.endsWith(key)) {
      actualRes = mapping[key];
      break;
    }
  }

  return actualRes;
}
```

The `fake-dialogs.js` file is a mock implementation that console logs the prompts; that is, it doesn't show the alert message, but instead logs to the console:

```
(function(window) {
  window.dialogs = {
    alert: function(msg) {
      console.log('alert:', msg);
    },

    confirm: function(msg) {
      console.log('confirm:', msg);
      return true;
    },
```

```
    prompt: function(msg) {
        console.log('prompt:', msg);
        return 'development';
    }
  };
})(window);
```

The `real-dialogs.js` file instead generates an alert message:

```
(function(window) {
  window.dialogs = {
    alert: function(msg) {
      window.alert(msg);
    },

    confirm: function(msg) {
      return window.confirm(msg);
    },

    prompt: function(msg) {
      return window.prompt(msg);
    }
  };
})(window);
```

The `production-sw.js` file imports the default mapping, as well as the injector. We also wire the event listeners for the events:

```
importScripts('injector.js');
importScripts('default-mapping.js');

self.onfetch = onFetch;
self.oninstall = onInstall;
self.onactivate = onActivate;
```

The `development-sw.js` file imports the default mapping and the injector as well. But the difference is it overrides `utils/dialogs` to serve the mockup instead:

```
importScripts('injector.js');
importScripts('default-mapping.js');

mapping['utils/dialogs'] = 'fake-dialogs.js';

self.onfetch = onFetch;
self.oninstall = onInstall;
self.onactivate = onActivate;
```

Forcing immediate control

Usually, a service worker will take control of a page when a navigation event is fired. In this recipe, we are looking at how we can take control of a page without waiting for any kind of navigation event.

Getting ready

To get started with service workers, you will need to have the service worker experiment feature turned on in your browser settings. If you have not done this yet, refer to the first recipe of *Chapter 1, Learning Service Worker Basics*: *Setting up service workers*. Service workers only run across HTTPS. To find out how to set up a development environment to support this feature, refer to the following recipes: *Setting up GitHub pages for SSL, Setting up SSL for Windows*, and *Setting up SSL for Mac*.

How to do it...

Follow these instructions to set up your file structure:

1. Download all the files from the following location:

   ```
   https://github.com/szaranger/szaranger.github.io/blob/master/
   service-workers/05/08/
   ```

2. Open up a browser and go to the `index.html` file.

3. Now refresh the page. You will see that there is no registration and no controller change event fired.

4. Open up the DevTools (*Cmd + Alt + I* or *F12*) and refresh the page. Check out the log details on the console. You will see the image has been served from the cache.

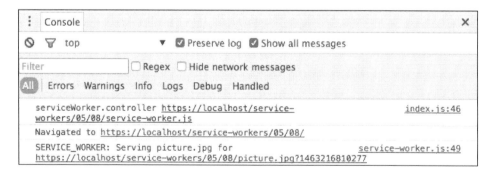

How it works...

In the `index.js` file, the `fetchServiceWorkerUpdate` method updates an image and the current version:

```
function fetchServiceWorkerUpdate() {
  var img = document.getElementById('picture');
  img.src = 'picture.jpg?' + Date.now();

  fetch('./version').then(function(res) {
    return res.text();
  }).then(function(text) {
    debug(text, 'version');
  });
}
```

The service worker will take control of the site on loading and handles offline fallbacks:

```
if (navigator.serviceWorker.controller) {
  var url = navigator.serviceWorker.controller.scriptURL;
  console.log('serviceWorker.controller', url);
  debug(url, 'onload');
  fetchServiceWorkerUpdate();
} else {
  navigator.serviceWorker.register('service-worker.js', {
    scope: './'
  }).then(function(registration) {
    debug('REFRESH for the Service Worker to control this client',
    'onload');
    debug(registration.scope, 'register');
  });
}
```

The `skipWaiting()` method will force the waiting service worker to become active by triggering the `onactivate` event. Along with `Clients.claim()`, this will allow the service worker to take effect immediately in the clients:

```
  }).then(function() {
    console.log('SERVICE_WORKER: Skip waiting on install');
    return self.skipWaiting();
  })
```

Usually, the `onactivate` method is called once a worker has been installed and the page is refreshed. However, because of the fact that we call `skipWaiting()` at the point of `oninstall`, the `onactivate` method is called immediately:

```
self.addEventListener('activate', function(evt) {
  self.clients.matchAll({
    includeUncontrolled: true
  }).then(function(clientList) {
    var urls = clientList.map(function(client) {
      return client.url;
    });
    console.log('SERVICE_WORKER:  Matching clients:', urls.join
    (', '));
  });

  evt.waitUntil(
    caches.keys().then(function(cacheNames) {
      return Promise.all(
        cacheNames.map(function(cacheName) {
          if (cacheName !== VERSION) {
            console.log('SERVICE_WORKER: Deleting old cache:',
            cacheName);
            return caches.delete(cacheName);
          }
        })
      );
    }).then(function() {
      console.log('SERVICE_WORKER: Claiming clients for version',
      VERSION);
      return self.clients.claim();
    })
  );
});
```

Implementing fallback responses

Generally, you can trust the API endpoints your application is connecting to, but there is always a chance that those services could go down. It is good to have a plan B for situations such as this. In this recipe, we are going to use the service worker to provide us with a fallback response in such a situation.

Getting ready

To get started with service workers, you will need to have the service worker experiment feature turned on in your browser settings. If you have not done this yet, refer to the first recipe of *Chapter 1, Learning Service Worker Basics*: *Setting up service workers*. Service workers only run across HTTPS. To find out how to set up a development environment to support this feature, refer to the following recipes: *Setting up GitHub pages for SSL*, *Setting up SSL for Windows*, and *Setting up SSL for Mac*.

How to do it...

Follow these instructions to set up your file structure:

1. Download all the files from the following location:

   ```
   https://github.com/szaranger/szaranger.github.io/blob/master/
   service-workers/05/09/
   ```

2. Open up a browser and go to the `index.html` file.

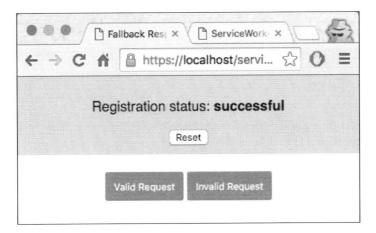

3. Click on the **Valid Request** button. You will see a list of three brands.

4. Now click on the **Invalid Request** button. You will see a list of three brands.

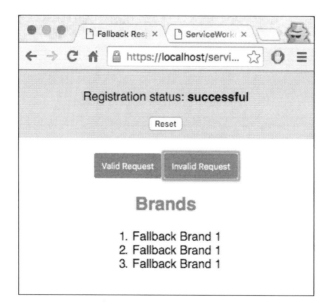

5. Open up the DevTools (*Cmd + Alt + I* or *F12*) and refresh the page. Check out the log details on the console. You will see the fallback response in action.

```
Navigated to https://localhost/service-
workers/05/09/
▶ Fetch complete: GET                        index.js:49
"https://raw.githubusercontent.com/szaranger/szaran
ger.github.io/master/service-
workers/05/09/brands.json".
⊗ GET                                        blah.json:1
https://raw.githubusercontent.com/szarang
er.github.io/master/service-workers/05/09/blah.json
404 (Not Found)
⚠ RESPONSE: Error in                  service-worker.js:20
constructing a fallback response  —  Error: response
status 404(…)
▶ Fetch complete: GET                        index.js:49
"https://raw.githubusercontent.com/szaranger/szaran
ger.github.io/master/service-
workers/05/09/blah.json".
⟩
```

How it works...

We are adding a section to the `index.html` file with two buttons, one for valid requests and the other for invalid requests:

```
<section id="actions">
    <button id="valid-call" disabled>Valid Request</button>
    <button id="invalid-call" disabled>Invalid Request</button>
    <div id="output"></div>
</section>
```

In the `index.js` file, the `enableRequestLinks` method wires up the event handlers for the buttons. Both handlers will fire a `fetchApiRequest` method with a link as a parameter:

```
function enableRequestLinks() {
  var validButton = document.querySelector('#valid-call');
  validButton.addEventListener('click', function() {
    fetchApiRequest('https://raw.githubusercontent.com/
    szaranger/szaranger.github.io/master/service-
    workers/05/09/brands.json');
  });
  validButton.disabled = false;
```

```
    var invalidButton = document.querySelector('#invalid-call');
    invalidButton.addEventListener('click', function() {
      fetchApiRequest('https://raw.githubusercontent.com/
      szaranger/szaranger.github.io/master/service-
      workers/05/09/blah.json');
    });
    invalidButton.disabled = false;
}
```

We have a mock API response prepared for this recipe at the following location:

```
https://github.com/szaranger/szaranger.github.io/blob/master/service-
workers/05/09/brands.json
```

It's a simple JSON object with few brand names:

```
{
    "brands": [
        {
          "name": "Apple"
        },
        {
          "name": "Google"
        },
        {
          "name": "Facebook"
        }
    ]
}
```

The `fetchApiRequest` method calls fetch to get a promise that will return the result in turn. We will use the response to build the list we need:

```
function fetchApiRequest(url) {
  fetch(url).then(function(res) {
    return res.json();
  }).then(function(res) {
    var brands = res.brands.map(function(brand) {
      return '<li>' + brand.name + '</li>';
    }).join('');

    brands = '<ol>' + brands+ '</ol>';

    document.querySelector('#output').innerHTML =
    '<h1>Brands</h1>' + brands;
  });
}
```

The service worker is where we implement the fallback response if the API is not available. But first, we need tell the service worker to take control of the page immediately:

```
self.addEventListener('install', function(evt) {
  evt.waitUntil(self.skipWaiting());
});

self.addEventListener('activate', function(evt) {
  evt.waitUntil(self.clients.claim());
});
```

In the fetch handler, we are checking for the response to see whether it is successful by checking `res.ok`. Otherwise, we will construct a response on the fly as the fallback:

```
self.addEventListener('fetch', function(evt) {
  evt.respondWith(
    fetch(evt.request).then(function(res) {
      if (!res.ok) {
        throw Error('response status ' + res.status);
      }

      return res;
    }).catch(function(err) {
      console.warn('RESPONSE: Error in constructing a fallback
      response - ', err);

      var fallbackRes = {
        brands: [
          {
            name: 'Fallback Brand 1'
          },
          {
            name: 'Fallback Brand 1'
          },
          {
            name: 'Fallback Brand 1'
          }
        ]
      };

      return new Response(JSON.stringify(fallbackRes), {
        headers: {'Content-Type': 'application/json'}
      });
    })
  );
});
```

Deferring offline requests

Applications such as Gmail can enqueue requests in a buffer while the network is not available. When the connection is restored, it will perform the requests in order to complete the operation.

In this recipe, we are building an app, which can defer to-do items while offline.

Getting ready

To get started with service workers, you will need to have the service worker experiment feature turned on in your browser settings. If you have not done this yet, refer to the first recipe of *Chapter 1, Learning Service Worker Basics: Setting up service workers*. Service workers only run across HTTPS. To find out how to set up a development environment to support this feature, refer to the following recipes: *Setting up GitHub pages for SSL*, *Setting up SSL for Windows*, and *Setting up SSL for Mac*.

How to do it...

Follow these instructions to set up your file structure:

1. Download all the files from the following location:

    ```
    https://github.com/szaranger/szaranger.github.io/blob/master/
    service-workers/05/10
    ```

2. Open up a browser and go to the `index.html` file.

3. Add and delete to-do items, then go offline as instructed. Once you reconnect, the to-do items will automatically synchronize.

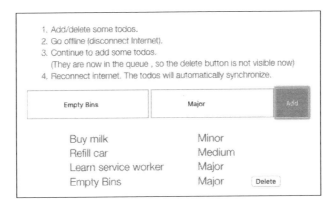

How it works...

We are adding a section to the index.html file with inputs and a button:

```
<section id="todo-area">
    <ol>
        <li>Add/delete some todos.</li>
        <li>Go offline (disconnect Internet).</li>
        <li>Continue to add some todos. <br/>(They are now in the
        queue, so the delete button is not visible now)</li>
        <li>Reconnect internet. The todos will automatically
        synchronize.</li>
    </ol>
    <form id="add-form">
        <input type="text" id="new-todo" placeholder="Add a task
        here"/>
        <input type="text" id="priority" placeholder="Priority"/>
        <input type="submit" value="Add" />
    </form>
    <table id="todos">
    </table>
</section>
```

In the service-worker.js file, we bring in two third-party libraries,
ServiceWorkerWare.js and localforage.js:

```
importScripts('./vendor/ServiceWorkerWare.js');
importScripts('./vendor/localforage.js');
```

Determine the root for the routes:

```
var root = (function() {
  var tokens = (self.location + '').split('/');
  tokens[tokens.length - 1] = '';
  return tokens.join('/');
})();
```

We are using Mozilla's `ServiceWorkerWare` library to build quick routes for the virtual server:

```
var worker = new ServiceWorkerWare();
```

In order to mock responses, we enqueue the original request:

```
function tryOrFallback(fakeResponse) {
  return function(req, res) {
    if (!navigator.onLine) {
      console.log('No network availability, enqueuing');
      return enqueue(req).then(function() {
      return fakeResponse.clone();
    });
  }
}
```

See also

▶   The *Logging API analytics* recipe of *Chapter 6, Working with Advanced Libraries*

6

Working with
Advanced Libraries

In this chapter, we will cover the following topics:

- ▶ Working with global APIs
- ▶ Implementing a circuit breaker
- ▶ Implementing a dead letter queue
- ▶ Logging API analytics
- ▶ Working with Google Analytics

Introduction

In this chapter, you will be introduced to some of the advanced libraries available to interface with the service worker. These topics will be pragmatic and you will be working with advanced libraries in real-world software development. We will also learn about advanced topics, such as circuit breakers and dead letter queues, which you might not come across in everyday programming, but are something new to learn.

Let's start off this chapter by looking at which global APIs are available for the service worker to work with.

Working with global APIs

Service workers can access some very useful global API methods. Let's look at a few of these methods; you might them find handy, and they can be used in your own projects. Some of these global API methods include `Cache`, `caches`, `getAll`, `Request`, `Response`, and `fetch`.

Getting ready

To get started with service workers, you will need to have the service worker experiment feature turned on in your browser settings. If you have not done this yet, refer to the first recipe of *Chapter 1, Learning Service Worker Basics: Setting up service workers*. Service workers only run across HTTPS. To find out how to set up a development environment to support this feature, refer to the following recipes of *Chapter 1, Learning Service Worker Basics: Setting up GitHub pages for SSL, Setting up SSL for Windows*, and *Setting up SSL for Mac*.

How to do it...

Follow these instructions to set up your file structure:

1. Copy the `index.html`, `index.js`, `service-worker.js`, and `style.css` files from the following location:

   `https://github.com/szaranger/szaranger.github.io/blob/master/service-workers/06/01/`

2. Open up a browser and go to `index.html`:

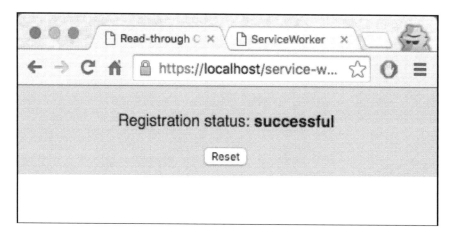

3. Open up the Developer Toolbar (*Cmd + Alt + I* or *F12*). Now refresh the page and look at the message in the console. You will see the global API functions logged into the console:

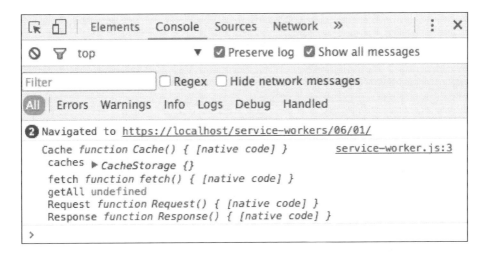

How it works...

We are simply printing some of the APIs available to the service worker to the console. Our `service-worker.js` file looks like the following:

```
'use strict';

console.log(
    'Cache', this.Cache, '\n',
    'caches', this.caches,'\n',
    'fetch', this.fetch,'\n',
    'getAll', this.getAll,'\n',
    'Request', this.Request,'\n',
    'Response', this.Response
);
```

Let's discuss some of these API methods in more detail.

Cache

The `Cache` interface is available for both service workers and windowed scopes. Its main purpose is to provide a storage mechanism for cached `Request` and `Response` object pairs.

caches

The service worker stores assets offline with the `CacheStorage` object, which is enabled by the `window.caches` read-only property.

fetch

The global `fetch` performs an asynchronous fetch across the network.

getAll

This is part of Chromium's command API. It gets passed into `Promise.then()` as an argument.

Implementing a circuit breaker

Imagine you run an application that polls an API every 5 seconds, but for some reason the service goes down, and you keep polling and getting timeouts. You would need to handle the error quickly and gracefully. The circuit breaker pattern detects failures and prevents your application from performing actions that are doomed to fail.

In this recipe, we will look at how to implement a circuit breaker library with the service worker.

Getting ready

To get started with service workers, you will need to have the service worker experiment feature turned on in your browser settings. If you have not done this yet, refer to the first recipe of *Chapter 1, Learning Service Worker Basics*: *Setting up service workers*. Service workers only run across HTTPS. To find out how to set up a development environment to support this feature, refer to the following recipes of *Chapter 1, Learning Service Worker Basics*: *Setting up GitHub pages for SSL, Setting up SSL for Windows*, and *Setting up SSL for Mac*.

How to do it...

Follow these instructions to set up your file structure:

1. Download all the files from the following location:

   `https://github.com/szaranger/szaranger.github.io/blob/master/service-workers/06/02/`

2. Open up a browser and go to the `index.html` file:

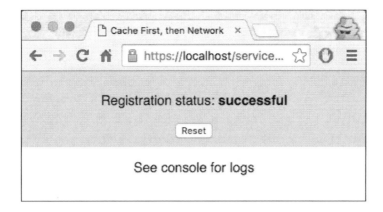

3. Now open up the DevTools (*Cmd + Alt + I* or *F12*) and make sure the **Preserve log** checkbox is clicked. Now refresh the page and you will see the log messages from the circuit breaker:

How it works...

Before looking at the implementation, let's try to understand how a circuit breaker goes about its business.

A circuit breaker monitors for failures. Whenever the failures hit the threshold, the circuit breaker trips and any calls to the circuit breaker will return with an error. After a suitable interval, the circuit breaker resets the breaker if the error no longer occurs.

As you can see, we need two thresholds for error handling and resetting at a certain time after the circuit breaker trips:

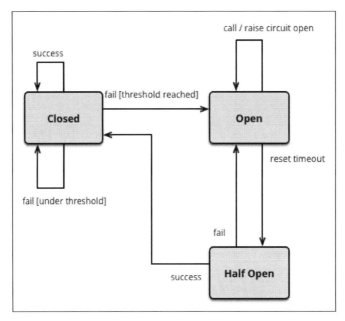

Image source: `http://martinfowler.com`

The majority of our work is going to be in the `circuit-breaker.js` file. If you want to learn more about the circuit breaker, follow this link:

`http://martinfowler.com/bliki/CircuitBreaker.html`

First, we need to configure the circuit breaker. Let's make 10 blocks with a 3-second timeout and a threshold of five. We also define the error threshold as fifty percent:

```
var TEN_SECONDS = 10000,
    TEN_BLOCKS = 10,
    THREE_SECONDS = 3000,
    FIFTY_PERCENT = 50,
    FIVE = 5;

  var CB = function(opts) {
    opts = opts || {};

    this.errorThreshold = opts.errorThreshold || FIFTY_PERCENT;
    this.numBlocks = opts.numBlocks || TEN_BLOCKS;
    this.timeoutDuration = opts.timeoutDuration || THREE_SECONDS;
    this.volumeThreshold = opts.volumeThreshold || FIVE;
```

```
        this.windowDuration = opts.windowDuration || TEN_SECONDS;

        this.hanldeCircuitOpen = opts.hanldeCircuitOpen ||
        function() {};
        this.handleCircuitClose = opts.handleCircuitClose ||
        function() {};

        this.$buckets = [this.$createBlock()];
        this.$state = CB.CLOSED;

        this.$startTicker();
    };
```

We then define a method for `run` as follows:

```
    CB.prototype.run = function(command, fallback) {
        if (this.isOpen()) {
            this.$executeFallback(fallback || function() {});
        } else {
            this.$execCmd(command);
        }
    };
```

This method executes the fallback function passed in as an argument if the circuit is open. Otherwise, it will execute the command. In the `service-worker.js` file, we pass in the `fetch` request as the fallback function for the `run` method:

```
    CircuitBreaker.prototype.fetch = function(request) {
        var unavailableRes = Response.error();

        return new Promise(function(resolve, reject) {
            this.run(function(success, fail) {
                fetch(request).then(function(res) {
                    if(res.status < 400) {
                        success();
                        console.log('FETCH: successful');
                    } else {
                        fail();
                        console.log('FETCH: failed');
                    }
                    resolve(res);
                }).catch(function(err) {
                    fail();
                    reject(unavailableRes);
                    console.log('FETCH: unavailable');
                });
```

```
        }, function() {
            resolve(unavailableRes);
        });
    }.bind(this));
};
```

The `forceClose`, `forceOpen`, and `unforce` methods change the state accordingly:

```
CB.prototype.forceClose = function() {
    this.$forced = this.$state;
    this.$state = CB.CLOSED;
};

CB.prototype.forceOpen = function() {
    this.$forced = this.$state;
    this.$state = CB.OPEN;
};

CB.prototype.unforce = function() {
    this.$state = this.$forced;
    this.$forced = null;
};
```

The `isOpen` function returns a value indicating whether the circuit is open or closed:

```
CB.prototype.isOpen = function() {
    return this.$state === CB.OPEN;
};
```

Query the cache first; if the request doesn't match, send the request to the network:

```
self.onfetch = function(evt) {
    evt.respondWith(openCache().then(function(cache) {
        var request = evt.request;

        return cache.match(request).then(function(res) {
            return res || fetch(request);
        });
    }));
};
```

We denote our private functions with a $ prefix. The $startTicker function starts the timer for us:

```
CB.prototype.$startTicker = function() {
    var me = this,
        bucketIndex = 0,
        bucketDuration = this.windowDuration / this.numBlocks;

    var tick = function() {
        if (me.$buckets.length > me.numBlocks) {
            me.$buckets.shift();
        }

        bucketIndex++;

        if (bucketIndex > me.numBlocks) {
            bucketIndex = 0;

            if (me.isOpen()) {
                me.$state = CB.HALF_OPEN;
            }
        }

        me.$buckets.push(me.$createBlock());
    };

    setInterval(tick, bucketDuration);
};
```

The $createBlock function gives us a fresh block to work with, and the $lastBlock function gives us the last block, as expected:

```
CB.prototype.$createBlock = function() {
    return {
        successes: 0,
        failures: 0,
        shortCircuits: 0,
        timeouts: 0
    };
};

CB.prototype.$lastBlock = function() {
    var numBlocks = this.$buckets.length,
        lastBlock = this.$buckets[numBlocks - 1];

    return lastBlock;
};
```

The $execCmd method updates the state by incrementing successes and failures:

```
CB.prototype.$execCmd = function(command) {
  var me = this,
    increment,
    timeout;

  increment = function(prop) {
    return function() {
      var bucket;

      if (!timeout) {
        return;
      }

      bucket = me.$lastBlock();
      bucket[prop]++;

      if (me.$forced === null) {
        me.$updateState();
      }

      clearTimeout(timeout);
      timeout = null;
    };
  };

  timeout = setTimeout(increment('timeouts'),
  this.timeoutDuration);

  command(increment('successes'), increment('failures'));
};
```

The $executeFallback function runs the fallback method we discussed before:

```
CB.prototype.$executeFallback = function(fallback) {
  var bucket;

  fallback();

  bucket = this.$lastBlock();
  bucket.shortCircuits++;
};
```

The `$calcMetrics` function returns the total number of errors, as well as the count of successes:

```
CB.prototype.$calcMetrics = function() {
    var totalCount = 0,
        totalErrors = 0,
        errorPerc = 0,
        bucket,
        errors,
        i;

        for (i = 0, len = this.$buckets.length; i < len; i++) {
          bucket = this.$buckets[i];
          errors = (bucket.failures + bucket.timeouts);

          totalErrors += errors;
          totalCount += (errors + bucket.successes);
        }

        errorPerc = (totalErrors / (totalCount > 0 ? totalCount : 1))
        * 100;

        return {
          totalErrors: totalErrors,
          errorPerc: errorPerc,
          totalCount: totalCount
        };
};
```

The `$updateState` method updates the state after a series of calculations:

```
CB.prototype.$updateState = function() {
    var metrics = this.$calcMetrics();

    if (this.$state == CB.HALF_OPEN) {
        var lastCmdFailed = !this.$lastBlock().successes &&
        metrics.totalErrors > 0;

        if (lastCmdFailed) {
          this.$state = CB.OPEN;
        } else {
          this.$state = CB.CLOSED;
          this.handleCircuitClose(metrics);
        }
    } else {
```

```
        var overErrorThreshold = metrics.errorPerc >
        this.errorThreshold,
          overVolumeThreshold = metrics.totalCount >
          this.volumeThreshold,
          overThreshold = overVolumeThreshold && overErrorThreshold;

      if (overThreshold) {
        this.$state = CB.OPEN;
        this.hanldeCircuitOpen(metrics);
      }
    }
  };
```

Inside our `service-worker.js` file, we are using our circuit-breaker library by passing the fetch request via a circuitBreaker object:

```
self.addEventListener('fetch', function(evt) {
    var url = evt.request.url;

    if(!circuitBreakers[url]) {
        circuitBreakers[url] = new CircuitBreaker(opt);
    }

    evt.respondWith(circuitBreakers[url].fetch(evt.request));
});
```

Implementing a dead letter queue

Dead letter queues are system-generated queues for one or many of the following reasons: for storing messages that could not be delivered, queue length limit exceeded, message length limit exceeded, or a message being rejected by another queue exchange.

In this recipe, we are implementing a dead letter queue in the service worker.

Getting ready

To get started with service workers, you will need to have the service worker experiment feature turned on in your browser settings. If you have not done this yet, refer to the first recipe of *Chapter 1, Learning Service Worker Basics: Setting up service workers*. Service workers only run across HTTPS. To find out how to set up a development environment to support this feature, refer to the following recipes: *Setting up GitHub pages for SSL, Setting up SSL for Windows*, and *Setting up SSL for Mac*.

How to do it...

Follow these instructions to set up your file structure:

1. Download all the files from the following location:

    ```
    https://github.com/szaranger/szaranger.github.io/blob/master/
    service-workers/06/03/
    ```

2. Open up a browser and go to `index.html`:

3. Now open up the DevTools (*Cmd + Alt + I* or *F12*) and make sure the **Preserve log** checkbox is clicked.

4. Select the offline option on the **Network** tab:

5. Now refresh the page and you will see the failed request messages, which are queued in the dead letter queue we implemented:

How it works...

The install event handler of the service worker caches the files we are passing into the addAll method in the `service-worker.js` file:

```
self.addEventListener('install', function(evt) {
    evt.waitUntil(
        caches.open(cacheName)
            .then(function(cache) {
                return cache.addAll([
                    'style.css',
                    'index.html',
                    'index.js',
                    'style.css'
                ]);
            })
            .then(function() {
                return self.skipWaiting();
            })
    );
});
```

When we request files over the wire, the `fetch` event handler queries the cache to find out whether the requests are matched, and if so, serves them from the cache:

```
self.addEventListener('fetch', function(evt) {
    evt.respondWith(
        caches.match(evt.request)
            .then(function(res) {
                if(res.status >= 500) {
                    console.log('RESPONSE: error');
                    return Response.error();
                } else {
                    console.log('RESPONSE: success');
                    replayQueuedRequests();
                    return res;
                }
            }).catch(function() {
                queueFailedRequest(evt.request);
            })
    );
});
```

Also, if the response is successful, then we call `replayQueuedRequests()` to run any outstanding requests in the queue:

```
function replayQueuedRequests() {
    Object.keys(queue).forEach(function(evt) {
        fetch(queue[evt]).then(function(){
            if(res.status >= 500) {
                console.log('RESPONSE: error');
                return Response.error();
            }
            console.log('DELETE: queue');
            delete queue[error];
        }).catch(function() {
            if (Date.now() - evt > expiration) {
                delete queue[error];
                console.log('DELETE: queue');
            }
        });
    });
}
```

If the fetch fails, we queue the request:

```
function queueFailedRequest(request) {
    queue[Date.now()] = request.url;
    console.log('QUEUED: failed request');
}
```

Logging API analytics

If you were asked to implement API logging for an existing application, what will your approach be? The most common approaches are to either change the client-side code or the server-side code, or both.

By using a service worker, we can intercept client requests and gather information, and then send them to a log API.

Getting ready

To get started with service workers, you will need to have the service worker experiment feature turned on in your browser settings. If you have not done this yet, refer to the first recipe of *Chapter 1, Learning Service Worker Basics*: *Setting up service workers*. Service workers only run across HTTPS. To find out how to set up a development environment to support this feature, refer to the following recipes: *Setting up GitHub pages for SSL*, *Setting up SSL for Windows*, and *Setting up SSL for Mac*.

How to do it...

Follow these instructions to set up your file structure:

1. Download all the files from the following location:

   ```
   https://github.com/szaranger/szaranger.github.io/blob/master/
   service-workers/06/04/
   ```

2. Run `npm install` on the command line:

   npm install

3. Run `npm start` on the command line:

   npm start

4. Open up a browser and go to the `index.html` file:

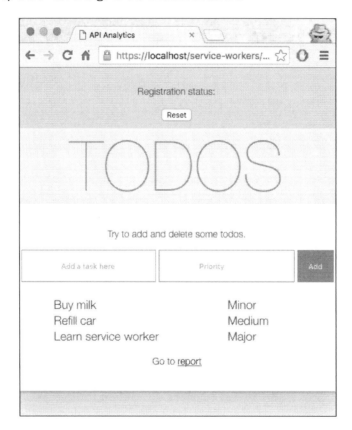

5. Add a task and a priority:

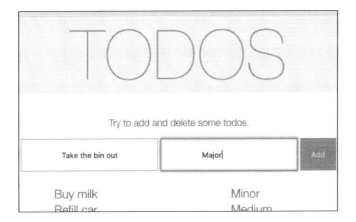

6. Now go to the reports page by clicking on the **reports** link:

How it works...

In the `index.html` file, we are adding a section with a form:

```
<section id="todo-area">
    <p>Try to add and delete some todos.</p>
    <form id="add-form">
      <input type="text" id="new-todo" placeholder="Add a task
      here"/>
```

```
          <input type="text" id="priority" placeholder="Priority"/>
          <input type="submit" value="Add" />
        </form>
        <table id="todos">
        </table>
        <p>Go to <a href="https://localhost:3011/report/"
        target="_blank">report</a></p>
      </section>
```

In the `service-worker.js` file, every time a fetch request is fired, we are logging it:

```
  self.onfetch = function(evt) {
    evt.respondWith(
      logRequest(evt.request).then(fetch)
    );
  };

  function logRequest(req) {
    var retRequest = function() {
      return req;
    };

    var data = {
      method: req.method,
      url: req.url
    };

    return fetch(URL, {
      method: 'POST',
      body: JSON.stringify(data),
      headers: { 'content-type': 'application/json' }
    }).then(retRequest, retRequest);
  }
```

The `index.js` file contains the logic for adding and deleting to-dos. We first show the list of to-dos at the point of registration:

```
  navigator.serviceWorker.oncontrollerchange = function() {
    this.controller.onstatechange = function() {
      if (this.state === 'activated') {
        loadTodos();
      }
    };
  };
```

By clicking on the add button, a new to-do is created and sent to the server:

```
  document.querySelector('#add-form').onsubmit = function(event) {
```

If a to-do was provided, skip it. If no priority is given, the default is `Minor`:

```
if (!newTodo) {
    return;
  }

priority = document.querySelector('#priority').value.trim()
                    || 'Minor';
```

We then send the API request, a `POST` request of to-do collection:

```
fetch(URL, {
    method: 'POST',
    body: JSON.stringify(todo),
    headers: headers,
  }).then(function(response) {
      return response.json();
    }).then(function(addedTodo) {
      document.querySelector('#todos').
      appendChild(getRowFor(addedTodo));
    });
};
```

In order to retrieve the collection of to-dos, we fire a fetch request with the `GET` method:

```
function loadTodos() {
  fetch(URL).then(function(res) {
      return res.json();
    }).then(showTodos);
}
```

Then we populate the to-dos table:

```
function showTodos(items) {
  var table = document.querySelector('#todos');

  table.innerHTML = '';
  for (var i = 0, len = items.length, todo; i < len; i++) {
    todo = items[i];
    table.appendChild(getRowFor(todo));
  }

  if (window.parent !== window) {
    window.parent.document.body.dispatchEvent(new
    CustomEvent('iframeresize'));
  }
}
```

A function is useful for creating rows for the table:

```javascript
function getRowFor(todo) {
  var tr = document.createElement('TR'),
    id = todo.id;

  tr.id = id;

  tr.appendChild(getCell(todo.todo));
  tr.appendChild(getCell(todo.priority));
  tr.appendChild(todo.isSticky ? getCell('') :
  getDeleteButton(id));

  return tr;
}
```

Build a helper function for the table data:

```javascript
function getCell(todo) {
  var td = document.createElement('TD');

  td.textContent = todo;
  return td;
}
```

Build a delete button:

```javascript
function getDeleteButton(id) {
  var td = document.createElement('TD'),
    btn = document.createElement('BUTTON');

  btn.textContent = 'Delete';
  btn.onclick = function() {
    deleteTodo(id).then(function() {
      var tr = document.getElementById(id);
      tr.parentNode.removeChild(tr);
    });
  };

  td.appendChild(btn);
  return td;
}
```

Make a DELETE request for deleting to-dos:

```javascript
function deleteTodo(id) {
  return fetch(URL + '/' + id, { method: 'DELETE' });
}
```

The `server.js` file consists of two APIs, of which one is for to-do management and the other is for logs.

We are providing a set of default to-dos to start with. These to-dos will appear on the top of our list as examples.

```
var todos = [
  {
    todo: 'Buy milk',
    priority: 'Minor'
  },
  {
    todo: 'Refill car',
    priority: 'Medium'
  },
  {
    todo: 'Learn service worker',
    priority: 'Major'
  }
].map(function(todo, index) {
  todo.id = index + 1;
  todo.isSticky = true;

  return todo;
});
```

The sticky flag will make sure that these to-dos are not removable.

The REST API endpoints will manage the requests for adding and deleting to-dos and the logs:

```
app.get('/report', function(req, res) {
  var stats = getLogSummary();
  var buffer = report({ stats: stats });
  res.send(buffer);
});

app.post('/report/logs', function(req, res) {
  var logEntry = logRequest(req.body);
  res.status(201).json(logEntry);
});

app.get('/api/todos', function(req, res) {
  res.json(todos.filter(function(item) {
    return item !== null;
  }));
});
```

```
app.get('/api/todos', function(req, res) {
  res.json(todos.filter(function(item) {
    return item !== null;
  }));
});

app.delete('/api/todos/:id', function(req, res) {
  var id = parseInt(req.params.id, 10) - 1;
  if (!todos[id].isSticky) {
    todos[id] = null;
  }
  res.sendStatus(204);
});

app.post('/api/todos', function(req, res) {
  var todo = req.body;
  todo.id = todos.length + 1;
  todos.push(todo);
  res.status(201).json(todo);
});
```

We create an aggregation function for the log report for GET, DELETE, and POST requests:

```
function getLogSummary() {
  var aggr = requestsLog.reduce(function(subSummary, entry) {
    if (!(entry.url in subSummary)) {
      subSummary[entry.url] = {
        url: entry.url,
        GET: 0,
        POST: 0,
        DELETE: 0,
      };
    }
    subSummary[entry.url][entry.method]++;
    return subSummary;
  }, {});

  return Object.keys(aggr).map(function(url) {
    return aggr[url];
  });
}
```

In the `report.html` file, we have a template for rendering log data. We use SWIG on the server side to render this template:

```html
<table id="todos">
    <tr>
      <th>url</th>
      <th>GET</th>
      <th>POST</th>
      <th>DELETE</th>
    </tr>
    {% for entry in stats %}
    <tr>
      <td>{{ entry.url }}</td>
      <td class="counter">{{ entry.GET }}</td>
      <td class="counter">{{ entry.POST }}</td>
      <td class="counter">{{ entry.DELETE }}</td>
    </tr>
    {% endfor %}
</table>
```

Working with Google Analytics

Google Analytics is a widely used tool today, and the majority of websites use it to collect various data from visitors. In this recipe, we are going to look at how we can benefit from the service worker when implementing Google Analytics.

Getting ready

To get started with service workers, you will need to have the service worker experiment feature turned on in your browser settings. If you have not done this yet, refer to the first recipe of *Chapter 1, Learning Service Worker Basics*: *Setting up service workers*. Service workers only run across HTTPS. To find out how to set up a development environment to support this feature, refer to the following recipes: *Setting up GitHub pages for SSL*, *Setting up SSL for Windows*, and *Setting up SSL for Mac*.

How to do it...

Follow these instructions to set up your file structure:

1. Download all the files from the following location:

    ```
    https://github.com/szaranger/szaranger.github.io/blob/master/
    service-workers/06/05/
    ```

2. Open up a browser and go to the `index.html` file:

3. Now open up the DevTools (*Cmd + Alt + I* or *F12*), and go to the **Network** tab. You will see the /collect requests have a **Status** of 200, which means they've been successful:

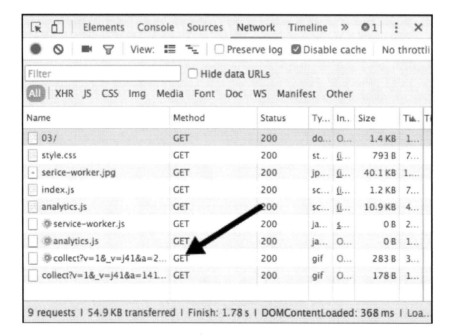

4. Refresh the page. You will see the following screen:

5. Go to the **Console** tab of the DevTools:

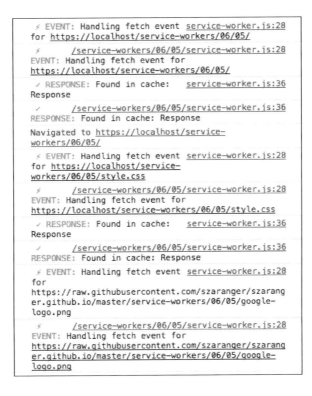

How it works...

In the `service-worker.js` file, at the point of activation, `caches.delete(cacheName)` will find and delete redundant out of date caches by checking the cache name:

```
var version = 1,
  currentCaches = {
    'google-analytics': 'google-analytics-v' + version
  };

self.addEventListener('activate', function(event) {
  var cacheNamesExpected = Object.keys(currentCaches)
  .map(function(key) {
    return currentCaches[key];
  });

  event.waitUntil(
    caches.keys().then(function(cacheNames) {
      return Promise.all(
        cacheNames.map(function(cacheName) {
          if (cacheNamesExpected.indexOf(cacheName) === -1) {
            console.log('DELETE: Out of date cache:', cacheName);
            return caches.delete(cacheName);
          }
        })
      );
    })
  );
});
```

The service worker will cache the initial requests; the subsequent requests to the same resource will be handled by the `fetch()` event handler of the service worker. The `fetch` event handler queries the cache for the requests in the `currentCaches` cache and sends back the response to the browser:

```
event.respondWith(
  caches.open(currentCaches['google-
  analytics']).then(function(cache) {
    return cache.match(event.request).then(function(res) {
      if (res) {
        console.log(
          '%c ✓ RESPONSE: %c Found in cache: %s',
          'color: #5EBD00', 'color: #000000', res
        );

        return res;
      }
```

If the response was not found, it will send a fetch request to the network:

```
return fetch(event.request.clone()).then(function(res) {
    console.log('%c ✓ RESPONSE: %c For %s from network: %O',
        'color: #5EBD00', 'color: #000000',
        event.request.url, res);

    if (res.status < 400) {
        cache.put(event.request, res.clone());
    }
```

If the response for the preceding request was successful, the response will be cloned and added to the cache, with the request being the key and the response being the value:

```
promises = promises.map(function(promise) {
    return Promise.resolve(promise);
});
```

Next, we make sure that we resolve the current promise as soon as another on the array gets resolved:

```
if (res.status < 400) {
    cache.put(event.request, res.clone());
}
```

See also

▶   The *Implementing read-through caching* recipe in *Chapter 4, Accessing Offline Content with Advanced Techniques*

7

Fetching Resources

In this chapter, we will cover the following topics:

- ▸ Fetching remote resources
- ▸ Fetching with `FetchEvent`
- ▸ Fetching a JSON file during service worker installation
- ▸ Proxying
- ▸ Prefetching

Introduction

In this chapter, we will look at how to request files and resources from different sources, which in more technical terms perform fetch actions against different resources. We will look at fetching a JSON file during the service worker installation, using the service worker as a proxy middleware, and prefetching a list of specific resource URLs during the installation process, so that you have the resources handy before loading the page.

Let's start off this chapter by looking at a simple example of fetching a resource from two different resources.

Fetching remote resources

Fetching remote resources can be done in different ways. In this recipe, we are going to look at two standard ways of fetching a remote resource using a service worker, with and without **cross-origin HTTP requests (CORS)**.

You can learn more about CORS at the following link:

`https://developer.mozilla.org/en-US/docs/Web/HTTP/Access_control_CORS`

Getting ready

To get started with service workers, you will need to have the service worker experiment feature turned on in your browser settings. If you have not done this yet, refer to the first recipe of *Chapter 1, Learning Service Worker Basics: Setting up service workers*. Service workers only run across HTTPS. To find out how to set up a development environment to support this feature, refer to the *Setting up GitHub pages for SSL* recipe of *Chapter 1, Learning Service Worker Basics*.

How to do it...

Follow these instructions to set up your file structure:

1. Copy the `index.html`, `index.js`, `service-worker.js`, and `style.css` file from the following location:

   `https://github.com/szaranger/szaranger.github.io/blob/master/service-workers/07/01/`

2. Open up a browser and go to `index.html`. You will see two images fetched from two different protocols, `https` and `https-acao`:

How it works...

At the beginning of the `index.js` file, we are testing two different protocols for loading resources:

- ▶ `https`: HTTP with **Secure Socket Layer** (**SSL**) protocol
- ▶ `https-acao`: SSL protocol with the `Access-Control-Origin=*` header

We will use two different URLs, which will be loaded multiple times:

```
var protocols = {
  'https-acao': 'https://i942.photobucket.com/albums/ad261/
  szaranger/Packt/packt-logo.png',
  'https': 'https://dz13w8afd47il.cloudfront.net/sites/all/
  themes/packt_v4/images/packtlib-logo-dark.png'
};
```

We will also use two different methods for fetching resources, with or without CORS:

```
navigator.serviceWorker.getRegistration().then(function
(registration) {
  var fetchModes = ['cors', 'no-cors'];
```

Next, we will check to see whether the service worker is registered:

```
if (!registration || !navigator.serviceWorker.controller) {
    navigator.serviceWorker.register(
    './service-worker.js').then(function() {
      console.log('Service worker registered, reloading the
      page');
      window.location.reload();
    });
```

If that is not the case, we register it and reload the page to ensure that the client is under the service worker's control:

```
for (var protocol in protocols) {
  if (protocols.hasOwnProperty(protocol)) {
    buildImage(protocol, protocols[protocol]);

    for (var i = 0; i < fetchModes.length; i++) {
      var fetchMode = fetchModes[i],
      init = {
        method: 'GET',
        mode: fetchMode,
```

```
            cache: 'default'
        };


    }
  }
}
```

The two `for` loops go through the provided protocols array and make requests for each protocol. They also build a DOM image element with each URL and go through each mode of the `fetchModes` array.

The `init` object contains any custom settings that you may want to apply to the request. Let's look at the properties of the `init` object:

- ▸ `method`: The request method, for example, `GET`, and `POST`
- ▸ `mode`: The mode you want to use for the request, for example, `cors`, `no-cors`, or `same-origin`
- ▸ `cache`: The cache mode you want to use for the request, for example `default`, `no-store`, `reload`, `no-cache`, `force-cache`, or `only-if-cached`

The `buildImage` function takes two arguments, `protocol` and `url`. It creates an image element on the fly and attaches the URL as the source of that image. Then it goes on to add that image to the DOM tree, where the ID is one of `https-acao-image`, `https-image`, or `http-image`. JavaScript has no control over the URL handling at this point; the browser handles the URLs:

```
function buildImage(protocol, url) {
  var element = protocol + '-image',
    image = document.createElement('img');

  image.src = url;
  document.getElementById(element).appendChild(image);
}
```

Images will be rendered for HTTPS requests only, as service workers only support connections over SSL.

The requests over SSL with the `Access-Control-Origin=*` header (Access Control Allow Origin) will return results successfully.

By default, fetching a resource from a third-party URL will fail if CORS is not supported by it. You can add a non-CORS option to the Request to overcome this. However, this will cause an opaque response, which means that you won't be able to tell whether the response was successful or not.

The `fireRequest` function takes three arguments, `fetchMode`, `protocol`, and `init`. This function returns another function, which we can call as a composition. We start with fetching the given resource directly from the remote resource:

```
fetch(url, init).then(function(response) {
    printSuccess(response, url, section);
}).catch(function(error) {
    printError(error, url, section);
});
```

If the fetch was successful, we print it into the console as well as log it on the web page. The same applies if the request fails, only this time we print the error.

The helper function log finds the DOM element by the ID and adds a paragraph element, as well as a class attribute to depict the type of the message:

```
function log(id, message, type) {
  var type = type || 'success',
      sectionElement = document.getElementById(id),
      logElement = document.createElement('p');

  if (type) {
    logElement.classList.add(type);
  }
  logElement.textContent = message;
  sectionElement.appendChild(logElement);
}
```

In the `index.html` file, we have style declarations in the head section:

```
<style>
.error {
    color: #FF0000;
  }
  .success {
    color: #00FF00;
  }
</style>
```

In our `log()` function, we set the undefined type to success so that it will display the color green when we add it to `classList`. The error type will display red, as declared in the preceding styles.

Fetching with FetchEvent

The `FetchEvent` class is a fetch action dispatched on the service worker. It contains details about requests as well as responses. It provides all important `FetchEvent.reponseWith()` methods, which we can use to provide a response back to the page that is controlled by the service worker.

Getting ready

To get started with service workers, you will need to have the service worker experiment feature turned on in your browser settings. If you have not done this yet, refer to the first recipe of *Chapter 1, Learning Service Worker Basics: Setting up service workers*. Service workers only run across HTTPS. To find out how to set up a development environment to support this feature, refer to the following recipes of *Chapter 1, Learning Service Worker Basics: Setting up GitHub pages for SSL, Setting up SSL for Windows*, and *Setting up SSL for Mac*.

How to do it...

Follow these instructions to set up your file structure:

1. Copy the `index.html`, `index.js`, `service-worker.js`, `adeobe-log.png`, and `style.css` files from the following location:

   `https://github.com/szaranger/szaranger.github.io/blob/master/service-workers/07/02/`

2. Open up a browser and go to `index.html`:

3. Open up the Developer Toolbar (*Cmd + Alt + I* or *F12*). Now refresh the page and look at the messages in the console. You will see the fetch requests are logged in the console:

How it works...

We are simply printing out different stages within the fetch event handler of the service worker to the console. The fetch method of our `service-worker.js` file looks like the following:

```
var cacheName= 'fetch-event-cache';

self.addEventListener('install', function(event) {
  event.waitUntil(
    caches.open(cacheName)
      .then(function(cache) {
        return cache.addAll([
```

```
                    'adobe-logo.png',

                    'style.css',
                    'index.html',
                    'index.js',
                    'style.css'
                ]);
            })
            .then(function() {
                return self.skipWaiting();
            })
        );
    });

    self.addEventListener('fetch', function(event) {
        console.log('Handling fetch event for', event.request.url);

        event.respondWith(
            caches.match(event.request).then(function(res) {
                if (res) {
                    console.log('Fetching from cache:', res);

                    return res;
                }
                console.log('No response from cache. Fetching from
                network...');

                return fetch(event.request).then(function(res) {
                    console.log('Response from network:', res);

                    return res;
                }).catch(function(error) {
                    console.error('ERROR: Fetching failed:', error);

                    throw error;
                });
            })
        );
    });
```

Let's discuss some of these API methods in more detail.

Cache.addAll()

This method takes in a URL array, retrieves the response, and then adds that result to a specified cache. The specified cache in our example is `'fetch-event-cache'`:

```
var cacheName= 'fetch-event-cache';
```

ExtendableEvent.waitUntil()

This method extends the lifetime of an event. In our example, we are waiting until the resources are cached:

```
.then(function(cache) {
        return cache.addAll([
            'adobe-logo.png',
            'style.css',
            'index.html',
            'index.js',
            'style.css'
        ]);
    })
```

FetchEvent.respondWith()

This method resolves by returning a `Response` object or a network error to the `Fetch` object:

```
event.respondWith(
    caches.match(event.request).then(function(res) {
```

Fetching a JSON file during service worker installation

In this recipe, we are going to learn how to cache resource files using a JSON file by specifying the names of the resource files in it. Usually, this is done by keeping an array in the service worker JavaScript file, but you might want them in a separate location, for reasons such as versioning, for example.

Getting ready

To get started with service workers, you will need to have the service worker experiment feature turned on in your browser settings. If you have not done this yet, refer to the first recipe of *Chapter 1, Learning Service Worker Basics: Setting up service workers*. Service workers only run across HTTPS. To find out how to set up a development environment to support this feature, refer to the following recipes of *Chapter 1, Learning Service Worker Basics: Setting up GitHub pages for SSL, Setting up SSL for Windows*, and *Setting up SSL for Mac*.

How to do it...

Follow these instructions to set up your file structure:

1. Download all the files from the following location:

2. `https://github.com/szaranger/szaranger.github.io/blob/master/service-workers/07/03/`

3. Open up a browser and go to the `index.html` file:

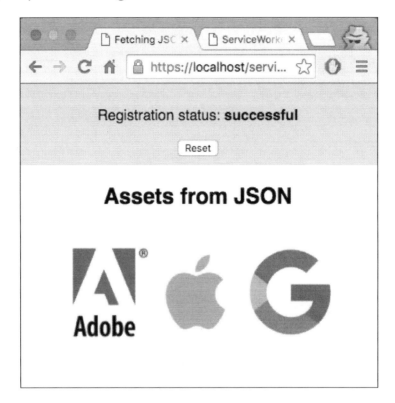

4. Now open up the DevTools (*Cmd + Alt + I* or *F12*) and make sure the **Preserve log** checkbox is clicked. Now refresh the page and you will see the log messages retrieving files from the cache:

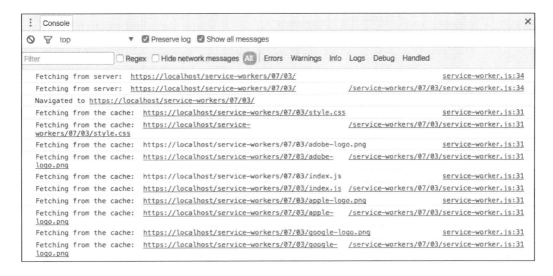

5. If you look at the **Resources** tab, you will see the cached resources:

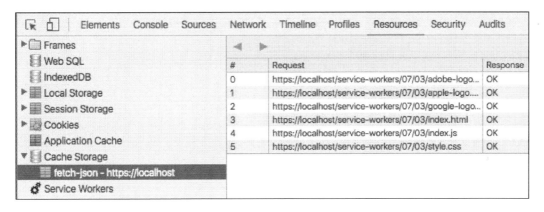

How it works...

We only require one action, which is at the time of the initial load for caching the assets and registering the service worker. So at the time of installation, we load the JSON file, parse JSON, and add the files to the cache. Our `service-worker.js` file looks like this:

```
var cacheName= 'fetch-json';

self.addEventListener('install', function(event) {
  event.waitUntil(
    caches.open(cacheName)
      .then(function(cache) {
```

```
            return fetch('files.json').then(function(response) {
                return response.json();
            }).then(function(files) {
                console.log('Installing files from JSON file: ', files);
                return cache.addAll(files);
            });
        })
        .then(function() {
            console.log(
                'All resources cached'
            );

            return self.skipWaiting();
        })
    );
});
```

Return a response from the cache if it was found:

```
self.addEventListener('fetch', function(event) {
    event.respondWith(
        caches.match(event.request)
            .then(function(response) {
                if (response) {
                    console.log('Fetching from the cache: ',
                    event.request.url);
                    return response;
                } else {
                    console.log('Fetching from server: ',
                    event.request.url);
                }
                return fetch(event.request);
            }
        )
    );
});
```

The client claims the service worker:

```
self.addEventListener('activate', function(event) {
    console.log('Activating the service worker!');
    event.waitUntil(self.clients.claim());
});
```

We will list the resource file names in the `files.json` file:

```
[
    "adobe-logo.png",
    "apple-logo.png",
    "google-logo.png",
    "style.css",
    "index.html",
    "index.js",
    "style.css"
]
```

We will add a section to our `index.html` file for the images:

```
<section>
    <h2>Assets from JSON</h2>
    <img src="adobe-logo.png" alt="adobe logo">
    <img src="apple-logo.png" alt="apple logo">
    <img src="google-logo.png" alt="google logo">
</section>
```

Proxying

A proxy is an intermediary between a web browser and the Internet. In this recipe, we will learn how to use the service worker as a proxy middleware.

Getting ready

To get started with service workers, you will need to have the service worker experiment feature turned on in your browser settings. If you have not done this yet, refer to the first recipe of *Chapter 1, Learning Service Worker Basics*: *Setting up service workers*. Service workers only run across HTTPS. To find out how to set up a development environment to support this feature, refer to the following recipes: *Setting up GitHub pages for SSL*, *Setting up SSL for Windows*, and *Setting up SSL for Mac*.

How to do it...

Follow these instructions to set up your file structure:

1. Download all the files from the following location:

   ```
   https://github.com/szaranger/szaranger.github.io/blob/master/
   service-workers/07/04/
   ```

2. Open up a browser and go to `index.html`:

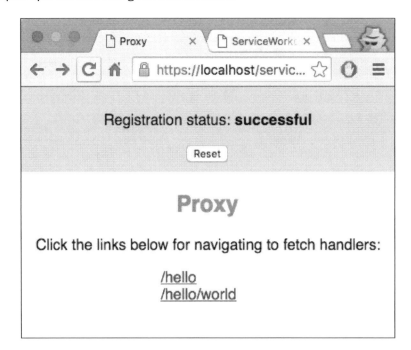

3. Now click on the first link to navigate to the `/hello` link:

4. Now open up DevTools (*Cmd + Alt + I* or *F12*) to see the log messages on the **Console** tab:

5. Now click on the first link to navigate to the /hello/world link:

How it works...

We are adding two links to the `index.html` file where we are planning to create a proxy:

```
<section >
    <h1>Proxy</h1>
    <p>Click the links below for navigating to fetch handlers:</p>
    <div class="links">
      <a href="/service-workers/07/04/hello">/hello</a><br />
      <a href="/service-
      workers/07/04/hello/world">/hello/world</a>
    </div>
</section>
```

We create a proxy for requests to the local URLs, inside the `service-worker.js` file, containing a `hello` string as well as `hello/world`. The client will recognize this as a local resource:

```
var helloFetchHandler = function(event) {
  if (event.request.url.indexOf('/hello') > 0) {
    console.log('DEBUG: Inside the /hello handler.');
    event.respondWith(new Response('Fetch handler for /hello'));
  }
};

var helloWorldFetchHandler = function(event) {
  if (event.request.url.endsWith('/hello/world')) {
    console.log('DEBUG: Inside the /hello/world handler.');
    event.respondWith(new Response('Fetch handler for
    /hello/world'));
  }
};
```

We pass these handlers into the fetch event listener as callbacks:

```
var fetchHandlers = [helloWorldFetchHandler, helloFetchHandler];

fetchHandlers.forEach(function(fetchHandler) {
  self.addEventListener('fetch', fetchHandler);
});
```

Prefetching

Prefetching resources during the service worker installation phase can easily enable offline viewing of a website. In this recipe, we will look into be prefetching resources including pages and images.

Getting ready

To get started with service workers, you will need to have the service worker experiment feature turned on in your browser settings. If you have not done this yet, refer to the first recipe of *Chapter 1, Learning Service Worker Basics: Setting up service workers*. Service workers only run across HTTPS. To find out how to set up a development environment to support this feature, refer to the following recipes: *Setting up GitHub pages for SSL, Setting up SSL for Windows*, and *Setting up SSL for Mac*.

How to do it...

Follow these instructions to set up your file structure:

1. Download all the files from the following location:

2. `https://github.com/szaranger/szaranger.github.io/blob/master/service-workers/07/05/`

3. Open up a browser and go to the `index.html` file:

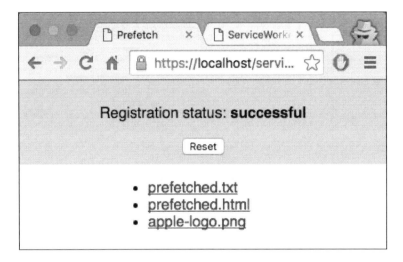

4. Open up the Developer Toolbar (*Cmd + Alt + I* or *F12*) and look at the messages in the console. You will see the resources have been successfully cached:

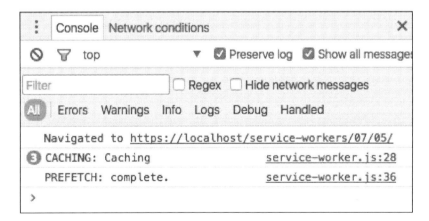

5. Now go offline by selecting offline on the DevTools **Network** tab:

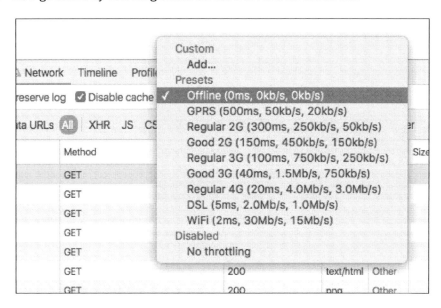

6. Now click on the **prefetched.txt** link. The linked text file will open in a new tab:

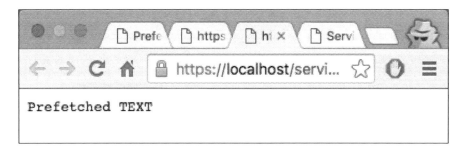

7. Click on the **prefetched.html** link. The linked page will open in a new tab:

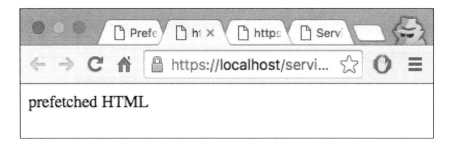

8. Click on the **apple-log.png** link. The linked image will open in a new tab:

9. If you examine the console, you will find the links have been served from the cache:

```
FETCH: Handling fetch event for  https://localhost/service-workers/07/05/prefetched.html  service-worker.js:45
FETCH: Handling fetch event for  https://localhost/service-                                service-worker.js:45
workers/07/05/prefetched.html
RESPONSE: found in cache:                                                                    service-worker.js:50
▼ Response {type: "basic", url: "https://localhost/service-workers/07/05/prefetched.html?cache-
  bust=1466590983526", status: 200, ok: true, statusText: "OK"…} ⊡
RESPONSE: found in cache: ▶ Response                                                         service-worker.js:50
```

How it works...

In the `index.html` file, we are adding a section with links to the prefetched files:

```html
<section id="prefetched">
  <ul>
    <li><a href="prefetched.txt"
    target="_blank">prefetched.txt</a></li>
    <li><a href="prefetched.html"
    target="_blank">prefetched.html</a></li>
    <li><a href="apple-logo.png" target="_blank">apple-
    logo.png</a></li>
  </ul>
</section>
```

In the `service-worker.js` file, we start with declaring the cache version at the top in case you have to force pages controlled by the service worker to use a new cache:

```
var cacheName= 'cache';
var currentCaches = {
  prefetch: 'prefetch-' + cacheName
};
```

We also list the resources to be cached:

```
var prefetchedURLs = [
    'prefetched.txt',
    'prefetched.html',
    'apple-logo.png'
];
```

The following line will construct a new URL from the list we have given it, using the service worker's script location as its base:

```
var url = new URL(prefetchedURLs, location.href);
```

Next, we add a cache busting timestamp to the query string:

```
url.search += (url.search ? '&' : '?') + 'cache-bust=' +
Date.now();
```

We have to make sure to specify `{mode: 'no-cors'}` if there is a possibility that the server delivering the resource does not support CORS:

```
var request = new Request(url, {mode: 'no-cors'});
```

Next, we fetch the resources and cache them:

```
return fetch(request).then(function(res) {
    if (res.status >= 400) {
        throw new Error('FAIL: request for ' + prefetchedURLs +
            ' failed, status ' + res.statusText);
    }
    console.log('CACHING: Caching');
    return cache.put(prefetchedURLs, res);
}).catch(function(err) {
    console.error('CACHING: Not caching ' + prefetchedURLs + ' due
    to ' + err);
});
```

Now let's look at the activate event handler. We make sure to delete all the caches that aren't in the `currentChaches` object we declared at the start:

```
self.addEventListener('activate', function(evt) {
    var expectedCacheNames =
    Object.keys(currentCaches).map(function(key) {
        return currentCaches[key];
    });

    evt.waitUntil(
        caches.keys().then(function(cacheNames) {
          return Promise.all(
            cacheNames.map(function(cacheName) {
              if (expectedCacheNames.indexOf(cacheName) === -
              1) {
                console.log('DELETE: out of date cache:',
                cacheName);
                return caches.delete(cacheName);
              }
            })
          );
        })
    );
});
```

The fetch event listener is where the service worker looks for the cached resources:

```
self.addEventListener('fetch', function(evt) {
  console.log('FETCH: Handling fetch event for ',
  evt.request.url);

  evt.respondWith(
    caches.match(evt.request).then(function(res) {
      if (res) {
        console.log('RESPONSE: found in cache:', res);

        return res;
      }

      console.log('RESPONSE: not found in cache. Fetching from
      network.');
```

```
        return fetch(evt.request).then(function(res) {
          console.log('RESPONSE: from network:', res);

          return res;
        }).catch(function(error) {
          console.error('FAIL: fetching :', error);

          throw error;
        });
      })
    );
  });
```

8

Experimenting with Web Push

In this chapter, we will cover the following topics:

- ▶ Implementing a simple push notification
- ▶ Showing rich push notifications
- ▶ Using the notification tag
- ▶ Implementing push clients
- ▶ Subscribing to push notifications
- ▶ Managing push notification quotas

Introduction

Push notifications have been popular with the features in mobile phone applications for the last few years. Regardless of whether you have an app opened, running in the foreground, or not running at all, push notifications will pop a message on your mobile phone. Similar to this, there is a new API available for the web called **Push API**, which is an experimental technology at the time of writing. In order to make Push API work, we need to have an active service worker running and must have subscribed to push notifications.

Let's start off this chapter by looking at how to implement a simple push notification.

Implementing a simple push notification

Fetching remote resources can be done in different ways. In this recipe, we are going to look at two standard ways of fetching a remote resource using a service worker with and without **cross-origin HTTP requests** (**CORS**).

If you want to learn more about CORS, follow this link:

`https://developer.mozilla.org/en-US/docs/Web/HTTP/Access_control_CORS`

Getting ready

To get started with service workers, you will need to have the service worker experiment feature turned on in your browser settings. If you have not done this yet, refer to the *Setting up service workers* recipe of *Chapter 1, Learning Service Worker Basics*. Service workers only run across HTTPS. To find out how to set up a development environment to support this feature, refer to the *Setting up GitHub pages for SSL* recipe of *Chapter 1, Learning Service Worker Basics*.

How to do it...

Follow these instructions to set up your file structure:

1. Copy the `index.html`, `index.js`, `service-worker.js`, `manifest.json`, `server.js`, `package.json`, and `style.css` files from the following location:

   `https://github.com/szaranger/szaranger.github.io/blob/master/service-workers/08/01/`

2. Run `npm install` from the command line.

3. Go to `https://console.developers.google.com/project` and create an API project. Obtain a sender ID (project number) and replace `gcm_sender_id` in the `manifest.json` file. Also replace the `<GCM API KEY>` placeholder in the `server.js` file.

   ```
   webPush.setGCMAPIKey(/*GCM API KEY*/);
   ```

4. Run `npm start` to kick off a server.

5. Open a browser and go to `index.html`. Make sure that you don't open the browser in the incognito mode. Click on the **Send Notification!** button to send a notification.

6. Open the Developer Toolbar (*Cmd + Alt + I* or *F12*). Now refresh the page and look at the messages in the console. You will see that the fetch requests are logged out into the console.

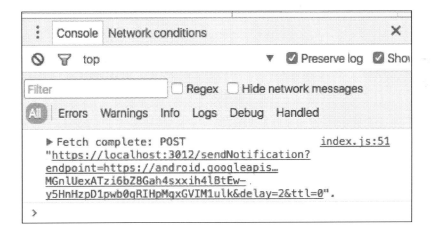

7. You will be prompted by your browser to allow notifications.

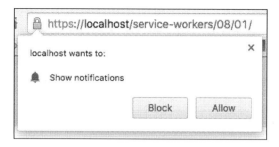

8. Soon you will receive the notification. (It might also take some time depending on your configuration.)

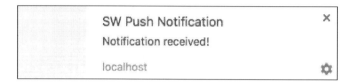

How it works...

At the beginning of the `index.js` file, we specify the base URL we use for the server.

```
var baseURL = 'https://localhost:3012/';
```

Next, in order to get the user subscription to the push service, we use `pushManager`.

```
return registration.pushManager.getSubscription()
```

If a subscription was found, it will be returned. Otherwise, the user is subscribed.

```
return registration.pushManager.getSubscription()
  .then(function(subscription) {
    if (subscription) {
      return subscription;
    }

    return registration.pushManager.subscribe({ userVisibleOnly:
    true });
  });
```

Next, we will send subscription details to the server.

```
fetch(baseURL + 'register', {
    method: 'post',
    headers: {
      'Content-type': 'application/json'
    },
    body: JSON.stringify({
      endpoint: subscription.endpoint,
    }),
  });
```

This will make the server send a notification to the client.

```
document.querySelector('#send').onclick = function() {
  var delay = document.querySelector('#notification-delay').value;
  var ttl = document.querySelector('#notification-ttl').value;

  fetch(baseURL + 'sendNotification?endpoint=' + endpoint +
  '&delay=' + delay +
        '&ttl=' + ttl,
    {
      method: 'post',
    }
  );
};
```

We will add a section to the `index.html` file for the input fields for the delay as well as the active time.

```
<section id="notification-input">
    <form>
      <h1>Notification</h1>
      Delay Time <input id='notification-delay' type='number'
      value='2'></input> <small>s</small><br/>
      <br/>
      Active Time <input id='notification-ttl' type='number'
      value='0'></input> <small>s</small><br/>
    </form>
    <button id="send">Send Notification!</button>
</section>
```

We will use a `manifest.json` file for Google Chrome support.

```
{
  "name": "Simple Push Notification",
  "short_name": "push-simple",
  "start_url": "./index.html",
  "display": "standalone",
  "gcm_sender_id": "46143029380",
  "gcm_user_visible_only": true
}
```

In the `service-worker.js` file, we will add an event listener for registering the push event.

```
'use strict';

self.addEventListener('push', function(event) {
  event.waitUntil(
    self.registration.showNotification('SW Push Notification', {
      body: 'Notification received!',
    })
  );
});
```

Showing rich notifications

Rich push notifications can send images, vibration patterns, and localized notifications. Let's look at how we can achieve this.

Getting ready

To get started with service workers, you will need to have the service worker experiment feature turned on in your browser settings. If you have not done this yet, refer to the *Setting up service workers* recipe of *Chapter 1, Learning Service Worker Basics*. Service workers only run across HTTPS. To find out how to set up a development environment to support this feature, refer to the *Setting up GitHub pages for SSL* recipe of *Chapter 1, Learning Service Worker Basics*.

How to do it...

Follow these instructions to set up your file structure:

1. Copy the `index.html`, `index.js`, `service-worker.js`, `manifest.json`, `server.js`, `package.json`, `amazon-logo.png`, and `style.css` files from the following location:

   `https://github.com/szaranger/szaranger.github.io/blob/master/service-workers/08/03/`

2. Open a browser and go to `index.html`.

3. You can change the delay time as well as the active time by changing them in the input fields.

4. You may be prompted to allow push notifications.

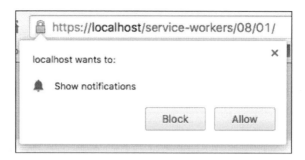

5. Soon you will receive the notification. (It might also take some time depending on your configuration.)

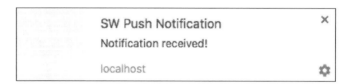

6. Open the Developer Toolbar (*Cmd + Alt + I* or *F12*). Now refresh the page and look at the messages in the console.

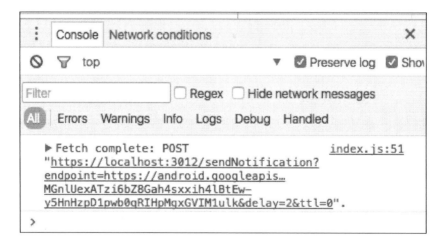

How it works...

In the `index.js` file, we will handle the click event when the user clicks on the button.

This will make the server send a notification to the client.

```
document.querySelector('#send').onclick = function() {
    var delay = document.querySelector('#notification-delay').value;
    var ttl = document.querySelector('#notification-ttl').value;

    fetch(baseURL + 'sendNotification?endpoint=' + endpoint +
    '&delay=' + delay +
        '&ttl=' + ttl,
    {
        method: 'post',
    }
    );
};
```

In the `service-worker.js` file, we will add an event listener to register the push event.

```
'use strict';

self.addEventListener('push', function(event) {
    event.waitUntil(
        self.registration.showNotification('SW Rich Push
        Notification', {
            body: 'Richer than richest',
            icon: 'amazon-logo.png',
            vibrate: [300, 100, 300]
        })
    );
});
```

Using the notification tag

In order to replace old notifications, we can use the notification tag. This will help us show up-to-date information to the user.

This recipe will show you how to manage a queue of notifications and discard previous notifications or merge them into a single notification.

Getting ready

To get started with service workers, you will need to have the service worker experiment feature turned on in your browser settings. If you have not done this yet, refer to the first recipe of *Chapter 1, Learning Service Worker Basics*: *Setting up service workers*. Service workers only run across HTTPS. To find out how to set up a development environment to support this feature, refer to the *Setting up GitHub pages for SSL* recipe of *Chapter 1, Learning Service Worker Basics*.

How to do it...

Follow these instructions to set up your file structure:

1. Copy the `index.html`, `index.js`, `service-worker.js`, `manifest.json`, `server.js`, `package.json`, and `style.css` files from the following location:

   `https://github.com/szaranger/szaranger.github.io/blob/master/service-workers/08/04/`

2. Open a browser and go to `index.html`.

3. Soon you will receive the notification. (It might also take some time depending on your configuration.)

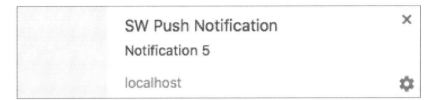

How it works...

In the `service-worker.js` file, we will add an event listener to register the push event. Note the `tag` element passed into the `showNotification` method.

```
'use strict';

self.addEventListener('push', function(event) {
  event.waitUntil(
      self.registration.showNotification('SW Push Notification', {
        body: 'Notification ' + count++,
        tag: 'swc'
      })  );
});
```

Implementing push clients

Push clients enables us to focus on the tab that our app is running on when the user clicks on a notification message. We can even reopen our app if it was closed.

Getting ready

To get started with service workers, you will need to have the service worker experiment feature turned on in your browser settings. If you have not done this yet, refer to the first recipe of *Chapter 1, Learning Service Worker Basics, Setting up service workers*. Service workers only run across HTTPS. To find out how to set up a development environment to support this feature, refer to the following recipes of *Chapter 1, Learning Service Worker Basics: Setting up GitHub pages for SSL, Setting up SSL for Windows*, and *Setting up SSL for Mac*.

How to do it...

Follow these instructions to set up your file structure:

1. Copy the `index.html`, `index.js`, `service-worker.js`, `manifest.json`, `server.js`, `package.json`, and `style.css` files from the following location:

   `https://github.com/szaranger/szaranger.github.io/blob/master/service-workers/08/05/`

2. Run `npm install` from the command line.

3. Go to `https://console.developers.google.com/project` and create an API project. Obtain a sender ID (project number) and replace `gcm_sender_id` in the `manifest.json` file. Also replace the `<GCM API KEY>` placeholder in the `server.js` file.

   ```
   webPush.setGCMAPIKey(/*GCM API KEY*/);
   ```

4. Run `npm start` to kick off a server.

5. Open a browser and go to `index.html`. Make sure that you don't open the browser in the incognito mode. Insert some text in the **Payload** field and click on the **Send Notification!** button to send a notification.

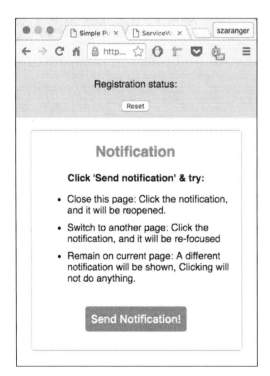

6. Open the Developer Toolbar (*Cmd + Alt + I* or *F12*). Now refresh the page and look at the messages in the console. You will see that the fetch requests are logged out into the console.

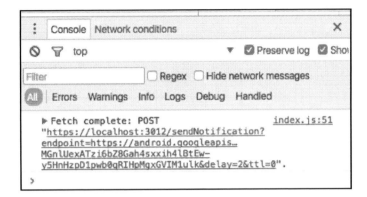

7. You will be prompted by your browser to allow notifications.

8. Soon you will start to receive notifications. (It might also take some time depending on your configuration.)

9. Clicking on this first notification will take you to the page your app is running.

10. Clicking on the second notification will not do anything.

11. Clicking on the third notification will open a new page with your app running.

How it works...

At the beginning of the `index.js` file, we will specify the base URL we use for the server.

```
var baseURL = 'https://localhost:3012/';
```

Next, in order to get the user subscription to the push service, we use `pushManager`.

```
return registration.pushManager.getSubscription()
```

If a subscription was found, this will be returned. Otherwise the user will be subscribed.

```
return registration.pushManager.getSubscription()
  .then(function(subscription) {
    if (subscription) {
      return subscription;
    }

    return registration.pushManager.subscribe({ userVisibleOnly:
    true });
});
```

Next, we will send subscription details to the server.

```
fetch(baseURL + 'register', {
    method: 'post',
    headers: {
      'Content-type': 'application/json'
    },
    body: JSON.stringify({
      endpoint: subscription.endpoint,
    }),
});
```

The send button enables the server to send a notification to the client with the payload we specified in the form.

```
document.querySelector('#send').onclick = function() {
  fetch(baseURL + 'sendNotification?endpoint=' + endpoint, {
      method: 'post',
  });
};
```

We will add a section to the index.html file for instructing the user about the notification messages.

```
<section id="notification-input">
    <form>
      <h1>Notification</h1>
      <p><strong>Click 'Send notification' &amp; try:</strong></p>
      <ul>
        <li>Close this page: Click the notification, and it will
        be reopened.</li>
        <li>Switch to another page: Click the notification, and it
        will be re-focused</li>
        <li>Remain on current page: A different notification will
        be shown, Clicking will not do anything.</li>
      </ul>
    </form>
    <button id="send">Send Notification!</button>
</section>
```

We use a `manifest.json` file for Google Chrome support.

```json
{
  "name": "SW Push Clients Notification",
  "short_name": "push-clients",
  "start_url": "./index.html",
  "display": "standalone",
  "gcm_sender_id": "46143029380",
  "gcm_user_visible_only": true
}
```

In the `service-worker.js` file, we will receive the payload and add an event listener for registering the push event.

```javascript
'use strict';

self.addEventListener('push', function(event) {
  event.waitUntil(
    self.clients.matchAll().then(function(clients) {

      var focused = clients.some(function(client) {
        return client.focused;
      });

      var notificationMessage;

      if (focused) {
        notificationMessage = 'Same Page';
      } else if (clients.length > 0) {
        notificationMessage = 'Diffrerent Page, ' +
                              'click here to gain focus';
      } else {
        notificationMessage = 'Page Closed, ' +
                              'click here to re-open it!';
      }

      return self.registration.showNotification('ServiceWorker
      Cookbook', {
        body: notificationMessage,
      });
    })
  );
});
```

Subscribing to push notifications

This recipe will teach you how to use push notifications with subscription management, enabling users to subscribe for features that your app will expose to keep in touch.

Getting ready

To get started with service workers, you will need to have the service worker experiment feature turned on in your browser settings. If you have not done this yet, refer to the first recipe of *Chapter 1*, *Learning Service Worker Basics*, *Setting up service workers*. Service workers only run across HTTPS. To find out how to set up a development environment to support this feature, refer to the following recipes of *Chapter 1*, *Learning Service Worker Basics*: *Setting up GitHub pages for SSL*, *Setting up SSL for Windows*, and *Setting up SSL for Mac*.

How to do it...

Follow these instructions to set up your file structure:

1. Copy the `index.html`, `index.js`, `service-worker.js`, `manifest.json`, `server.js`, `package.json`, and `style.css` files from the following location:

   `https://github.com/szaranger/szaranger.github.io/blob/master/service-workers/08/06/`

2. Run `npm install` from the command line.

3. Go to `https://console.developers.google.com/project` and create an API project. Obtain a sender ID (project number) and replace `gcm_sender_id` in the `manifest.json` file. Also replace the `<GCM API KEY>` placeholder in the `server.js` file.

   ```
   webPush.setGCMAPIKey(/*GCM API KEY*/);
   ```

4. Run `npm start` to kick off a server.

5. Open a browser and go to `index.html`. Make sure that you don't open the browser in the incognito mode. Click on the **Subscribe** button. The button will change into **Unsubscribe**.

6. Open the Developer Toolbar (*Cmd + Alt + I* or *F12*). Now refresh the page and look at the messages in the console. You will see that the fetch requests are logged out into the console.

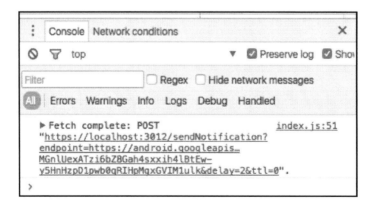

7. You might be prompted by your browser to allow notifications.

8. Soon you will receive notifications. (It might also take some time depending on your configuration.) Once you click on the **Unsubscribe** button, the notifications will no longer appear.

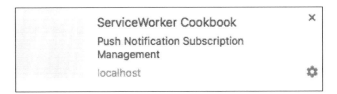

How it works...

At the beginning of the `index.js` file, we will specify the base URL we use for the server.

```
var baseURL = 'https://localhost:3012/';
```

Next, in order to get the user subscription to the push service, we use `pushManager`.

```
return registration.pushManager.getSubscription()
```

If a subscription was found, it will be returned. Otherwise the user is subscribed.

```
return registration.pushManager.getSubscription()
  .then(function(subscription) {
    if (subscription) {
```

```
        return subscription;
    }

    return registration.pushManager.subscribe({ userVisibleOnly:
    true });
});
```

Next, we will send subscription details to the server.

```
fetch(baseURL + 'register', {
    method: 'post',
    headers: {
      'Content-type': 'application/json'
    },
    body: JSON.stringify({
      endpoint: subscription.endpoint,
    }),
  });
```

The button enables the server to send a notification to the client with the payload we specified in the form.

```
document.querySelector('#subscription-button').onclick =
function() {
  fetch(baseURL + 'sendNotification?endpoint=' + endpoint, {
      method: 'post',
  });
};
```

In order to manage subscriptions we will add toggle logic.

```
function unsubscribe() {
  getSubscription().then(function(subscription) {
    return subscription.unsubscribe()
      .then(function() {
        console.log('Unsubscribed', subscription.endpoint);
        return fetch('unregister', {
          method: 'post',
          headers: {
            'Content-type': 'application/json'
          },
          body: JSON.stringify({
            endpoint: subscription.endpoint
          })
        });
```

```
    });
  }).then(setSubscribeButton);
}

function setSubscribeButton() {
  subscriptionBtn.onclick = subscribe;
  subscriptionBtn.textContent = 'Subscribe!';
}

function setUnsubscribeButton() {
  subscriptionBtn.onclick = unsubscribe;
  subscriptionBtn.textContent = 'Unsubscribe!';
}
```

We will add a section to the `index.html` file for instructing the user about the notification messages.

```html
<section id="notification-input">
    <form>
      <h1>Notification</h1>
      <p>Click to subscribe</p>
    </form>
    <button id="subscription-button" disabled=true></button>
</section>
```

We will use a `manifest.json` file for Google Chrome support.

```json
{
  "name": "SW Push Notification Subscription Management",
  "short_name": "push-with_subscription",
  "start_url": "./index.html",
  "display": "standalone",
  "gcm_sender_id": "46143029380",
  "gcm_user_visible_only": true
}
```

In the `service-worker.js` file, we will receive the payload and add an event listener for registering the push event.

```js
'use strict';

self.addEventListener('push', function(event) {
  event.waitUntil(self.registration.
  showNotification('ServiceWorker Cookbook', {
```

```
      body: 'Push Notification Subscription Management'
    }));
  });


  self.addEventListener('pushsubscriptionchange', function(event) {
    console.log('Subscription expired');
    event.waitUntil(
      self.registration.pushManager.subscribe({ userVisibleOnly:
      true })
      .then(function(subscription) {
        console.log('Subscribed after expiration',
        subscription.endpoint);
        return fetch('register', {
          method: 'post',
          headers: {
            'Content-type': 'application/json'
          },
          body: JSON.stringify({
            endpoint: subscription.endpoint
          })
        });
      })
    );
  });
```

In the `server.js` file, we will send notifications to the push service.

```
  function sendNotification(endpoint) {
    webPush.sendNotification(endpoint).then(function() {
      console.log('Push Application Server - Notification sent to '
      + endpoint);
    }).catch(function() {
      console.log('ERROR in sending Notification, endpoint removed '
      + endpoint);
      subscriptions.splice(subscriptions.indexOf(endpoint), 1);
    });
  }
```

For the purpose of demonstration, we will simulate the event that has occurred by sending a notification in every `pushInterval` to the registered end point. So, you will see notifications coming in rapidly.

```
setInterval(function() {
  subscriptions.forEach(sendNotification);
}, pushInterval * 1000);

function isSubscribed(endpoint) {
  return (subscriptions.indexOf(endpoint) >= 0);
}
```

Managing push notification quotas

In this recipe, we are going to experiment with the quota management policies of different browsers. We will attempt to send as many notifications as possible to test against opened and closed tabs, clicking on notifications as well as ignoring them.

Getting ready

To get started with service workers, you will need to have the service worker experiment feature turned on in your browser settings. If you have not done this yet, refer to the *Setting up service workers* recipe of *Chapter 1, Learning Service Worker Basics*. Service workers only run across HTTPS. To find out how to set up a development environment to support this feature, refer to the following recipes of *Chapter 1, Learning Service Worker Basics*: *Setting up GitHub pages for SSL, Setting up SSL for Windows*, and *Setting up SSL for Mac*.

How to do it...

Follow these instructions to set up your file structure:

1. Copy the `index.html`, `index.js`, `service-worker.js`, `manifest.json`, `server.js`, `package.json`, and `style.css` files from the following location:

   `https://github.com/szaranger/szaranger.github.io/blob/master/service-workers/08/07/`

2. Run `npm install` from the command line.

3. Go to `https://console.developers.google.com/project` and create an API project. Obtain a sender ID (project number) and replace `gcm_sender_id` in the `manifest.json` file. Also, replace the `<GCM API KEY>` placeholder in the `server.js` file.

   `webPush.setGCMAPIKey(/*GCM API KEY*/);`

4. Run `npm start` to kick off a server.

5. Open a browser and go to `index.html`. Make sure that you don't open the browser in the incognito mode. Click on either the **Visible notifications** or **Invisible notifications** button.

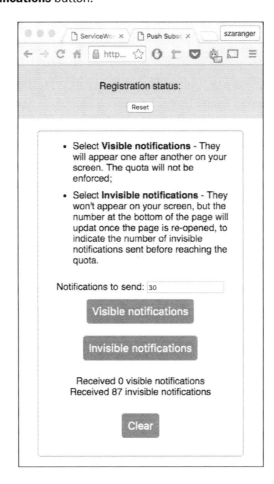

6. Open the Developer Toolbar (*Cmd* + *Alt* + *I* or *F12*). Now refresh the page and look at the messages in the console. You will see that the fetch requests are logged out into the console.

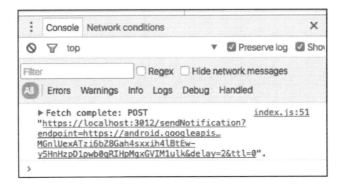

7. You may be prompted by your browser to allow notifications.

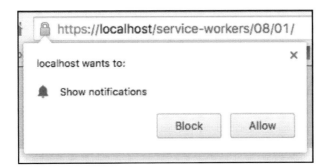

How it works...

At the beginning of the `index.js` file, we will specify the base URL we use for the server.

```
var baseURL = 'https://localhost:3012/';
```

Next, in order to get the user subscription to the push service, we use `pushManager`.

```
return registration.pushManager.getSubscription()
```

If a subscription was found, that will be returned. Otherwise the user is subscribed.

```
return registration.pushManager.getSubscription()
  .then(function(subscription) {
    if (subscription) {
      return subscription;
    }

    return registration.pushManager.subscribe({ userVisibleOnly:
    true });
});
```

We will also retrieve the user's public key.

```
var rawKey = subscription.getKey ? subscription.getKey('p256dh') :
'';
key = rawKey ?
btoa(String.fromCharCode.apply(null,
new Uint8Array(rawKey))) : '';
var rawAuthSecret = subscription.getKey ?
subscription.getKey('auth') : '';
authSecret = rawAuthSecret ?
btoa(String.fromCharCode.apply(null, new
Uint8Array(rawAuthSecret))) : '';

    endpoint = subscription.endpoint;
```

Next, we will send subscription details to the server.

```
fetch(baseURL + 'register', {
    method: 'post',
    headers: {
      'Content-type': 'application/json'
    },
    body: JSON.stringify({
      endpoint: subscription.endpoint,
      key: key,
      authSecret: authSecret
    }),
  });
```

We will ask the server to send the client a notification for testing purposes.

```
fetch(baseURL + 'sendNotification', {
    method: 'post',
    headers: {
      'Content-type': 'application/json'
    },
    body: JSON.stringify({
      endpoint: endpoint,
      key: key,
      visible: visible,
      num: notificationNum,
    }),
});
```

The `clear` button clears the notification cache, which stores the number of notifications received.

```
document.querySelector('#clear').onclick = function() {
  window.caches.open('notifications').then(function(cache) {
    Promise.all([
      cache.put(new Request('invisible'), new Response('0', {
        headers: {
          'content-type': 'application/json'
        }
      })),
      cache.put(new Request('visible'), new Response('0', {
        headers: {
          'content-type': 'application/json'
        }
      })),
    ]).then(function() {
      updateNotificationNumbers();
    });
  });
};
```

Update the UI by reading the number of notifications received.

```
function updateNotificationNumbers() {
  window.caches.open('notifications').then(function(cache) {
    ['visible', 'invisible'].forEach(function(type) {
```

```
        cache.match(type).then(function(res) {
          if(res) {
            res.text().then(function(text) {
              document.getElementById('sent-' + type).textContent =
              text;
            });
          }
        });
      });
    });
}
```

Also, update the number of notifications received periodically.

```
window.onload = function() {
  updateNotificationNumbers();
  setInterval(updateNotificationNumbers, 1000);
};
```

We will add a section to the `index.html` file for instructing the user about the notification messages.

```
<section id="notification-input">
    <ul>
        <li>Select <strong>Visible notifications</strong> - They
        will appear one after another on your screen. The quota will
        not be enforced;</li>
        <li>Select <strong>Invisible notifications</strong> - They
        won't appear on your screen, but the number at the bottom of
        the page will update once the page is re-opened, to indicate
        the number of invisible notifications sent before reaching
        the quota.</li>
    </ul>

    <form>
    Notifications to send: <input id="notification-count"
    type="number" value="30"></input>
    </form>

    <button id="visible">Visible notifications</button>
    <button id="invisible">Invisible notifications</button>

    <p>Received <span id="sent-visible">0</span> visible
    notifications<br />
```

```
      Received <span id="sent-invisible">0</span> invisible
      notifications</p>
      <button id="clear">Clear</button>
   </section> id="subscription-button" disabled=true></button>
</section>
```

We will use a `manifest.json` file for Google Chrome support.

```
{
   "name": "SW Push Quota",
   "short_name": "push-quota",
   "start_url": "./index.html",
   "display": "standalone",
   "gcm_sender_id": "46143029380",
   "gcm_user_visible_only": true
}
```

In the `service-worker.js` file, we keep the service worker alive until the notifications cache is updated.

```
self.addEventListener('push', function(event) {

   var visible = event.data ? event.data.json() : false;

   if (visible) {
     event.waitUntil(updateNumber('visible').then(function(num) {
       return self.registration.showNotification('SW', {
         body: 'Received ' + num + ' visible notifications',
       });
     }));
   } else {
     event.waitUntil(updateNumber('invisible'));
   }
});
```

We will create a notifications cache to store the notifications received.

```
self.addEventListener('install', function(event) {
   event.waitUntil(
     caches.open(cacheName).then(function(cache) {
       return Promise.all([
         cache.put(new Request('invisible'), new Response('0', {
           headers: {
             'content-type': 'application/json'
           }
         })),
```

```
        cache.put(new Request('visible'), new Response('0', {
          headers: {
            'content-type': 'application/json'
          }
        })),
      ]);
    })
  );
});
```

In the `server.js` file, we will send notifications to the push service.

```
app.post('/sendNotification', function(req, res) {
  var num = 1;
  var promises = [];

  var intervalID = setInterval(function() {
    promises.push(webPush.sendNotification(req.body.endpoint, {
      TTL: 200,
      payload: JSON.stringify(req.body.visible),
      userPublicKey: req.body.key,
      userAuth: req.body.authSecret,
    }));

    if (num++ === Number(req.body.num)) {
      clearInterval(intervalID);

      Promise.all(promises)
      .then(function() {
        res.sendStatus(201);
      });
    }
  }, 1000);
});
```

9
Looking at General Usage

In this chapter, we will cover the following topics:

- ▶ Taking immediate control of the page
- ▶ Working with slow responses
- ▶ Relaying messages
- ▶ Using a service worker as a proxy middleware
- ▶ Using a service worker with a live flowchart

Introduction

In this chapter, we will look into some of the scenarios where the service worker can become useful. These scenarios may fall into the general-use category. The examples we will look at here can be used as the foundation to build other service worker features.

Taking immediate control of the page

This simple recipe will demonstrate how to have the service worker immediately take control of the page without having to wait for a navigation event.

Getting ready

To get started with service workers, you will need to have the service worker experiment feature turned on in your browser settings. If you have not done this yet, refer to the *Setting up service workers* recipe of *Chapter 1, Learning Service Worker Basics*. Service workers only run across HTTPS. To find out how to set up a development environment to support this feature, refer to the *Setting up GitHub pages for SSL* recipe of *Chapter 1, Learning Service Worker Basics*.

How to do it...

Follow these instructions to set up your file structure:

1. Copy the `index.html`, `index.js`, `service-worker.js`, and `style.css` files from the following location:

    `https://github.com/szaranger/szaranger.github.io/blob/master/`
    `service-workers/09/01/`

2. Open a browser and go to `index.html`.

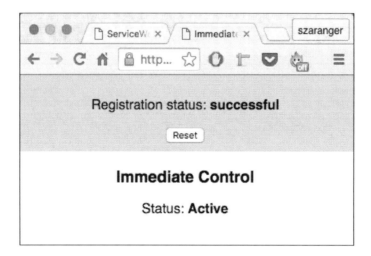

3. Refresh the page. The status of the service worker will be displayed on the screen.

How it works...

In our `index.html` file, we will add a section to display the service worker status.

```
<section>
    <h3>Immediate Control</h3>
    <p>Status:
        <strong><span id="control-status"></span></strong>
    </p>
</section>
```

At the beginning of the `index.js` file, we will inspect the registration status and print it to the screen.

```
if (registration.installing) {
    serviceWorker = registration.installing;
    document.querySelector('#control-status')
    .textContent = 'Installing';
} else if (registration.waiting) {
    serviceWorker = registration.waiting;
    document.querySelector('#control-status')
    .textContent = 'Waiting';
} else if (registration.active) {
    serviceWorker = registration.active;
    document.querySelector('#control-status')
    .textContent = 'Active';
}
```

Next, in the `service-worker.js` file, we will call `skipWaiting()` to enable an updated service worker to be immediately active when there is an existing service worker that differs from the updated version.

```
if (typeof self.skipWaiting === 'function') {
  console.log('self.skipWaiting()');
  self.addEventListener('install', function(evt) {
    evt.waitUntil(self.skipWaiting());
  });
} else {
  console.log('self.skipWaiting() is unsupported.');
}
```

```
if (self.clients && (typeof self.clients.claim === 'function')) {
  console.log('self.clients.claim()');
  self.addEventListener('activate', function(evt) {
    evt.waitUntil(self.clients.claim());
  });
} else {
  console.log('self.clients.claim() is unsupported.');
}
```

Working with slow responses

Slow updates from the service worker are a good way to mock slow response times from the servers. In this recipe, we are going to use a timeout to mock slow responses.

Getting ready

To get started with service workers, you will need to have the service worker experiment feature turned on in your browser settings. If you have not done this yet, refer to the first recipe of *Chapter 1, Learning Service Worker Basics*: *Setting up service workers*. Service workers only run across HTTPS. To find out how to set up a development environment to support this feature, refer to the following recipes in *Chapter 1, Learning Service Worker Basics*: *Setting up GitHub pages for SSL, Setting up SSL for Windows*, and *Setting up SSL for Mac*.

How to do it...

Follow these instructions to set up your file structure:

1. Copy the `index.html`, `index.js`, `service-worker.js`, `manifest.json`, `server.js`, `package.json`, and `style.css` files from the following location:

   `https://github.com/szaranger/szaranger.github.io/blob/master/service-workers/09/02/`

2. Open a browser and go to index.html.

3. Open the Developer Toolbars (*Cmd + Alt + I* or *F12*). Now refresh the page and look at the messages in the console. You will see the service worker life cycle methods are logged out into the console.

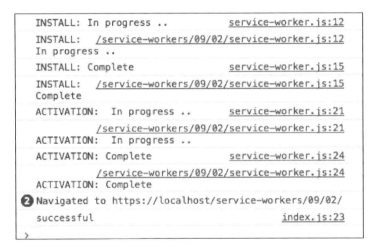

4. Refresh the page. A message from the service worker will be displayed on the screen.

How it works...

In the `index.js` file, we will append the console message to the screen at the point of service worker registration.

```
function printStatus(status) {
    document.querySelector('#status').innerHTML = status;
    document.body.appendChild(document.
    createTextNode(Array.prototype.join.call(arguments, ", ") +
    '\n'));

    console.log.apply(console, arguments);
}
```

Next, in the `service-worker.js` file we will create a function to delay any new promise we receive.

```
function wait(ms) {
  return new Promise(function(resolve) {
    setTimeout(resolve, ms);
  });
}
```

The usual lifecycle methods will call the `wait` function in order to delay the `install`, `activate`, and `fetch` statuses.

```
self.addEventListener('install', function(evt) {
  console.log('INSTALL: In progress ..');
  evt.waitUntil(
    wait(DELAY).then(function() {
      console.log('INSTALL: Complete');
    })
  );
});

self.addEventListener('activate', function(evt) {
  console.log('ACTIVATION: In progress ..');
  evt.waitUntil(
    wait(DELAY).then(function() {
      console.log('ACTIVATION: Complete');
    })
  );
});

self.addEventListener('fetch', function(evt) {
  evt.respondWith(new Response("Service workers says Hello!"));
});
```

Relaying messages

Service workers can be used to build a small chat message feature into your browser. This recipe demonstrates how to communicate between a page and the service worker by relaying messages between pages we are going to use to build our little chat app.

Getting ready

To get started with service workers, you will need to have the service worker experiment feature turned on in your browser settings. If you have not done this yet, refer to the *Setting up service workers* recipe of *Chapter 1, Learning Service Worker Basics*. Service workers only run across HTTPS. To find out how to set up a development environment to support this feature, refer to the *Setting up GitHub pages for SSL* recipe of *Chapter 1, Learning Service Worker Basics*.

How to do it...

Follow these instructions to set up your file structure:

1. Copy the `index.html`, `index.js`, `service-worker.js`, `manifest.json`, `package.json`, and `style.css` files from the following location:

    `https://github.com/szaranger/szaranger.github.io/blob/master/service-workers/09/03/`

2. Open a browser and go to `index.html`.

3. Now open another browser and go to `index.html`. Type something in the text area.

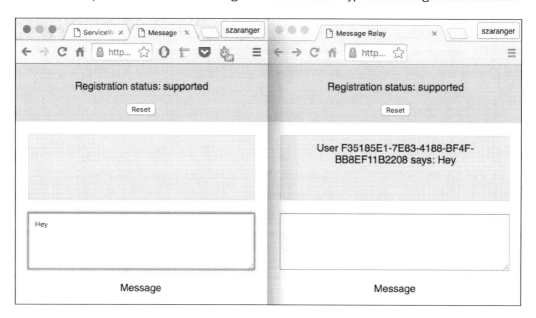

4. Now open another browser and go to `index.html`. Type something in the text area.

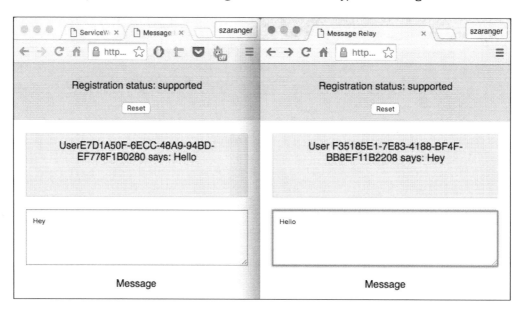

How it works...

At the beginning of the `index.js` file, we query the DOM nodes for the UI.

```
if (navigator.serviceWorker) {
  var message = document.querySelector('#message');
  var received = document.querySelector('#received');
  var status = document.querySelector('#status');
  var inbox = {};
```

We then listen to any service worker messages. When a message is received, we specify a DOM element to display it.

```
navigator.serviceWorker.addEventListener('message', function(evt)
{

    var userId = evt.data.client;
    var node;

    if (!inbox[userId]) {
      node = document.createElement('div');
      received.appendChild(node);
      inbox[userId] = node;
    }

    node = inbox[userId];
    node.textContent = 'User ' + userId + ' says: ' +
    evt.data.message;
});
```

When a page is force-reloaded, for example, the service worker will not send any messages.

```
message.addEventListener('input', function() {
    if (!navigator.serviceWorker.controller) {
      status.textContent = 'ERROR: no controller';
      return;
    }

    navigator.serviceWorker.controller.
    postMessage(message.value);
});
```

The `service-worker.js` file has the event handler for the message.

```javascript
self.addEventListener('message', function(event) {

    var promise = self.clients.matchAll()
    .then(function(clientList) {
        var senderID = event.source ? event.source.id : 'unknown';

        if (!event.source) {
            console.log('Unsure about the sender');
        }

        clientList.forEach(function(client) {
            if (client.id === senderID) {
                return;
            }
            client.postMessage({
                client: senderID,
                message: event.data
            });
        });
    });

    if (event.waitUntil) {
        event.waitUntil(promise);
    }
});
```

An immediate claim will make sure that the user doesn't have to refresh the page.

```javascript
self.addEventListener('activate', function(event) {
    event.waitUntil(self.clients.claim());
});
```

In the `index.html` file, we add a div, a text area, and a paragraph tag for the messages.

```html
<section class="message">
    <div id="received"></div>

    <textarea id="message" style="width: 90%;padding: 10px;"
    rows="5"></textarea>
    <p>Message</p>
</section>
```

Using a service worker as a proxy middleware

A proxy is an intermediary between a web browser and the Internet. In this recipe, you will learn how to use a service worker as a proxy middleware.

Getting ready

To get started with service workers, you will need to have the service worker experiment feature turned on in your browser settings. If you have not done this yet, refer to the first recipe of *Chapter 1, Learning Service Worker Basics: Setting up service workers*. Service workers only run across HTTPS. To find out how to set up a development environment to support this feature, refer to the following recipes in *Chapter 1, Learning Service Worker Basics: Setting up GitHub pages for SSL, Setting up SSL for Windows*, and *Setting up SSL for Mac*.

How to do it...

Follow these instructions to set up your file structure:

1. Download all the files from the following location:

   ```
   https://github.com/szaranger/szaranger.github.io/blob/master/
   service-workers/09/04/
   ```

2. Open a browser and go to `index.html`.

3. Now click on the first link to navigate to the `/hello` link.

4. Now open DevTools (*Cmd + Alt + I* or *F12*) to see the log messages on the **Console** tab.

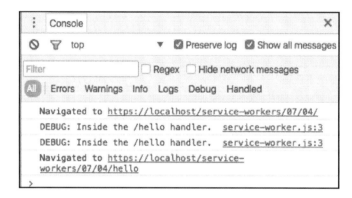

5. Now click on the first link to navigate to the `/hello/world` link.

How it works...

We will add two links to the `index.html` file where we are planning to create a proxy.

```html
<section >
    <h1>Proxy</h1>
    <p>Click the links below for navigating to fetch handlers:</p>
    <div class="links">
       <a href="/service-workers/07/04/hello">/hello</a><br />
       <a href="/service-workers/
       07/04/hello/world">/hello/world</a>
    </div>
</section>
```

We will create a proxy for requests to the local URLs inside the `service-worker.js` file containing a `hello` string as well as `hello/world`. The client will recognize this as a local resource.

```javascript
var helloFetchHandler = function(event) {
  if (event.request.url.indexOf('/hello') !== -1) {
    console.log('DEBUG: Inside the /hello handler.');
    event.respondWith(new Response('Fetch handler for /hello'));
  }
};

var helloWorldFetchHandler = function(event) {
  if (event.request.url.endsWith('/hello/world')) {
    console.log('DEBUG: Inside the /hello/world handler.');
    event.respondWith(new Response('Fetch handler for
    /hello/world'));
  }
};
```

We will pass these handlers into the fetch event listener as callbacks.

```javascript
var fetchHandlers = [helloWorldFetchHandler, helloFetchHandler];

fetchHandlers.forEach(function(fetchHandler) {
  self.addEventListener('fetch', fetchHandler);
});
```

Using a service worker with a live flowchart

In this recipe, you will learn how to use a service worker by demonstrating the workflow and logging the steps so we can follow the flow.

The features we are going to implement are as follows:

- A button to register a service worker
- A button to reload the document
- A button to unregister the service worker

The buttons can be pressed in any order. You can also specify the service worker script URL and scope to simulate different test cases.

Getting ready

To get started with service workers, you will need to have the service worker experiment feature turned on in your browser settings. If you have not done this yet, refer to the *Setting up service workers* recipe of *Chapter 1, Learning Service Worker Basics*. Service workers only run across HTTPS. To find out how to set up a development environment to support this feature, refer to the *Setting up GitHub pages for SSL* recipe of *Chapter 1, Learning Service Worker Basics*.

How to do it...

Follow these instructions to set up your file structure:

1. Download files from the following location:

   ```
   https://github.com/szaranger/szaranger.github.io/blob/master/
   service-workers/08/05/
   ```

2. Open a browser and go to `index.html`.

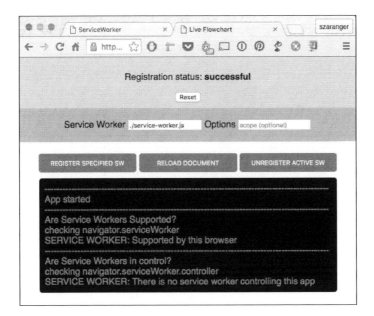

3. Now open DevTools (*Cmd + Alt + I* or *F12*) to see the log messages on the **Console** tab.

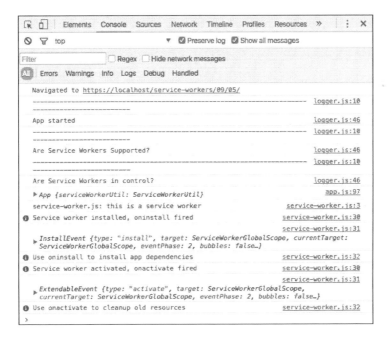

4. Now click on the **REGISTER SPECIFIED SW** button.

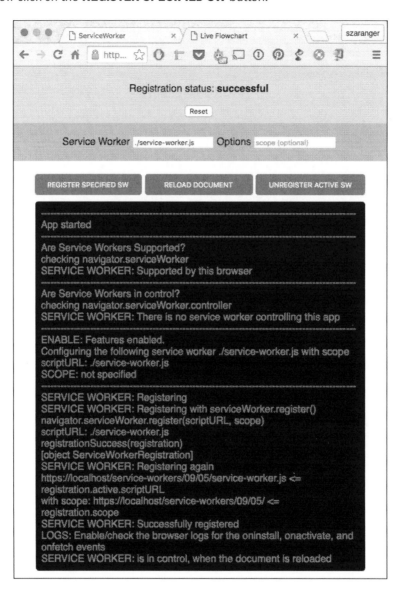

5. Now open DevTools (*Cmd + Alt + I* or *F12*) to see the log messages on the **Console** tab.

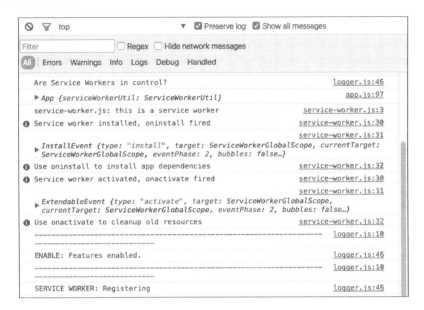

6. Now click on the **RELOAD DOCUMENT** button.

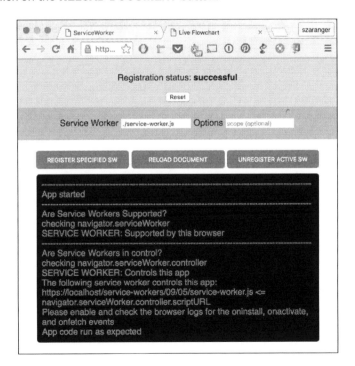

7. Now open up DevTools (*Cmd + Alt + I* or *F12*) to see the log messages on the **Console** tab.

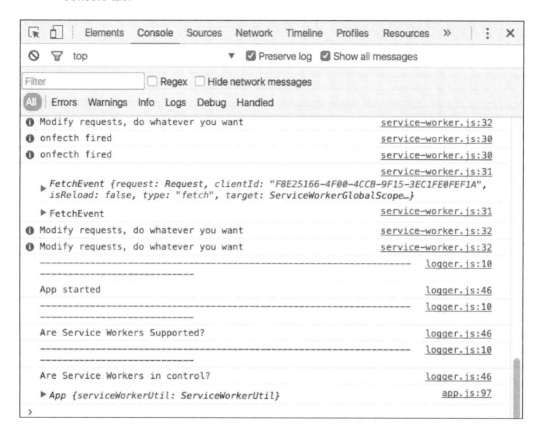

8. Now click on the **UNREGISTER ACTIVE SW** button.

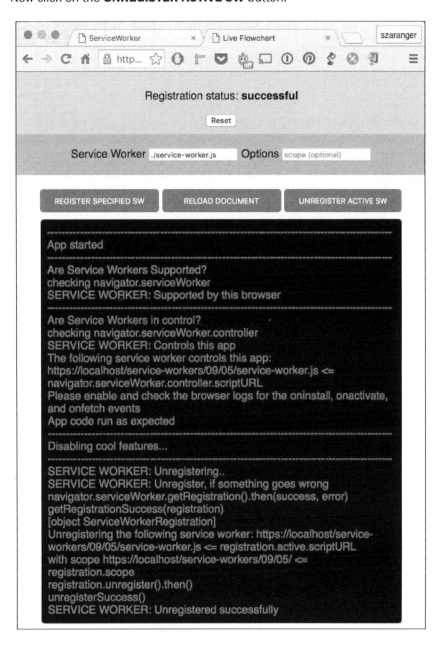

9. Now open up DevTools (*Cmd + Alt + I* or *F12*) to see the log messages on the **Console** tab.

How it works...

At the beginning of the `app.js` file, we initiate a helper for the service worker.

```
this.serviceWorkerUtil = new ServiceWorkerUtil();
```

To register a service worker, we perform the following steps:

```
document.getElementById('reloadapp').addEventListener('click',
function() {
    window.location.reload();
});
```

Then, we check if the service worker is supported.

```
if (this.serviceWorkerUtil.isServiceWorkerSupported()) {
    document.getElementById('swinstall').addEventListener('click',
        function() {
            self.enableFeatures();
        }
    );

    document.getElementById('swuninstall').
    addEventListener('click',
        function() {
            self.disableFeatures();
        }
    );
```

Next, we check if the service worker is in control.

```
if (this.serviceWorkerUtil.isServiceWorkerControllingThisApp()) {
    Logger.info('App code run as expected');

    this.disableSWRegistration();
  } else {
    this.enableSWRegistration();
  }
```

Now we try to register the service worker in order to enable features.

```
App.prototype.enableFeatures = function enableFeatures() {
  var scriptURL;
  var scope;

  Logger.newSection();
  Logger.log('ENABLE: Features enabled.');

  scriptURL = document.getElementById('swscripturl');
  scope = document.getElementById('swscope');

  Logger.debug(
    'Configuring the following service worker ' +
    scriptURL.value +
    ' with scope ' + scope.value
  );

  if (scriptURL.value !== '') {
    Logger.debug('scriptURL: ' + scriptURL.value);
  } else {
    Logger.error('No SW scriptURL specified');
    return;
  }

  if (scope.value !== '') {
    Logger.debug('SCOPE: ' + scope.value);
  } else {
    Logger.warn('SCOPE: not specified');
  }
```

```
    this.serviceWorkerUtil.registerServiceWorker(scriptURL.value,
    scope.value).then(
        this.disableSWRegistration,
        this.enableSWRegistration
    );
};
```

We will disable the possibility of the user unregistering the service worker.

```
App.prototype.enableSWRegistration = function() {
    document.getElementById('swinstall').disabled = false;
    document.getElementById('swuninstall').disabled = true;
};
```

```
App.prototype.disableSWRegistration = function() {
    document.getElementById('swinstall').disabled = true;
    document.getElementById('swuninstall').disabled = false;
};
```

So the application gets started.

```
var app = new App();
```

```
console.debug(app);
```

In the `service-worker.js` file, we receive the payload and add an event listener for registering the push event.

```
'use strict';
```

```
self.addEventListener('push', function(event) {
    event.waitUntil(
        self.clients.matchAll().then(function(clients) {

            var focused = clients.some(function(client) {
                return client.focused;
            });

            var notificationMessage;

            if (focused) {
                notificationMessage = 'Same Page';
            } else if (clients.length > 0) {
```

```
                notificationMessage = 'Diffrerent Page, ' +
                                      'click here to gain focus';
          } else {
            notificationMessage = 'Page Closed, ' +
                                  'click here to re-open it!';
          }

          return self.registration.showNotification('ServiceWorker
          Cookbook', {
            body: notificationMessage,
          });
        })
    );
  });
```

In the `index.html` file, we will add a section to display the buttons and the console.

```html
<section class="playground">
    <div class="inputs">
        <span class="title">Service Worker</span>
        <input id="swscripturl" placeholder="SW path"
        value="./service-worker.js" />
        <span class="title">Options </span>
        <input id="swscope" placeholder="scope (optional)" />
    </div>
    <div class="actions">
        <button id="swinstall" disabled>Register specified
        SW</button>
        <button id="reloadapp">Reload document</button>
        <button id="swuninstall" disabled>Unregister active
        SW</button>
    </div>
    <div id="log" class="log"></div>
</section>
```

10

Improving Performance

In this chapter, we will cover the following topics:

- ▶ Performing network requests from a cache
- ▶ Performing network requests from a network
- ▶ Testing `waitUntil`
- ▶ Implementing background sync
- ▶ Sending forward requests
- ▶ Avoiding model fetching and render times

Introduction

In this last chapter, we will explore improving performance with the help of the service worker. Now, we are going to look into the areas around improving network requests from a cache and network, implementing background sync, sending forward requests, and avoiding model fetching and render times.

Performing network requests from a cache

If you are a regular visitor to a certain website, chances are that you may be loading most of the resources such as CSS and JavaScript files from your cache rather than the server itself. This saves us necessary bandwidth for the server as well as requests over the network. Having control over which content we deliver from the cache and server is a great advantage. The server worker provides us this powerful feature by giving us programmatic control over the content. In this recipe, we are going to look at the methods that enable us to do so by creating a performance art event viewer web app.

Getting ready

To get started with service workers, you will need to have the service worker experiment feature turned on in your browser settings. If you have not done this yet, refer to the *Setting up service workers* recipe of *Chapter 1, Learning Service Worker Basics*. Service workers only run across HTTPS. To find out how to set up a development environment to support this feature, refer to the following recipes of *Chapter 1, Learning Service Worker Basics*: *Setting up GitHub pages for SSL, Setting up SSL for Windows*, and *Setting up SSL for Mac*.

How to do it...

Follow these instructions to set up your file structure.

1. Download files from the following location:

   ```
   https://github.com/szaranger/szaranger.github.io/blob/master/
   service-workers/10/01/
   ```

2. Open a browser and go to `index.html`.

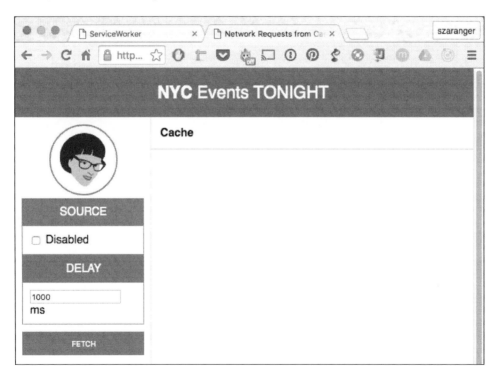

3. First we will request data from the network with the cache enabled. Click on the
   FETCH button.

4. Now we are going to select the **Disabled** checkbox under the **SOURCE** label and click on the **FETCH** button again in order to fetch data only from the cache. An error will be shown on the page. Since the cache is disabled, data cannot be fetched.

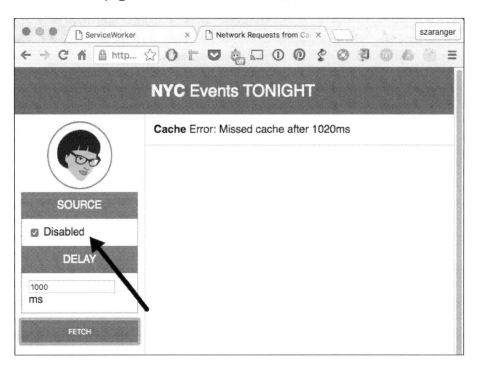

How it works...

In the `index.js` file, we will set a page-specific name for the cache as the caches are per origin-based and no other page should use the same cache name.

```
var CACHE_NAME = cache-only';
```

If you inspect the **Resources** tab of the development tools, you can find the cache inside **Cache Storage**.

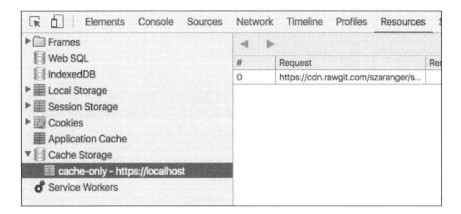

We will store the elapsed time for the cache in variables.

```
var cacheFetchStartTime;
```

The source URL, for example, points to a file location in GitHub via RawGit.

```
var SOURCE_URL = 'https://cdn.rawgit.com/szaranger/
szaranger.github.io/master/service-workers/10/01/events';
```

If you want to set up your own source URL, you can easily do so by creating a gist or a repository in GitHub and creating a file with your data in the JSON format (you don't need the `.json` extension). Once you've done that, copy the URL of the file and head over to `https://rawgit.com`.

Paste the link there to obtain another link with a content type header as shown in the following screenshot:

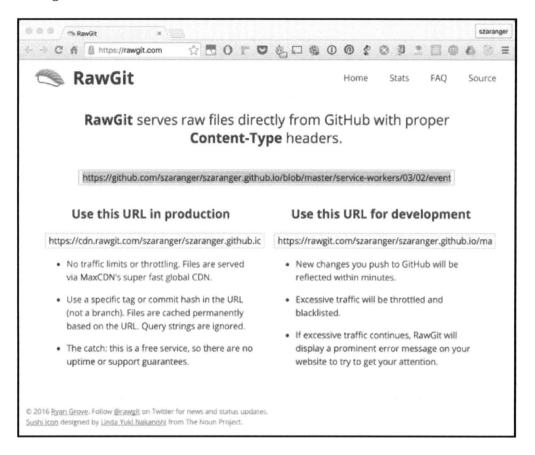

Between the time we click on the fetch button and all the data being received, we have to make sure that the user doesn't either change the criteria for searching or click on the fetch button again. To handle this situation, we will disable the controls.

```
function clear() {
  outlet.textContent = '';
  cacheStatus.textContent = '';
}

function disableEdit(enable) {
  fetchButton.disabled = enable;
```

```
  cacheDelayText.disabled = enable;
  cacheDisabledCheckbox.disabled = enable;

  if(!enable) {
    clear();
  }
}
```

The returned data will be rendered to the screen in rows.

```
function displayEvents(events) {

  events.forEach(function(event) {
    var tickets = event.ticket ?
      '<a href="' + event.ticket + '" class="tickets">Tickets</a>'
      : '';

    outlet.innerHTML = outlet.innerHTML +
      '<article>' +
      '<span class="date">' + formatDate(event.date) +
      '</span>' +
      ' <span class="title">' + event.title + '</span>' +
      ' <span class="venue"> - ' + event.venue + '</span> ' +
      tickets +
      '</article>';
  });

}
```

Each item of the `events` array will be printed to the screen as rows.

03-25-2016 East Village: Lens on the Lower East Side - **Fourth Arts Block** `Tickets`	
04-05-2016 Land Use Workshop: Panel Discussion on Preservation & Local Issues - **Museum**	
04-11-2016 David Gilmour at Madison Square Garden - **Madison Square Garden**	

The `handleFetchComplete` function is the callback for the cache.

Because request bodies can only be read once, we have to clone the response.

```
cloned = response.clone();
```

We will place the cloned response in the cache using `cache.put` as a key value pair. This helps subsequent cache fetches to find this updated data.

```
caches.open(CACHE_NAME).then(function(cache) {
    cache.put(SOURCE_URL, cloned); // cache.put(URL, response)
});
```

Now we will read the response in the JSON format.

```
response.json().then(function(data) {
    displayEvents(data);
});
```

When the user clicks on the fetch button, we will make nearly simultaneous requests from the cache for data. This would happen on a page load in a real-world application instead of as a result of a user action.

```
fetchButton.addEventListener('click', function handleClick() {
...
}
```

To simulate cache delays, we wait before calling the cache fetch callback. In case the callback errors out, we will make sure that we reject `Promise` we got from the original call to match.

```
return new Promise(function(resolve, reject) {
        setTimeout(function() {
            try {
               handleCacheFetchComplete(response);
               resolve();
            } catch (err) {
               reject(err);
            }
        }, cacheDelay);
});
```

The `formatDate` function is a helper function for us to convert the date format we receive in the response into a much more readable format on the screen.

```
function formatDate(date) {
  var d = new Date(date),
      month = (d.getMonth() + 1).toString(),
      day = d.getDate().toString(),
      year = d.getFullYear();
  if (month.length < 2) month = '0' + month;
  if (day.length < 2) day = '0' + day;

  return [month, day, year].join('-');
}
```

If you prefer a different date format, you can shuffle the position of the array in the return statement to your preferred format.

See also

▶   The *Showing cached content first* recipe in *Chapter 3, Accessing Offline Content*

Performing network requests from a network

In the previous recipe, we looked at how we can fetch requests from the cache. In this recipe, we are going to demonstrate how we can fetch requests from the server/network using the service worker. To demonstrate network fetch, we are going to build an interface similar to the previous recipe, but catered to show network interactions.

Getting ready

To get started with service workers, you will need to have the service worker experiment feature turned on in your browser settings. If you have not done this yet, refer to the first recipe of *Chapter 1, Learning Service Worker Basics, Setting up service workers*. Service workers only run across HTTPS. To find out how to set up a development environment to support this feature, refer to the following recipes of *Chapter 1, Learning Service Worker Basics: Setting up GitHub pages for SSL, Setting up SSL for Windows*, and *Setting up SSL for Mac*.

How to do it...

Follow these instructions to set up your file structure:

1. Download files from the following location:

   ```
   https://github.com/szaranger/szaranger.github.io/blob/master/
   service-workers/10/02/
   ```

2. Open a browser and go to `index.html`.

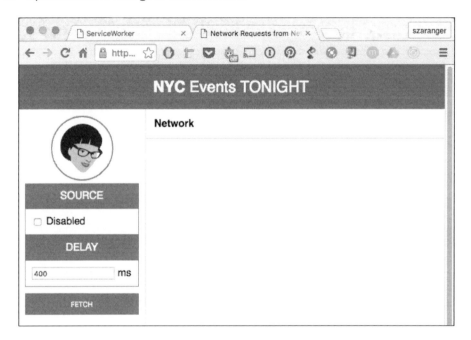

3. First, we will request data from the network with the cache enabled. Click on the **FETCH** button.

4. Now we are going to select the **Disabled** checkbox under the **SOURCE** label and click on the **FETCH** button again in order to fetch data only from the cache. An error will be shown on the page. Since the cache is disabled, data cannot be fetched.

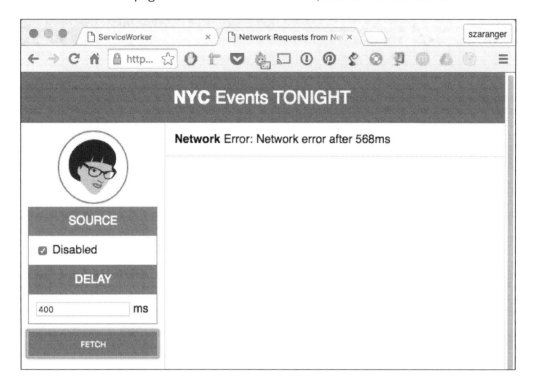

How it works...

In the `index.js` file, we will set a page-specific name for the cache as the caches are per origin-based and no other page should use the same cache name.

```
var CACHE_NAME = 'network-only';
```

If you inspect the **Resources** tab of the development tools, you can find the cache inside **Cache Storage**.

We will store the elapsed time for both networks in variables.

```
var networkFetchStartTime;
```

The source URL, for example, points to a file location in GitHub via RawGit.

```
var SOURCE_URL = 'https://cdn.rawgit.com/szaranger/
szaranger.github.io/master/service-workers/10/02/events';
```

If you want to set up your own source URL, you can easily do so by creating a gist or a repository in GitHub and creating a file with your data in the JSON format (you don't need the `.json` extension). Once you've done that, copy the URL of the file and head over to `https://rawgit.com`. Paste the link there to obtain a another link with a content type header as shown in the following screenshot:

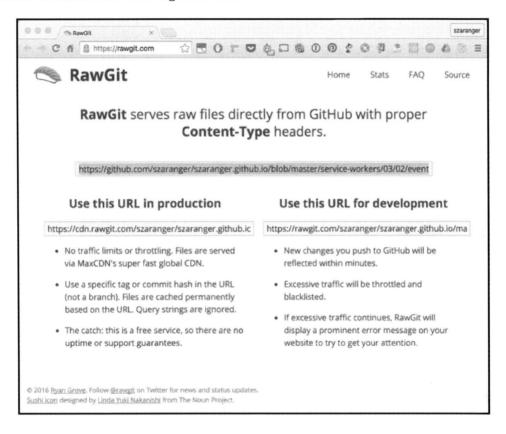

Between the time we click on the fetch button and all the data being received, we have to make sure that the user doesn't either change the criteria for searching or click on the fetch button again. To handle this situation, we will disable the controls.

```
function clear() {
    outlet.textContent = '';
    networkStatus.textContent = '';
    networkDataReceived = false;
}
```

```
function disableEdit(enable) {
  fetchButton.disabled = enable;
  networkDelayText.disabled = enable;
  networkDisabledCheckbox.disabled = enable;

  if(!enable) {
    clear();
  }
}
```

The returned data will be rendered to the screen in rows.

```
function displayEvents(events) {

  events.forEach(function(event) {
    var tickets = event.ticket ?
      '<a href="' + event.ticket + '" class="tickets">Tickets
      </a>' : '';

    outlet.innerHTML = outlet.innerHTML +
      '<article>' +
      '<span class="date">' + formatDate(event.date) +
      '</span>' +
      ' <span class="title">' + event.title + '</span>' +
      ' <span class="venue"> - ' + event.venue + '</span> ' +
      tickets +
      '</article>';
  });

}
```

Each item of the `events` array will be printed to the screen as rows.

03-25-2016 East Village: Lens on the Lower East Side - **Fourth Arts Block** Tickets	
04-05-2016 Land Use Workshop: Panel Discussion on Preservation & Local Issues - **Museum**	
04-11-2016 David Gilmour at Madison Square Garden - **Madison Square Garden**	

The `handleFetchComplete` function is the callback for both the cache and network.

If the **Disabled** checkbox is checked we will simulate a network error by throwing an error.

```
var shouldNetworkError = networkDisabledCheckbox.checked,
    cloned;

  if (shouldNetworkError) {
    throw new Error('Network error');
  }
```

Because request bodies can only be read once, we have to clone the response.

```
cloned = response.clone();
```

Now we will read the response in the JSON format.

```
response.json().then(function(data) {
    displayEvents(data);
    networkDataReceived = true;
});
```

When the user clicks on the fetch button, we will make nearly simultaneous requests from the network and the cache for data. This would happen on a page load in a real-world application instead of as the result of a user action.

```
fetchButton.addEventListener('click', function handleClick() {
  ...
}
```

We will start with disabling any user input while the network fetch requests are initiated.

```
disableEdit(true);

networkStatus.textContent = 'Fetching events...';
networkFetchStartTime = Date.now();
```

We will request data with the fetch API with a cache-busting URL as well as a no-cache option in order to support Firefox, which hasn't implemented the caching options yet.

```
networkFetch = fetch(SOURCE_URL + '?cacheBuster=' + now, {
    mode: 'cors',
    cache: 'no-cache',
    headers: headers
})
```

In order to simulate network delays, we wait before calling the network fetch callback. In situations where the callback errors out, we have to make sure that we reject `Promise` we received from the original fetch.

```
return new Promise(function(resolve, reject) {
    setTimeout(function() {
        try {
            handleFetchComplete(response);
            resolve();
        } catch (err) {
            reject(err);
        }
    }, networkDelay);
});
```

The `formatDate` function is a helper function for us to convert the date format we receive in the response into a much more readable format on the screen.

```
function formatDate(date) {
    var d = new Date(date),
        month = (d.getMonth() + 1).toString(),
        day = d.getDate().toString(),
        year = d.getFullYear();

    if (month.length < 2) month = '0' + month;
    if (day.length < 2) day = '0' + day;

    return [month, day, year].join('-');
}
```

If you prefer a different date format, you can shuffle the position of the array in the return statement to your preferred format.

See also

▶ The *Showing cached content first* recipe in *Chapter 3, Accessing Offline Content*

Testing waitUntil

In this recipe, we are going to use the service worker to test the `waitUntil` method, which will delay the install method of the service worker life cycle until the process of opening caches and saving a page to the cache.

Getting ready

To get started with service workers, you will need to have the service worker experiment feature turned on in your browser settings. If you have not done this yet, refer to the *Setting up service workers* recipe of *Chapter 1, Learning Service Worker Basics*. Service workers only run across HTTPS. To find out how to set up a development environment to support this feature, refer to the following recipes of *Chapter 1, Learning Service Worker Basics*: *Setting up GitHub pages for SSL, Setting up SSL for Windows*, and *Setting up SSL for Mac*.

How to do it...

Follow these instructions to set up your file structure:

1. Download files from the following location:

   ```
   https://github.com/szaranger/szaranger.github.io/blob/master/
   service-workers/10/03/
   ```

2. Open a browser and go to `index.html`. You will see the **Registration status: successful** message.

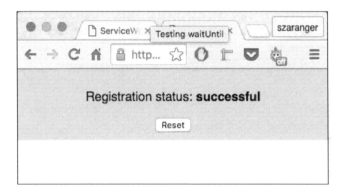

3. Now open DevTools (*Cmd + Alt + I* or *F12*), go to the **Network** tab, click on the dropdown displaying **No Throttling**, and select **Offline**.

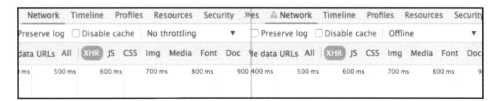

4. Now refresh your bowser, and you will see the offline message and the image.

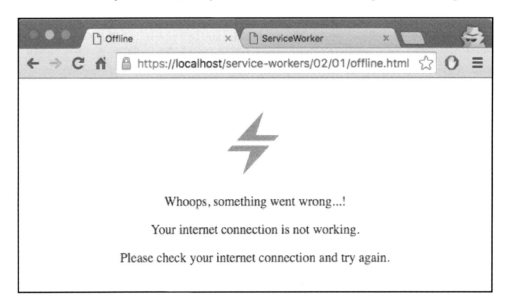

How it works...

The `waitUntil` event extends the lifetime of the install event until all the caches are populated. In other words, it delays treating the installing worker as installed until all the resources we specify are cached and the passed promise resolves successfully.

We saw an HTML and an image file getting cached and then retrieved when our website was offline. We can cache other resources as well, including CSS and JavaScript files.

```
caches.open(currentCache.offline)
.then(function(cache) {
        return cache.addAll([
            'offline.html',
            '/assets/css/style.css',
            '/assets/js/index.js'
        ]);
    })
);
```

When the registration is successful, we will instruct the service worker to intercept a request and provide resources from the cached content using the fetch event.

Inside the `index.html` file, when the registration is successful, we will inspect the state of the registration and print it to the browser. Otherwise, we will print the error message returned by the service worker.

```
navigator.serviceWorker.register(
        'service-worker.js',
        { scope: './' }
    ).then(function(serviceWorker) {
        document.getElementById('status').innerHTML =
            'successful';
    }).catch(function(error) {

        document.getElementById('status').innerHTML = error;

});
```

The service worker script file will intercept network requests, check for connectivity, and provide the content for the user.

We will add an event listener to the install event, and inside the callback we will fire a request to get this offline page with its resources, which gets added to the cache when the result is successful.

```
self.addEventListener('install', function(event) {
    event.waitUntil(
        caches.open(currentCache.offline)
        .then(function(cache) {
            return cache.addAll([
            offlineUrl
                ]);
            })
        );
});
```

Now we can retrieve this page whenever we need to, because the offline page is stored in the cache. We need to add the logic to return the offline page if we don't have connectivity in the same service worker.

```
self.addEventListener('fetch', function(event) {
    var request = event.request,
        isRequestMethodGET = request.method === 'GET';

    if (request.mode === 'navigate' || isRequestMethodGET) {
        event.respondWith(
```

```
      fetch(createRequestWithCacheBusting
      (request.url)).catch(function(error) {
         console.log('OFFLINE: Returning offline page.', error);
         return caches.match(offlineUrl);
      })
    );
  } else {
    event.respondWith(caches.match(request)
        .then(function (response) {
        return response || fetch(request);
      })
    );
  }
});
```

We are listening out for the fetch event in the preceding source code, and we simply return the offline page from the cache if we detect that the user is trying to navigate to another page, resulting in an error. Now we have our offline page working.

Implementing background sync

The background synchronization feature of the service worker is responsible for managing background synchronization processes. This feature, as of writing this book, is still nonstandard and you should avoid using it in the production.

Getting ready

To get started with service workers, you will need to have the service worker experiment feature turned on in your browser settings. If you have not done this yet, refer to the *Setting up service workers* recipe of *Chapter 1, Learning Service Worker Basics*. Service workers only run across HTTPS. To find out how to set up a development environment to support this feature, refer to the *Setting up GitHub pages for SSL* recipe of *Chapter 1, Learning Service Worker Basics*.

How to do it...

Follow these instructions to set up your file structure:

1. Copy files from the following location:

   ```
   https://github.com/szaranger/szaranger.github.io/blob/master/
   service-workers/10/04/
   ```

2. Open a browser and go to `index.html`.

3. Click on the **Register Background Sync** button. A message will appear at the bottom displaying **Sync registered**.

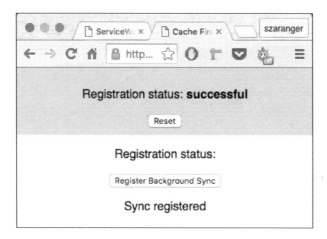

4. A notification message will also appear on the screen.

How it works...

In our `index.html` file, we will add a section for the button and the message.

```html
<section>
  <p>Registration status: <strong id="status"></strong></p>
  <button id="register">Register Background Sync</button>
  <div id="console"></div>
</section>
```

We will handle the button click in the `index.js` file. Notifications need permissions, so we will handle that here as well.

```js
document.getElementById('register').addEventListener('click',
function(event) {
    event.preventDefault();

    new Promise(function(resolve, reject) {
      Notification.requestPermission(function(result) {
        if (result !== 'granted') {
          return reject(Error('Notification permission
          denied'));
        }
        resolve();
      })
    }).then(function() {
      return navigator.serviceWorker.ready;
    }).then(function(reg) {
      return reg.sync.register('syncTest');
    }).then(function() {
      print('Sync registered');
    }).catch(function(err) {
      print('It broke');
      print(err.message);
    });
});
```

Our `service-worker.js` file is fairly simple. We show the notification when the sync event handler is called.

```js
self.addEventListener('sync', function(event) {
  self.registration.showNotification('Sync\'d');
});
```

Sending forward requests

In this recipe, we are going to implement a service worker that sends forward requests. Request forwarding is helpful when you want to temporarily forward a request to a different resource.

Getting ready

To get started with service workers, you will need to have the service worker experiment feature turned on in your browser settings. If you have not done this yet, refer to the first recipe of *Chapter 1, Learning Service Worker Basics, Setting up service workers*. Service workers only run across HTTPS. To find out how to set up a development environment to support this feature, refer to the following recipes of *Chapter 1, Learning Service Worker Basics: Setting up GitHub pages for SSL, Setting up SSL for Windows*, and *Setting up SSL for Mac*.

How to do it...

Follow these instructions to set up your file structure:

1. Download all the files from the following location:

   ```
   https://github.com/szaranger/szaranger.github.io/blob/master/
   service-workers/10/05/
   ```

2. Open a browser and go to `index.html`.

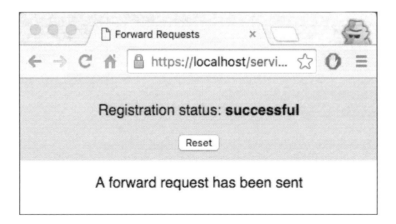

3. Now open DevTools (*Cmd + Alt + I* or *F12*) to see the log messages on the **Console** tab. A forward message will appear in a second.

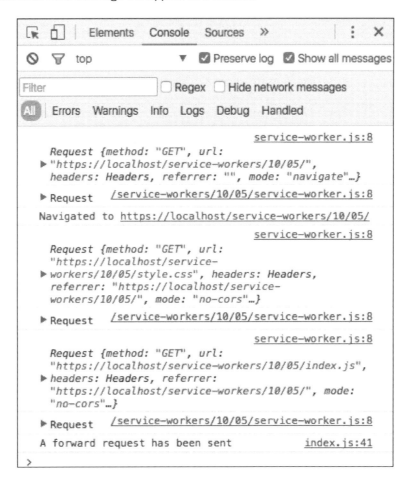

How it works...

We will add a `div` element to the `index.html` file where we are planning to log a message.

```
<section>
    <div id="console"></div>
</section>
```

We will handle the `active` and `fetch` events inside the `service-worker.js` file.

```
self.addEventListener('activate', _ => {
  clients.claim();
});

self.addEventListener('fetch', event => {
  console.log(event.request);
  event.respondWith(fetch(event.request));
});
```

The helper function for logging messages to the screen is in the `index.js` file.

```
var consoleEl = document.getElementById('console');

function print(message) {
  var p = document.createElement('p');

  p.textContent = message;
  consoleEl.appendChild(p);
  console.log(message);
}
```

Avoiding model fetching and render times

In order to avoid model fetching and render times upon successive requests, a cache containing the interpolated templates in order is saved, which we call as a render **store**.

According to Mozilla, the render store is intended to save/restore a serialized version of a particular view, mostly for the purpose of performance.

Getting ready

To get started with service workers, you will need to have the service worker experiment feature turned on in your browser settings. If you have not done this yet, refer to the *Setting up service workers* recipe of *Chapter 1, Learning Service Worker Basics*. Service workers only run across HTTPS. To find out how to set up a development environment to support this feature, refer to the *Setting up GitHub pages for SSL* recipe of *Chapter 1, Learning Service Worker Basics*.

How to do it...

Follow these instructions to set up your file structure:

1. Download files from the following location:

   `https://github.com/szaranger/szaranger.github.io/blob/master/`
   `service-workers/10/06/`

2. Open a browser and go to `index.html`.

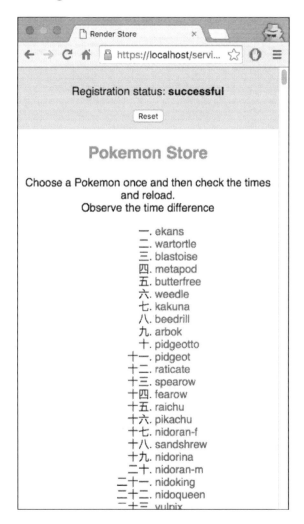

3. Click on any link in the list to go to the store.

How it works...

At the beginning of the `index.js` file, we specify the Pokemon API endpoint as well as a secure origin.

```
var proxy = 'https://crossorigin.me/';
var pokedex = proxy + 'http://pokeapi.co/api/v1/pokedex/1/';
...
```

Next, fetch the Pokemon list from `pokedex` and create a list of links.

```
function fetchPokemonList() {
  fetch(pokedex)
    .then(function(response) {
      return response.json();
    })
    .then(function(info) {
      populatePokemonList(info.pokemon);

      if (window.parent !== window) {
        window.parent.document.body
          .dispatchEvent(new CustomEvent('iframeresize'));
      }
    });
}
```

Subsequently, populate the list and create the links for the Pokemon list. These links will be intercepted by the service worker.

```
function populatePokemonList(pokemonList) {
  var el = document.querySelector('#pokemon');
  var buffer = pokemonList.map(function(pokemon) {
    var tokens = pokemon.resource_uri.split('/');
    var id = tokens[tokens.length - 2];
    return '<li><a href="pokemon.html?id=' + id + '">' +
    pokemon.name +
           '</a></li>';
  });
  el.innerHTML = buffer.join('\n');
}
```

Next, let's look at the `service-worker.js` file. It tries to recover a cached copy of the document. If not found, it responds from the network.

```
function getResponse(request) {
  return self.caches.open('render-store').then(function(cache) {
    return cache.match(request).then(function(match) {
      return match || fetch(request);
    });
  });
}
```

The `cacheResponseInRenderStore` function gets the interpolated HTML contents of a PUT request from `pokemon.js` and creates an HTML response for the interpolated result.

```
function cacheResponseInRenderStore(request) {
  return request.text().then(function(contents) {
    var headers = { 'Content-Type': 'text/html' };
    var response = new Response(contents, { headers: headers });

    return self.caches.open('render-store').then(function(cache) {
      return cache.put(request.referrer, response);
    });
  });
}
```

In the `pokemon.js` file, we initialize timers to start with.

```
var startTime = performance.now();
var interpolationTime = 0;
var fetchingModelTime = 0;
```

We are going to create a template for a Pokemon, which is responsible for rendering by obtaining data requested from the URL's query string. This template will fetch the given Pokemon and fill the template. Once the template has been filled, we will mark the document as cached and then we will send it to the render store by sending the contents to the service worker.

```
if (document.documentElement.dataset.cached) {
  logTime();
} else {
  var pokemonId = window.location.search.split('=')[1];

  getPokemon(pokemonId).then(fillCharSheet).
  then(logTime).then(cache);
}
```

```
function getPokemon(id) {
  var fetchingModelStart = getStartTime();

  return fetch(getURL(id)).then(function(response) {
    fetchingModelTime = getStartTime() - fetchingModelStart;
    return response.json();
  });
}
```

Next, we mark the documents as cached, get all the HTML content, and send it to the service worker using a PUT request into the `./render-store/` URL.

```
function interpolateTemplate(template, pokemon) {
  var interpolationStart = performance.now();
  var result = template.replace(/{{(\w+)}}/g, function(match,
  field) {
    return pokemon[field];
  });
  interpolationTime = performance.now() - interpolationStart;
  return result;
}
```

Index

fetch() function
 no credentials by default 88
 non-CORS fail by default 88, 89
Firefox
 service worker, enabling 5, 6
Firefox Nightly
 URL 5
font family, from Google
 reference 68
fonts
 loading offline 64-70
forward requests
 sending 357-359

G

GitHub pages
 setting up, for SSL 13-15
global APIs
 working with 232, 233
Google Analytics
 about 253
 working with 253-257
Google Developers Console page
 URL 35

H

handlebars library
 reference 146
**Hyper Text Transfer Protocol
 Secure (HTTPS) 4**

I

images
 loading offline 50-53
 responsive images, handling 54
immediate control
 forcing 219-221
IndexedDb
 references 158
index.html file
 reference 107

init object
 cache 84
 method 84
 mode 84
Internet Information Service (IIS) 6
issues with Chrome, service workers
 ERR_FILE_EXISTS error message 17
 stale console messages 18

J

JSON file
 fetching, during service worker
  installation 267-271

L

live flowchart
 service worker, using with 324-333

M

messages
 relaying 317-320
mock responses
 creating 30-35
model fetching
 avoiding 359-363
multiple fetch handlers
 implementing 71-76

N

network races
 implementing 117-124
network requests
 performing, from cache 336-343
 performing, from network 343-350
network responses
 receiving offline 186, 187
Node.js
 URL 194
notification tag
 using 289-291

O

offline Google Analytics
allowing 158-169
offline requests
deferring 228-230
offline user interaction
allowing 170-177

P

page
immediate control, taking of 311-313
Promise.reject(reason) 4
Promise.resolve(value) 4
promises 3
proxy 271
proxy middleware
service worker, using as 271-274
using 321-323
Push API 281
push clients
implementing 291-296
push notification quota
managing 303-309
push notifications
subscribing to 297-303

R

RawGit
URL 113
read-through caching
about 150
implementing 150-157
remote resources
fetching 76-88, 259-263
render times
avoiding 359-363
request
redirecting 198-204
request headers
setting 204-208
request timeouts
handling 36-40

resources
prefetching 274-279
responsive images
device-pixel ratio 55
handling 54
picture element 56-59
sizes attribute 55
srcset attribute 54
rich notifications
displaying 286-289

S

selective caching
implementing 178-184
service worker
about 2, 3
debugging 22
enabling, in Chrome 4
enabling, in Firefox 5
registering 15, 16
registering, in detail 18-20
setting up 4
using, as proxy middleware 271-274
using, with live flowchart 324-333
working, as dependency injector 213-218
working, as remote server 208-213
service worker, stages
activate 21
fetch 21
install 21
terminate 22
simple push notification
implementing 282-286
single page applications (SPA) 140
slow responses
working with 314-316
srcset attribute
about 54
device-pixel ratio 54
pixel density of device 54
zoom level of browser 54